鲁宾逊漂流记

Robinson
Crusoe

编 写	杜瑞清
主编 校译	方华文
副主审 改翻译	王富民

陕 西 出 版 集 团
陕 西 人 民 出 版 社

（陕）新登字001号

图书在版编目（CIP）数据

鲁宾逊漂流记／〔英〕狄福（Defoe,D.）著；王富民改
写．—西安：陕西人民出版社，2002

ISBN 978-7-224-06069-0

Ⅰ.鲁… Ⅱ.①狄…②王… Ⅲ.英语－语言
读物，小说 Ⅳ.H319.4：I

中国版本图书馆CIP数据核字（2001）第076473号

书　名：	鲁宾逊漂流记	
作　者：	原著 〔英〕Daniel Defoe	
	改写 翻译	王富民
出版发行：	陕西出版集团	
	陕西人民出版社（西安北大街147号　邮编：710003）	
印　刷：	安康天宝实业有限公司	
开　本：	787mm×1092mm　42开　10.875印张　2插页	
字　数：	189千字	
版　次：	2002年10月第1版　2013年1月第4次印刷	
书　号：	ISBN 978-7-224-06069-0/H·227	
定　价：	18.50元	

序

　　提高文化素质的最佳途径是读书，不少成名作家都是在读书中成长起来的。我喜欢文学，幼时特别爱读长篇小说。开始是在父亲单位的图书室借，像《西游记》、《三国演义》、《水浒传》等，我在十一岁时就统统读过。后来图书室的书不够看了，恰好新华书店开展租书业务，我便把不多的零用钱换了书来读，我看过全部的《沫若文集》、《巴金文集》、《茅盾文集》等，虽然是囫囵吞枣，但总觉得兴味无穷。这期间，我读的主要是中国的各种名著。

　　考上西安外国语学院以后，我更多地接触了外国名著。记得我看的第一部小说是《沉船》，泰戈尔那诗一般的语言，他描述的那田园诗一般的生活，深深地打动了我，使我受到了心灵的震撼，我初次感到了外国文学的巨大力量。恰好碰上了"文化大革命"，我就有更多的时间徜徉在外国图书的海洋中了。曾经给我国一代年轻人深刻教育的《牛虹》、《古丽雅的道路》、《卓娅和舒拉的故事》、《钢铁是怎样炼成的》等作品，便是在这时期读过的。此外，我还系统地阅读了狄更斯、巴尔扎克、雨果、莫泊桑、托尔斯泰、德莱赛、大仲马、陀思妥耶夫斯基、高尔基、果戈理等外国大师的著名作品，从此我与世界名著结下了不解之缘，而这些名著带给我的不仅是一种享受，更多的是一生受用不尽的精神财富。

世上新人换旧人，但世界文学名著却为一代代人青睐，你可以随之轻轻松松地走进异国他乡，去享受大师们驾驭语言的神奇魅力。而且，随着我国进一步的改革开放，只读译著已经不够，有条件的，还需要去涉猎原汁原味的外国文学，以回避译文中可能发生的种种不足。涉猎要一步步的来，原著，对于一般的外语学习者而言，是太难了，它会让人望而生畏，甚至丧失学习的信心和兴味。怎么办呢？思来想去，还是先搞一些英汉对照的改写本吧。让有一定外语基础的青少年读者，既了解了名著，又学习了语言，两全其美，何乐而不为呢？

本着这个初衷，我社约请著名学者、西安外国语学院英语学科带头人杜瑞清博士和著名翻译家方文华先生主编了这套丛书，第一辑十册：《飘》、《鲁宾逊漂流记》、《简·爱》、《雾都孤儿》、《蝴蝶梦》、《少年维特之烦恼》、《莎士比亚戏剧故事集》、《巴黎圣母院》、《汤姆·索耶历险记》和《金银岛》。"年年岁岁花相似"，愿经典名著这不败的鲜花，伴随着我们年轻的朋友成长。

这套丛书如果能受到广大青少年读者的喜欢，且对他们在名著与语言的学习上有一定的裨益，我们将陆续推出第二辑、第三辑……读者的需要就是我们的使命。值此出版前夕，抚今追昔，不由一笔在手，感慨系之。

　　但愿书长久，人间日月圆。

周鹏飞
二零零二年九月写于西安逍遥斋

ROBINSON CRUSOE

鲁宾逊漂流记

Chapter 1 My Father's Advice

My father was a businessman. After he married my mother, they lived happily at York. I was born in the year 1632. I had two elder brothers. I am the third son of the family. My father, a very old fashioned man, had given me a competent share of learning, as far as house education and a country free school generally goes, and designed me for the law; but I would be satisfied with nothing but going to sea. My inclination to this led me so strongly against my father's will, and against all the entreaties and persuasions of my mother and other friends, and there seemed to be something fatal in that pretension of nature tending directly to the life of misery which was to befall me.

My father, a wise and grave man, gave me serious and excellent counsel against what he foresaw was my design. He called me one morning into his chamber, where he was confined by the gout, and expostulated very

第一章　苦口婆心

我父亲是个生意人，结婚后和我母亲幸福地生活在约克郡。我一六三二年出生，有两个哥哥，我在家中排行老三，我父亲思想很保守，让我在家中学习，也让我上林间的免费学校，使我掌握了足够的知识，他想让我做一名律师，但我却只对航海感兴趣。既不愿意遵从父亲的意愿，也不听母亲和朋友们的恳求和劝告，出现了这种现象，似乎这一切都注定了我将遭受悲苦的生活。

我父亲勇敢而且聪明，发现了我的动机，经常诚恳地给我一些忠告，教我如何做人。一天，他把我叫进卧室——他因患病而呆在卧室——就

warmly with me upon this subject. he asked me what reasons I had for leaving my father's house and my native country, with a life of ease and pleasure. He told me it was for men of desperate fortunes on one hand, or for aspiring superior fortunes on the other, who went abroad upon adventures, to rise by enterprise, and make themselves famous in undertakings of a nature out of the common road; that these things were all either too far above me, or too far below me, that mine was the middle state, or what might be called the upper station of low life, which he had found by long experience was the best state in the world, the most suited to human happiness, not exposed to the miseries and sufferings of the mechanic part of mankind and not embarrassed with the pride, luxury, ambition, and envy of the upper part of mankind. He told me, I might judge the happiness of this state, that this was the state of life which all other people envy; that kings have frequently lamented the miserable consequences of being born to great things, and wish they had been placed in the middle of the two extremes, between the mean and the great; that the wise man gave his testimony to this, as the just standard of true felicity, when he prayed to have neither poverty nor riches.

He bade me observe that the calamities of life were shared among the upper and lower part of mankind; but

我想航海这件事，诚恳地规劝我，言辞热烈。他问我为什么要离开家，离开自己的祖国，以及这种舒适和快乐的生活。他还告诉我，有些人一方面因为贫穷，另一方面为了追求更多的财富，就想出去冒险，通过此举向上爬，或是不走平常人的路而去挑战大自然，使自己成名。对我来说这太遥远了，再说我也瞧不上，我的生活处于中等水平，也可以说是低等生活中的上层阶级，而且他也凭自己漫长的生活经历认定这是世界上最好的生活，也是人生最大的幸福，不用经历那些机械性工作的痛苦和折磨，也不会因上层人的骄傲、富裕、雄心勃勃和嫉妒而觉得难堪。他告诉我，我可以对这种状态是否幸福做出判断；他说这种幸福的生活是所有人都向往的，那些国王经常因为出生高贵而带来的不幸痛惜不已，希望他们自己处于两种极端的中间，出生在高贵与低贱之间，做个普通人，聪明的人祷告上帝让他们既不贫穷也不富裕，把这作为评判真正幸福的标准。

他试图让我明白上层人和下层人都遭受着生

that the middle station had the fewest disasters, and was not exposed to so many vicissitudes as the higher or lower part of mankind. They were not subjected to so many distempers and uneasiness either of body or mind, as those were who, by vicious living, luxury, and extravagances on one hand, or by hard labor, want of necessaries, and mean or insufficient diet on the other hand, bring distempers upon themselves by the natural sequences of their way of living; that the middle station of life was calculated for all kind of virtues and all kind of enjoyments; that peace and plenty were the handmaids of a middle fortune; that temperance, moderation, quietness, health, society, all agreeable diversions, and all desirable pleasures, were the blessings attending the middle station of life; that this way men went silently and smoothly through the world, and comfortably out of it, not sold to the life of slavery for daily bread, or harassed with perplexed circumstances, with the passion of secret burning lust of ambition for great things; but in easy circumstances sliding gently through the world, and sensibly tasting the sweets of living without the bitter, feeling that they are happy, and learning by every day's experience to know it more sensibly.

After this, he pressed me earnestly, in the most affectionate manner, not to play the young man, not to

活的磨难，但中等阶层的人灾难最少，不用遭受像上流阶层或下等人那样多的波折，他们无论在肉体上还是心理上都不会躁动不安，那些上层人过着奢侈、挥霍、残暴的生活，而那些下层人因贫穷不得不辛苦地劳作，生活拮据，食不果腹。这些生活道路的客观性给他们带来这样或那样的烦恼。但中等阶层的人可以具有各种美德，获得许多享受，安宁与富足属于他们，节制、温和、平静、健康、社交、各种惬意的消遣以及理想中的欢乐都是中庸人可以享受到的，这类人的生活道路风平浪静舒舒服服地远离世事，既不用为每天的生计成为生活的奴隶，不用周旋于复杂的环境之中也不用因利欲熏心而烦恼，他们的生活一帆风顺，安安逸逸，尝尽了生活带来的乐趣，感到很幸福，而且每过一天，都会对此有更清醒的认识。

后来，他又用最诚恳的语气，用关心的态度劝我说，不要凭着年轻人的一时冲动，鲁莽地反

precipitate myself into miseries which nature and the station of life I was born in, seemed to have provided against; that I was under no necessity of seeking my bread; that he would do well for me, and endeavor to enter me fairly into the station of life which he had been just recommending to me; and that if I was not very easy and happy in the world, it must be my mere fate or fault that must hinder it, and that he should have nothing to answer for, having thus discharged his duty in warning me against measures which he knew would be to my hurt; in a word, that as he would do very kind things for me if I would stay and settle at home as he directed, and to close all, he told me I had my elder brother for an example, to whom he had used the same earnest persuasions to keep him from going into the wars, but could not prevail, his young desires prompting him to run into the army, where he was killed; and though he said he would not cease to pray for me, yet he would venture to say to me, that if I did take this foolish step, God would not bless me, and I would have leisure hereafter to reflect upon having neglected his counsel when there might be none to assist in my recovery.

I observed in this last part of his discourse which was truly prophetic, though I suppose my father did not know it to be so himself, I observed the tears run down

叛我的天性与天命，这样必定会带来不尽的灾难。我不需要为生计而奔波，他会努力让我按他为我作的安排而过得幸福，让我进入他刚才所推荐的生活状态，如果我过得不十分轻松，不幸福，那就是我的命运不济或是我的过错使然，他将不负任何责任，这样也尽了他的责任，阻止我自我毁灭。总之，如果我能按照他的意愿呆在家中，他会把一切都做好。最后，他又拿我的哥哥作为例子，他也曾苦口婆心地劝过他不要去打仗，但白费口舌，他的一意孤行使他匆忙投军，最终战死疆场，他说他会一直祈求上帝保佑我，但又说，如果我要迈出那愚蠢的一步，上帝将不会保佑我，以后求助无门之时就不会有足够的时间来反思当初没听劝告所带来的灾难。

我发现他在说最后这段话的时候，脸上老泪纵横，他的话的确有先见之明，只可惜我一叶障

his face very plentifully, and especially when he spoke of my brother, and that when he spoke of my having leisure to repent, and none to assist me, he was so moved, that he broke off the discourse, and told me his heart was so full, he could say no more to me.

I was sincerely affected with this discourse, and I resolved not to think of going abroad any more, but to settle at home according to my father's desire. But, alas! A few days wore it all off; and, in short, to prevent any of my father's further importunities, in a few weeks I resolved to run quite way from him. However, I did not act so hastily, but I took my mother at a time when I thought her a little pleasanter than ordinary, and told her that my thoughts were so entirely bent upon seeing the world, that I should never settle to anything with resolution enough to go through with it, and my father had better give me his consent than force me to go without it; that I was now eighteen years old, which was too late to go apprentice to a trade, or clerk to an attorney; that I was sure, if I did, I should never serve out my time, and I should certainly run away from my master before my time was out, and go to sea; and if she would speak to my father to let me go but one voyage abroad, if I came home again and did not like it, I would go no more, and I would promise by a double diligence to

目，不知好歹。他在谈到我的哥哥时，更是痛心。当他说到我会后悔、将求助无门时，他又是那样的悲伤。他打住话头，说心里憋得慌，他就这样结束了谈话。

我被他这番话深深地感动了，我决定不再去想出海的事，呆在家中按父亲的意愿过稳定的生活，可是，天呀！几天以后那个决心又消失殆尽。总之，为了不再听父亲的唠叨，几星期后我决定悄悄地离开他。然而，我没有匆匆而去，有一段时间，看母亲的心情比平日好些，我跟她进行了一次谈话，告诉了她我的想法，就是我只想出去看看外面的世界，我从没有过这么大的决心去做一件事，父亲应该同意这件事而不该强迫我留下，我现在已十八岁了，学个手艺，或是当个律师已太晚了。我知道我也学不出个什么结果，未及学徒期满我便会抛弃师父逃走出海。如果她能说服父亲让我去航海，就这一次，我想，要是不适应航海我就回来，不再出海，而会加倍努力弥补那

recover that time I had lost.

This put my mother into a great passion: she told me, she knew it would be to no purpose to speak to my father upon any such subject; that he knew too well what was my interest to give his consent to anything so much for my hurt, and that she wondered how I could think of any such things after such a discourse as I had had from my father, and such kind and tender expressions as she knew my father had used to me, and that, in short, if I would ruin myself, there was no help for me; but I might depend I should never have their consent to it; that for her part she would not have so much hand in my destruction; and I should never have it to say, that my mother was willing when my father was not.

Though my mother refused to move it to my father, yet, she reported all the discourse to him, and that my father, after showing a great concern at it, said to her, with a sigh, "That boy might be happy if he would stay at home, but if he goes abroad, he will be the most miserable wretch that was ever born; I can give no consent to it."

It was not till almost a year after this that I broke loose, though in the mean time I continued obstinately deaf to all proposals of settling to business, and frequently expostulating with my father and mother. One day

段浪费的时光。

这次谈话使母亲很是不安，她知道针对这样的事情她无法说服父亲，十分惊讶在父亲那样温和的谆谆劝告下我却听不进去。父亲心里有数，知道怎样才有益于我，不会同意明知对我有害的事情。她说如果我执意要自我毁灭，大人也没有办法，他们永远不会同意我去冒险的，如果我一意孤行，必须后果自负，不可怨天尤人。她让我死了心，说他们决不同意我的作为。既然我执意要自取灭亡，她不愿有任何干系，她可不愿让人说，在父亲反对的情况下，是她同意我走的。

虽然母亲不愿意劝说父亲，可她还是将这次谈话转告给了父亲。我父亲听后忧心忡忡，叹气道："孩子如果呆在家里，他会幸福的，一旦出海，他将是世界上最不幸的家伙，我决不会同意这件事。"

此事大约过去一年之后，我终于逃离了家庭的束缚，那时我对众人让我去经商的建议充耳不闻，对父亲与母亲的忠告也听不进去。一天，我

at Hull, where I went casually, and without any purpose of making an elopement that time—but I say, being there, and one of my companions being about to sail to London, in his father's ship, and prompting me to go with them, with the common allurement of seafaring men, namely, that it should cost me nothing for my passage, I consulted neither father nor mother any more, nor so much as sent them word of it; but leaving them to hear of it as they might, without asking God's blessing, or my father's, without any consideration of circumstances or conjuncts, and in an ill hour—God knows—on the first of September, 1651, I went on board a ship bound for London. Never any young adventure's misfortunes, I believe, began sooner, or continued longer than mine. The ship was no sooner gotten out of the harbor, but the wind began to blow, and the waves to rise in a most frightful manner; and as I had never been at sea before, I was most inexpressibly sick in body, and terrified in mind. I began now seriously to reflect upon what I had done, and how justly I was overtaken by the judgment of Heaven for my wicked leaving my father's house, and abandoning my duty; all the good counsel of my parents, my father's tears and my mother's entreaties, came now fresh into my mind, and my conscience, which was not yet to the pith of hardness to which it has

去了赫尔，去的时候，我心里并没有出走的打算。可是到了那里，我的一位同伴正打算坐他父亲的船到伦敦去。他用一般船上人招引水手的方式，怂恿我跟他一块去，说我不用花一分钱，因此，我没有和父母商量，也没有给家里留下只言片语，只让他们自然而然地去听我的消息；既不求上帝或是父亲的祝福，也不考虑一下当时的处境和后果。那是一个黑色的日子。一六五一年九月一日，我登上了去伦敦的轮船。我想再没有什么人遇到的灾难会比我遇到的更早，持续的时间更长了，船刚离开海岸，就刮起了狂风，狂暴的大海危机四伏。因为这是我第一次出海，我晕船晕得厉害，非常害怕。我开始认真地反思我的出海，上帝是多么公正地惩罚了我擅自离开父母，放弃我做儿子的责任的行为，母亲的谆谆劝告，父亲悲伤的泪水以及母亲的恳求重新浮现在我脑海中，良心

been since, reproached me with the contempt of advise, and the breach of my duty to God and my father.

All this while the storm increased, and the sea, which I had never been upon before, went very high, though nothing like what I have seen many times since; no, nor like what I saw a few days after: but it was enough to affect me, a young sailor, who had never known anything of the matter. I expected every wave would have swallowed us up, and that every time the ship fell down, as I thought, in the trough of the sea, we should never rise more; and in this agony of mind I made many vows and resolutions, that if it would please God here to spare my life this one voyage, if ever I got once my foot upon dry land again I would go directly home to my father, and never set it into a ship again while I lived; that I would take his advice, and never run myself into such miseries as these any more. Now I saw plainly the goodness of his observations about the middle station of life, how easy, how comfortably he had lived all his days, and never had been exposed to tempests at sea, or troubles on shore; and I resolved that I would, like a true repenting prodigal, go home to my father. These wise and sober thoughts continued all the while the storm continued, and indeed some time after; but the next day the wind was abated and the sea calm-

的谴责使我十分后悔，怪自己不该无视别人的忠告，无视自己对上帝及父亲的责任。

就在这段时间里，暴风雨越来越大，海水涨得很高，这一切都是我从未遇到过的，虽然比起以后的几次还算不上什么，但这也足够使我恐惧万分了，对我这样一个从未见过这种场面的年轻水手来说，对于海上的事完全没有意识。我感觉每一次浪花都要把我吞没，每一次船从浪峰跌入海水里时，我都觉得它再也浮不起来了，船也快要沉没。在这种恐惧中我暗暗发誓，倘上帝能免我一死，让我逃过这一劫，一上陆地我会立马回家到父亲的身边去，这一生中再也不会出海航行了。我将接受父亲的忠告，不再自我折磨，让自己遭受这样的磨难了。现在我发现了中等阶层人美好的生活，多么舒适与安稳，没有遭受海上暴风袭击的恐惧，也不用为生活而烦恼，我决定要像一个忏悔者一样，回到父亲的身边。在暴风雨中，我一直保持着这种冷静的想法。等到第二天，风力减弱了，海面也恢复了往日的平静，我开始

er, and I began to be a little inured to it: however, I was very grave for all that day, being also a little sea – sick still; but towards night the weather cleared up, the wind was quite over, and a charming fine evening followed; the sun went down perfectly clear, and rose so the next morning; and having little or no wind, and a smooth sea, the sun shining upon it, the sight was, as I thought, the most delightful that ever I saw.

I had slept well in the night, and was now no more seasick, but very cheerful, looking with wonder upon the sea that was so rough and terrible the day before, and could be so calm and so pleasant in so little time after. And now, lest my good resolutions should continue, my companion, who had indeed enticed me away, came to me. "Well, Bob" says he, "how do you do after it? I warrant you were frightened, weren't you, when it blew but a cap full of wind?" "A cap full do you call it?" said I. "It was a terrible storm." "A storm, you fool," replies he; "do you call that a storm? Why it was nothing at all; give us but a good ship and sea – room, and we think nothing of such a squall of wind as that; but you're but a fresh – water sailor, Bob: come, let us make a bowl of punch, and we'll forget all that. Do you see what charming weather it is now?" To make short this sad part of my story, we went the old way of all

有些习惯海上的生活了——虽然在那一整天里，我晕船仍然晕得厉害。傍晚时，天空晴朗，大风停止了，一个美丽的夜晚降临了，万里无云，红日西坠；第二天早晨，阳光灿烂，海面上风平浪静，我认为这是我所见过的最美丽的景色。

晚上，我睡得很香甜，也不再晕船了，现在我感觉很快乐，惊奇地望着先前还是狂怒的大海，现在却是那样的平静而美丽，我先前的那些决心又不那么强烈了。我的朋友在一边又怂恿我，说："怎么样，伙计，现在觉得好点儿了吗？那一场小风，估计你吓呆了。""你叫它小风吗？""我说，"那是一场可怕的大风暴。""那不算风暴，傻瓜，"他回答说，"你叫它风暴吗？那算什么！只要船只坚固，海面宽阔，这点儿小风算不了什么！你那样想是因为你是一个新水手，来，让我们喝一杯，就会忘记它，现在不是一个很好的天气吗？"简单地描绘一下这段伤心的故事，就是我们走了普通

sailors; the punch was made, and I was made drunk with it, and in that night's wickedness I drowned all my repentance, all my reflections upon my past conduct, and all resolutions for my fortune. In a word, as the sea returned to its smoothness of surface and settled calmness by the abatement of that storm, so the hurry of my thoughts being over, my fears and apprehensions of being swallowed up by the sea being forgotten, and the current of my former desires returned, I entirely forgot the vows and promises that I made in my distress. I found indeed some intervals of reflection, and the serious thoughts did, as it were, endeavor to return again sometimes; but I shook them off, and roused myself from them as it were from a distemper, and applying myself to drink and company, soon mastered the return of those fits, for so I called them, and I had in five or six days got as complete a victory over conscience as any young fellow that resolved not to be troubled with it could desire. But I was to have another trial for it still. If I would not take this for a deliverance, the next was to be such a one as the worst and most hardened wretch among us would confess both the danger and mercy.

水手们的老路。我们调好了酒，喝得酩酊大醉；那一晚的恶行把我对过去行动的全部悔恨，全部反省，以及对未来的全部决心，通通淹没了。和朋友多喝了几杯，感觉好多了，于是忘记了自己对过去行为的反思以及对未来的坚定信念。总之，当海面恢复了平静，我那慌乱的心情一过去，我那担心被海水吞下去的恐怖和畏惧一忘记，我的旧有的欲望又涌上我的心头。我完全忘记了自己在灾难中发过的誓言，虽然有时那些决心又会出现，我也是尽力把它们置诸脑后，全当是心情不好的缘故。我不断地喝酒、与朋友聊天，很快克服了这种恐惧，过了五六天，我良心的谴责也慢慢消退了。也因了这缘故，我命定要再受一次灾。如果我这一回不肯乘机悔改，下一次大祸当然就要变本加厉，就连世界上最坏的人、最天不怕地不怕的人遇见它，也要害怕、求饶。

Chapter 2   The Storm

The sixth day of our being at sea came into Yarmouth Roads; the wind having been contrary, and the weather calm, we had made but little way since the storm. Here we were obliged to come to an anchor, and here we lay, the wind continuing contrary for seven or eight days.

By this time it blew a terrible storm indeed; and now I began to see terror and amazement in the faces even of the seamen themselves. The master, though vigilant in the business of preserving the ship, yet as he went in and out of his cabin, I could hear him softly to himself say several times, "Lord, be merciful to us; we shall be all lost, we shall be all undone," and the like. During these first hurries, I was stupid, lying still in my cabin, which was in the steerage, and could not describe my temper. I could ill reassume the first penitence which I had so apparently trampled upon, and hardened myself again: I thought the bitterness of death had been past, and that this would be nothing like the first. But when the master himself came by me and said we should be all lost, I was dreadfully frightened. I got up out of my cabin, and looked; but such a dismal sight I never saw: the

第二章　暴风骤雨

我们在海上航行的第六天，来到了亚摩斯港湾，天气很平静，但海上一直吹着逆风。自暴风雨来临后，我们无法前进，最后不得不在这儿停航抛锚，逆风一直吹了七八天，我们也一直在这里呆着。

事实上这次刮了一场猛烈的暴风雨，我开始在海员们的脸上发觉到了恐惧与惊讶的表情。船长虽然在保护轮船上显得十分警惕，但当他进出他的船舱时，我几次听到他喃喃自语道："上帝啊，发发慈悲吧，我们会迷失方向的，让我们解脱吧！"等等。在这初始的慌乱中，我很迟钝，我一动不动地躺在船舱里，船舱处于统舱内，我几乎无法描述我当时的心情。我愚蠢地对这些忏悔毫不在乎，变得麻木不仁。我以为死亡的威胁已经过去，不会发生什么事的，不会再出现先前的那种严重情况。但当船长走到我身边说我们已迷失了方向时，我是那样的恐惧。我从船舱里爬起来，向外望去。我从来没见过如此令人恐惧的景

sea went mountains high, and broke upon us every three or four minutes. When I could look about, I could see nothing but distress round us: two ships that rid near had cut their masts by the board, being deep laden; and our men cried out that a ship which rid about a mile of us was foundered. Two more ships being driven from their anchors were run out of the roads to sea at all adventures, and that with not a mast standing. The light ships fared the best, as not much laboring in the sea; but two or three of them drove, and came close by us. Towards evening the mate boatswain begged the master of our ship to let them cut away the foremast, which he was very unwilling to do; but the boatswain protesting to him, that if he did not, the ship would founder, he consents; and when they had cut away the foremast, the mastermast stood so loose, shook the ship so much, they were obliged to cut her away also, and make a clear deck

Any one may judge what a condition I must be in all this, who was but a young sailor, and who had been in such a fright before but a little. But if I can express at this distance the thoughts I had about me at that time, I was in ten – fold more horror of mind upon account of my former convictions, and the having returned from them to the resolutions I had wickedly taken at first, than I was at death itself; and these, added to the terror of the

况，海水涨到山一般高，每隔三四分钟就会冲到我们的船上。当我向四周望去，看到的只是围绕着我们的灾难，两艘船，两艘在近旁行驶的船，上边的桅杆已折断，吃水很深。我们的人又大喊着说另一艘被冲出一海里远的轮船也沉没了。又有两艘船已脱锚，驶离了航线，正在往下沉，没有一个船桅能支撑得住。载重轻的船情况比较好些，在海上还不是很费力地航行，有两三艘在我们周围缓慢地行进着。到了黄昏时分，水手长乞求船长把前桅杆给切断，这是船长极不愿意做的事。但水手长说如不这样做，船将沉没。最后船长同意了。前桅杆切断后，主桅也开始松散了，船摇摆得厉害，最后只好把主桅杆也卸下来，整艘船只剩下光秃秃的甲板了。

像我这样一个没有经验的水手，以前遇见那样一点儿风浪还吓得不得了，现在处在这种情形之下，我那心情也就可想而知了。现在回忆起来，我当时对于自己悔罪之后重萌恶念的恐惧，比对死的恐惧还大十倍。这种恐惧，再加上风暴所给

storm, put me into such a condition, that I can by no words describe it. But the worst was not come yet: the storm continued with such fury, that the seamen themselves acknowledged they had never known a worse. We had a good ship, but she was deep laden, and wallowed in the sea, that the seaman every now and then cried out she would founder. It was my advantage in one respect that I did not know what they meant by founder, till I inquired. However, the storm was so violent that I saw what is not often seen, the master, the boatswain, and some others more sensible than the rest, at their prayers, and expecting every moment the ship would go to the bottom. In the middle of the night, and under all the rest of our distresses, one of the men that had been down on purpose to see, cried out, we had sprung a leak; another said there was four foot water in the hold. Then all hands were called to the pump. At that very word my heart, as I thought, died wit me, and I fell backyards off the side of my bed where I sat, into the cabin. However, the men roused me, and told me that I who was able to do nothing before, was as well able to pump as another; at which I stirred up, and went to the pump and very heartily. While this was going, the master seeing some light colliers, who, not able to ride out the storm, were obliged to slip and run away past our ship to

予我的恐惧，使我陷入一种无法用语言形容的境地。但最糟的情况还没到来，暴风雨仍在怒吼，海员们自己也不知道将要发生什么更糟的事。我们的船虽然是条好船，但它载重太大，在海上颠簸着，海员们不时地大喊它会沉掉。我的优势只表现在一个方面：我压根就不明白他们喊的沉船是怎么回事，向别人了解之后心里才知道了。然而，暴风雨是这样的猛烈，我从没遇到过这样的情形。船长、水手长还有另外几个海员比其他人都要明智，知道轮船随时都可能沉到海底，他们都在祈求上帝。午夜时分，看到大家心情都非常沮丧，一位船员下到舱里去，想了解一下那儿的情况。只听他大声叫喊，船进水了，另一个人在洞里说水已涨到四英尺高了。后来所有的人都接到命令去抽水。在那一刻，我的心与我一起死掉了，我坐着的身子向后倒去，从床沿掉下来，摔在了地上。然而有人把我唤醒，告诉我先前我什么事也做不了，现在可以和其他人一样去抽水。我被鼓动了起来，热心地去抽水，当我在做这一切的时候，船长看到一些小煤船因经不起风暴，

sea, ordered his men to fire a gun as a signal. I who knew nothing what that meant, was so surprised that I thought the ship had broken, or some dreadful thing happened. In a word I was so surprised that I fell down in a swoon. As this was a time when everybody had his own life to think of, nobody minded me, or what was become of me; but another man stepped up to the pump, and thrusting me aside with his foot, let me lie, thinking I had been dead, and it was a great while before I came to myself.

We worked on, but the water increasing in the hold, it was apparent that the ship would founder; and though the storm began to abate a little, yet as it was not possible she could swim till we might run into a port, so the master continued firing guns for help; and a light ship who had rid it out just ahead of us, ventured a boat out to help us. It was with the utmost hazard the boat came near us, but it was impossible for us to get on board, or for the boat to lie near the ship's side; till at last, the men rowing very heartily, and venturing their lives to save ours, our men cast them a rope over the stern with the buoy to it, and then veered it out a great length, which they, after great labor and hazard, took-hold of, and we hauled them close under our stern and got all into their boat. It was to no purpose for them or

不得不顺着风向海上飘去，要从我们的船边经过，便下令放一响枪，作为求救的讯号。我不知道那枪声意味着什么，大吃一惊，以为肯定是船坏了或发生了一些可怕的事情。总之，我惊骇万分，处于昏迷不醒中。这一刻每一个人都想的是自己的生命，没有人在意我的存在或死活。这时另一个人走进来，冲到水泵跟前，把我踢到一旁，让我躺在那里，还以为我已经死了，过了好大一会儿，我才苏醒过来。

　　我们工作着，同时海水从洞里不断涌入，很明显船即将沉没。虽然暴风雨开始减缓了一些，但这艘船是不可能支撑到下一个海港的。船长一直在鸣枪以寻求支援，这时有一艘轮船驶在我们前面脱离了险境，放出一只小船来营救我们，冒着极大的危险，这艘小船靠近了我们，但我们无法上去，小船也无法挨近。船员们用力地划着，他们冒着生命危险来救我们，我们的人把一根带浮标的绳子从船艉抛下了海，尽量把它放长，他们费了很大的劲儿，冒了很大的危险，终于抓住了绳子。我们将他们的船拉近我们的船艉，然后都跳进他们的船中。进入船中，我们以及他们的

us after we were in the boat to think of reaching to their own ship, so all agreed to let her drive, and only to pull her in towards shore as much as we could, and our master promised them that if the boat was staved upon shore he would make it good to their master; so partly rowing and partly driving, our boat went away to the northward, sloping towards the shore almost as far as Winterton – Ness.

We were not much more than a quarter of an hour out of our ship before we saw her sink, and then I understood for the first time what was meant by a ship foundering in the sea. I must acknowledge I had hardly eyes to look up when the seamen told me she was sinking; from that moment they rather put me into the boat than that I might be said to go in: my heart was as it were dead within me, partly with fright, partly with horror of mind, and the thoughts of what was yet before me.

While we were in this condition, the men yet laboring at the oars to bring the boat near the shore, we could see a great many people running along the shore to assist us when we should come near; but we made but slow way towards the shore, nor were we able to reach the shore, till, being past the light – house at Winterton, the shore falls off to the westward toward Cromer, and so the land broke off a little the violence of the wind: here

船员都知道无望靠拢他们的船了，都同意由他们驾驶，使尽平生力量把它划向岸边。我们的船长向他们保证如果船被海岸撞破，他会修好的。最后，一部分人划着，一部分人驾驶，颠簸着顺着海岸朝北驶去，几乎驶到了温特顿岬角。

我们离船不到一刻钟，就眼睁睁地看着它沉没了。这时我才第一次明白海上的"船沉"是怎么回事。老实说，当水手们告诉我大船要沉了的时候，我几乎无心去看它，因为那时节我与其说是自己走上了小艇，不如说是被人丢进了小艇。我的心似乎也和船一起沉没了，部分是由于害怕，也有些是因为脑海中的恐惧以及不知后边还会发生怎样的事情。

在这样的处境中，大家都飞桨荡橹，在使劲划着小船。能够看到许多人沿着岸边跑来帮助我们。当我们靠近时，行驶得是这样慢，我们简直无法登岸，直到通过温特顿的灯塔时，才在海岸朝着西边的克罗默安全上了岸。因为这儿的海岸

we got in, and, though not without much difficulty, got all safe on shore, and walked afterwards on foot to Yarmouth, where, as unfortunate men, we were used with great humanity, as well by the magistrates of the town, who assigned us good quarters, as by particular merchants and owners of ships, and had money given us sufficient to take us either to London or back to Hull, as we thought fit.

Had I now had the sense to have gone back to Hull, and have gone home, I had been happy, and my father had even killed the fatted calf for me; for hearing the ship I went away in was cast away in Yarmouth Roads, it was a great while before he had any assurance that I was not drowned. But my ill fate pushed me on now with an obstinacy that nothing could resist; and though I had several times loud calls from my reason and my more composed judgment to go home, yet I had no power to do it. I know not what to call this, nor will I urge that it is a secret overruling decree that hurries us on to be the instruments of our own destruction, even though it be before us, and that we rush upon it with our eyes open. Certainly nothing but some such decreed unavoidable misery attending, and which it was impossible for me to escape, could have pushed me forward against the calm reasonings and persuasions of my most retired

西倾，减弱了些许风势。虽然有些困难，总算安全到达。步行朝亚摩斯走，在那儿，作为不幸的人，我们得到了人道主义援助。那个镇上的治安法官给我们以极大的同情，他给我们安排了很好的栖身之地，一些商人和轮船主解囊相助，给我们足够的钱，或去伦敦，或回赫尔，由我们自己选择。

如果我当时聪明一点儿，回到赫尔或返回家里，我一定会很幸福，父亲准会为我杀了那头喂肥了的牛，因为我所乘的那艘船已在亚摩斯路那沉没了，而他是过了好久才确信我没有被淹死的。但厄运促使我固执地不想回家，任什么都阻止不了我的顽固决定。尽管好几次我理性地劝说自己做出了一些较平静的决断，要回家去，却都失败了——我无力执行自己的决定，我不知道这应该称之为什么，也不知是否有一种秘密的主宰命运的东西在催促着我们，使我们走向毁灭即便大限在即，我们也会睁着眼睛朝前冲。这种东西非同小可，而是一种无法避免的悲惨命运，我逃也逃不掉。它推波助澜，使我盲目地朝前走，违背了自己的内心深处的那种理智的思考和警示，与我

thoughts, and against two such visible instructions as I had met with in my first attempt.

My friend who had helped to harden me before, and who was the master's son, was now less forward than I. Looking very melancholy, and shaking his head, he asked me how I did, and told his father who I was, and how I had come this voyage only for a trial, in order to go farther abroad. His father, turning to me with a very grave and concerned tone, "Young man," says he, "you ought never to go to sea any more; you ought to take this for a plain and visible token that you are not to be a sea – faring man." "Why, sir," said I, "will you go to sea no more?" "That is another case," said he; "it is my calling, and therefore my duty; but as you made this voyage for a trial, you see what a taste Heaven has given you of what you are to expect if you persist; perhaps this is all befallen us on your account," continued he, "what are you? And on what account did you go to sea?" Upon that I told him some of my story; at the end of which he burst out with a strange kind of passion: "What had I done," says he, "that such an unhappy wretch should come into my ship? I would not set my foot in the same ship with you again for a thousand pounds." However, he afterwards talked very gravely to me, and exhorted me to go back to my father and not tempt Providence to my

第一次尝试出海时所接受的教训背道而驰。

　　我的朋友，船长的儿子曾那样地帮助和鼓动我，现在也有些畏缩不前了，他目光忧郁，不停地摇头。他问我将怎样做，把我介绍给他父亲，并告诉他父亲我随同这次出航只是出于好奇和新鲜，以便能到国外逛逛。他父亲非常严肃而关心地说："年轻人，你应把这作为一次教训，你不适合航海，永远都不要在海上漂泊了。""为什么，先生？"我问道，"难道你也不再出海了吗？""这是另一码子事，"他说，"这是对我的召唤，也是我的责任，你已尝试到了航海的滋味，应该看到上帝所给予你的这次机会，也许由于你的缘故，这次灾难才会降临到我们身上。"他继续问："那么，是什么原因促使你出来航海呢？"我告诉他一些关于我的故事，最后，他突然莫名其妙地激动了起来，说道："我究竟造了什么孽，竟然让这么个扫帚星上到了我的船上！怎么会是这么不幸的一艘船呢，再给我一千英镑，我也不会与你同行了。"后来他非常严肃地跟我谈了谈，劝我回到父

ruin; told me I might see a visible hand of Heaven against me. "And, young man," said he, "depend upon it if you do not go back, wherever you go, you will meet with nothing but disasters and disappointments, till your father's words are fulfilled upon you."

We parted soon after, and I saw him no more. As for me, having some money in my pocket, I traveled to London by land; and there, as well on the road, had many struggles with myself: what course of life I should take, and whether I should go home, or go to sea.

As to going home, shame opposed the best motions that offered to my thoughts; and it immediately occurred to me how I should be laughed at among the neighbors, and should be ashamed to see, not my father and mother only, but even everybody else. In this state of life, I remained some time, uncertain what measure to take. An irresistible reluctance continued to going home; and as I stayed a while, the remembrance of the distress I had been in wore off, and as that abated, the little motion I had in my desires to a return wore off with it, till at last I quite laid aside the thoughts of it, and looked out for a voyage.

That evil influence which carried me first away from my father's house, that hurried me into the wild notion of raising my fortune, and that impressed those conceits

亲那里，而且说上帝在反对我出航，否则我会毁掉自己的，他说，"年轻人，如果你坚持航行，执意不回家，那么不管你到哪儿，你将遇到的是灾难与失望，直到你父亲的话在你身上应验。"

我们不久便分开了，我也没有再见过他。我的衣兜里有一些钱，就从陆地去了伦敦。在路上，以及到了伦敦之后，我一直在与自己作斗争，我应该选择什么样的生活道路，回家？或是出海？

一想到回家，我深感羞耻，这种想法老和理智的念头作对。我立即想到邻居们一定会嘲笑我。我不仅羞于见父母，而且还担心会成为别人的笑柄。在这种情况下，我迟疑了一些时间，不知如何是好，可是有一种不可抗拒的力量阻止我回到家里。我呆了一些日子，痛苦的记忆慢慢减轻了，关于回归故乡的念头也随之烟消云散。最后，我摒弃了一切杂念，一心一意要扬帆于大海了。

当时那种让我第一次离开父亲，使我产生赚大钱的野心，使我想入非非，对别人的建议根本

so forcibly upon me as to make me deaf to all good advice, presented the most unfortunate of all enterprises to my view; and I went on board a vessel bound for the coast of Africa, or, as our sailors vulgarly call it, a voyage to Guinea.

Chapter 3   The Misfortunes

It was my great misfortune that in all these adventures I did not ship myself as a sailor, and it was always my fate to choose for the worse. It was my lot first of all to fall into pretty company in London, which does not always happen to such loose and unguided young fellows as I then was. I fell acquainted with the master of a ship who had been on the coast of Guinea, and who, having had very good success there, resolved to go again; and who, taking a fancy to my conversation, which was not all disagreeable at that time, hearing me say I had a mind to see the world, told me if I would go the voyage with him I should be at no expense; I should be his messmate and his companion, and if I could carry anything with me, I should have all the advantage of it that the trade would admit, and perhaps I might meet with some encouragement.

I embraced the offer. The captain was an honest

充耳不闻的邪恶力量，使我看上了一种最不幸的事业。后来，我登上了一艘驶往非洲海岸的轮船，海员们风趣地把这次航行叫去圭尼亚的旅游。

第三章　祸从天降

没有当过水手，这是我在所有历险中最大的不幸，也可能我时乖运蹇，命该如此。我在伦敦结交了一个朋友。这样的机会是像我这样放荡不羁、误入歧途的年轻小伙子很难碰到的。我与一位船长熟识了，他曾去过几内亚，到过那儿的海岸线，生意做得不错，决定再去一趟。他十分乐于与我交谈，在当时这种谈话还是令人愉快的。他听说我有周游世界的愿望，他说如果我能与他同行，无需任何花费，我将成为他的伙伴并与他共餐，如我能随便带点货，还能赚钱，或许会赚很多的钱。

我接受了他的提议，船长是个诚实和很容易

and plain – dealing man. I went the voyage with him, and carried a small fortune with me, which, by the disinterested honesty of my friend the captain, I increased very considerably; for I carried about 40 pounds. in such toys and trifles as the captain directed me to buy. This 40 pounds. I had mustered together by the assistance of some of my relations whom I corresponded with, and who, I believe, got my father, or at least my mother, to contribute so much as that to my first adventure.

This was the only voyage which I may say was successful in all my adventures, and which I owe to the integrity and honesty of my friend the captain, under whom I also got a competent knowledge of the mathematics, and the rules of the navigation, learned how to keep an account of the ship's course, take an observation, and, in short, to understand some things that were needful to be understood by a sailor; for, as he took delight to instruct me, I took delight to learn, and, in a word, this voyage made me both a sailor and a merchant; for I brought home five pounds nine ounces of gold dust for my adventure, which yielded me in London at my return, almost 300 pounds, and this filled me with those aspiring thoughts which have since so completed my ruin.

Yet even in this voyage I had my misfortunes too, particularly, that I was continually sick, being thrown

相处的人，我怀着一种去冒险的心态和船长一同出航，由于这位船长的正直无私，我赚了不少钱。因为在他的劝说下，我花了约四十镑买了些玩具和其他小玩意儿。这些钱是我用通信的方式靠几位亲戚的帮助筹划出来的，我想他们又是从我父亲或我母亲那里弄到的，送给我作第一次出海的资本。

在我所有的历险中，这是惟一一次成功的航行。这得归功于我那正直与诚实的船长朋友，在他的指引下我掌握了良好的数学知识以及航海的规则，也学会了怎样作航海记录、观察天象、辨别方向等。总之学到了一些做水手必要的基础知识。当然，他很乐意教导我，我也很高兴去学，总之，这次航海我既当了一名水手又成了一个商人，历经风险总算赚了五磅九盎司的金沙。回到伦敦，我把金沙兑换了三百多镑。这样我又踌躇满志起来，却也因此断送了我的一生。

然而即便在这次航行中，我也遇到了一些麻烦，我一直都晕船，由于天气太热，我患了重感

into a violent fever by the excessive heat of the climate; our principal trading being upon the coast, from the latitude of fifteen degrees north even to the line itself.

I was now set up for a Guinea trader; and my friend, to my great misfortune, dying soon after his arrival, I resolved to go the same voyage again, and I embarked in the same vessel with one who was his mate in the former voyage, and had now got the command of the ship. This was the unhappiest voyage that ever man made; for though I did not carry quite 100 pounds. of my new gained wealth, so that I had 200 pounds. left, which I lodged with my friend's widow, who was just to me, yet I fell into terrible misfortunes in this voyage; and the first was this: our ship, making her course towards the Canary Island, or rather between those islands and the African shore, was surprised in the gray of the morning by a Turkish rover of Sallee, who gave chase to us with all the sail she could make. We crowded also as much canvas as our yards would spread. but finding the pirate gained upon us, and would certainly come up with us in a few hours. We prepared; our ship having twelve guns, and the rogue eighteen. To cut short this melancholy part of our story, our ship being disabled, and three of our men killed, and eight wounded, we were obliged to yield, and were carried all prisoners into

冒，发高烧，我们主要在岸上做着贸易，从北纬15度一直到赤道附近都有生意可做。

我俨然成了一个做几内亚生意的商人，极为不幸的是，我的朋友回来后不久便去世了。我决定再出一次海，和上次的路线一样，我和他的一个同伴登上了上次那条船，并且拥有了那艘船的指挥权。这是人类历史上最不幸的一次航行，我只带了不到一百镑的货物，我把新获得的财富中剩余的二百镑存放在我朋友的寡妇那里，她对我公正无私。这是最不幸的一次航行，就是这次出航，使我陷入了极大的灾难中。事情的开端是这样的：我们的船朝着卡那利岛航行，或更确切地说在这些岛屿及非洲海岸间航行时，一个灰蒙蒙的早晨，我们遇上了一伙土耳其萨利海盗，他们扬帆加速追赶我们，我们也扯起帆开足马力竭力逃命。我们发现海盗航行的速度比我们快，几小时后，他们肯定会追上我们的船只。我们开始做战斗准备，我们的船上只有十二门炮，而那些海盗有十八门。我真不想给你们讲那血肉横飞的惨景。总之，我们的船失去了战斗力，抵挡不住，我们死了三个，伤了八个，不得不投降。我们和所有的犯人

Sallee, a port belong-ing to the Moors.

I was kept by the captain of the rover as his proper prize, and made his slave, being young and nimble, and fit for his business. At this surprising change of my circumstances, from a merchant to a miserable slave, I was perfectly overwhelmed; and now I looked back upon my father's prophetic discourse to me, that I should be miserable, and had none to relieve me, which, I thought, was now so effectually brought to pass, that I could not be worse; that now the hand of Heaven had overtaken me, and I was undone without redemption. But, alas! This was but a taste of the misery I was to go through.

As my new master had taken me home to his house, I was in hopes that he would take me with him when he went to sea again, believing that it would some time or other be his fate to be taken by a Spanish or Portuguese man – of – war, and that then I should be set at liberty. But this hope of mine was soon taken away; for when he went to sea, he left me on shore to look after his little garden, and do the common drudgery of slaves about his house; and when he came home again from his cruise, he ordered me to lie in the cabin to look after the ship.

Here I meditated nothing but my escape, and what method I might take to effect it, but found no way that had the least probability in it, for I had nobody to com-

一起被囚运到萨利，一个属于摩尔人的港口。

因我年轻伶俐，就被这群海盗的首领作为他的战利品留下了，当了他的奴隶，我年轻，手脚麻利，很适合为他做事。我的境况发生了巨大变化，从一个富有的商人沦为一个可悲的奴隶，我真是悲痛欲绝。现在我回想起父亲对我说的那些具有先见之明的话，即我应该受苦难，且不会解脱，简直灵验极了。我的情况糟得不能再糟了。我既然受到了上帝的惩罚，任何人也不会解救我脱离苦海。天哪！谁料想到这才是我苦难的开始。

当我的新主人带我到了他的房子，我还存有一丝希望，就是他能带我一起出海，或是某一天，命运会安排他被西班牙或葡萄牙人在战斗中打死，那样我就可以获得自由了。但我的这个希望不久就破灭了，因为每当他出海的时候，就留我在岸上照看他的小花园，或做一些最乏味的事情，作为奴隶为他效力。当他从海上回来后，他又命令我睡在船舱里替他看船。

这时候我惟一想的就是如何逃走，我在思量哪一种方法更有效一些，但却没找到任何可行的办法，因为我没有同我商量的人。就这样过了两

municate it to, so that for two years, though I often pleased myself with the imagination, yet I never had the least encouraging prospect of putting it in practice.

After about two years an odd circumstance presented itself, which put the old thought of making some attempt for my liberty again in my head: my patron lying at home longer than usual, without fitting out his ship, which, as I heard, was for want of money, he used constantly, once or twice a week, sometimes oftener, if the weather was fair, to take the ship's pinnace, and go out into the road a fishing; and as he always took me and a young man with him to row the boat, we made him very merry, and I proved very dexterous in catching fish: insomuch, that sometimes he would send me with a Moor, one of his kinsmen, to catch a dish of fish for him.

It happened one time, that going a fishing in a stark calm morning, a fog rose so thick, that though we were not half a league from the shore, we lost sight of it; and rowing we knew not where or which way, we labored all day, and all the next night, however, we got well in again, though with a great deal of labor, and some danger; for the wind began to blow pretty fresh in the morning, but particularly we were all very hungry.

We went frequently out a fishing, and as I was most dexterous to catch fish for him, he never went without

年，虽然我常常用想象的办法自慰，然而我却没有一点勇气把它们付诸实施。

两年以后，一次奇怪的机会使我那些企图逃跑以获得自由的念头又复苏了。我的主人在家的时间比往常更长了，没有装备他的船。我听说是因为缺钱。他过去经常出海，每周一两次，有时甚至更频繁。如果天气好的话，他带上轮船的小艇，到外边去钓鱼，他总是让我和一个年轻人去划小船，我们使他很快乐，在抓鱼的时候，我表现得十分灵巧。因此，有时他会派我跟他的一个摩尔人亲戚出海为他捕鱼吃。

有 次，那是一个风平浪静的早晨，我们出去钓鱼，雾特别大，虽然刚驶出半海里远，我们却看不到海岸了。我们胡乱地划着，不知到哪儿去，也不知朝哪儿划，整整划了一天一夜，最后，我们费了很大的劲，冒了很大的危险，总算踏上了归途。因为那天早晨风吹得很硬，而且我们都饿得要命，但总算是划了回来。

我们经常出去钓鱼，由于我捕鱼的技巧特别好，所以他出去时总带着我。一天，他让我为他

me. One day he ordered me to get ready three fuses with powder and shot, for he wanted to go out for pleasure with two or three Moors. I got all things ready as he directed, and waited the next morning with the boat washed clean. Then my patron came and told me his guests had put off going, upon some business that fell out, and ordered me with the man and boy, as usual to go and catch them some fish, for his friends were to sup at his house.

This moment my former notions of deliverance darted into my thoughts, for now I found I was about to have a little ship at my command; and my master being gone, I prepared to furnish myself, not for a fishing business, but for a voyage; though I knew not, neither did I so much as consider, where I should steer; for anywhere to get out of that place was my way.

My first contrivance was to make a pretense to speak to this Moor, to get something for our subsistence on board; for I told him we must not presume to eat our patron's bread; so he brought a large basket biscuit of their kind, and three jars with fresh water, into the boat. I knew where my patron's case of bottles stood, and I conveyed them into the boat while the Moor was on shore. I conveyed also a great lump of bees – wax into the boat, which weighed above half a hundredweight,

准备三根导火索以及弹药，因为他想与他的几个摩尔朋友出去游乐。我按他的指示把所有的东西都准备好了，把船也洗干净了，一直等到第二天早晨。后来我的主人告诉我他的客人去不成了，由于商业上出了些问题。所以他就派我、那个青年人和摩尔男孩，像往常一样出去为他捕鱼，因为他的朋友要在这里吃晚饭。

机不可失，时不再来。强烈的逃生欲望控制了我，现在我即将有一艘小船听我指挥，我的主人离去了，我为自己准备了一些必需品，不是为钓鱼，而是为一次航行，虽然我并不知道，也没有去细想我该向哪个方向行驶，也不知道哪儿才是我逃离的道路。

我的第一个计划就是假装和这个摩尔男孩说话，获取我们在甲板上生存所需的东西。我对他说我们不能吃我们主人的面包，所以他带上了一大篮子他们吃的那种饼干，三罐淡水，我知道主人装酒的箱子所在的地方，趁着摩尔人到岸上的时候，偷偷把它运到了船上。我又运了一块蜂蜡到船里，大约五十公斤重，还有一卷尼龙线，一

with a parcel of twine or thread, a hatchet, a saw, and a hammer, all which were of great use to us afterwards; especially the wax to make candles. Another trick I tried upon him, which he innocently came into also. "Moley," said I, "our patron's guns are on board the boat; can you not get a little powder and shot, we may kill some birds for ourselves," and accordingly he brought a great leather pouch which held about a pound and a half of powder, and another with shot, at the same time I had found some powder of my master's in the great cabin, with which I filled one of the large bottles in the case, and thus furnished with everything needful, we sailed out of the port to fish. The wind blew from the N. N.E. which was contrary to my desire; for had it blown southerly I had been sure to have made the coast of Spain, and at least reached the bay of Cadiz; but my resolutions were, blow which way it would, I would be gone from that horrid place where I was, and leave the rest to fate.

After we had fished some time we caught nothing, for when I had fish on my hook I would not pull them up, that he might not see them, I said to the Moor, "This will not do; our master will not be thus served; we must stand farther off," he thinking no harm agreed, and being in the head of the boat set the sails; and as I had

把斧头，一把锯，一把榔头。所有这些在以后都派上了很大的用场，特别是用蜂蜡制成的蜡烛。我又对他施了一个小小的诡计，他也相信了，我说，"伙计，主人的枪放在船上，你可以弄些弹药来，我们可以射几只鸟自己吃。"因而他带了一个大皮革袋，可装约一磅半的火药，另一个装着枪弹。与此同时，我在大的船舱里找到一些主人用的火药，我装了一大瓶。就这样，我们准备好了一些所需的东西，便驶出海港去捕鱼。风从东北方向吹来，这与我的愿望相反，因为如果它向南吹，我一定会朝着西班牙海岸的方向驶去，至少会到卡迪斯湾，我最后决定，不管风朝哪边吹，我也要逃离那个可怕的地方，其余的一切听天由命吧。

我们一边航行着，一边钓着鱼，但没有捕到一条。因为当有鱼咬鱼钩时，我却不收鱼线，我对摩尔小孩说："这恐怕不行，钓不到鱼，主人吃不上鱼会不高兴的，我们必须划得远一些。"他没有意识到什么恶意，便同意了，他站在船头便起

the helm I ran the boat out near a league farther, and then brought her to as if I would fish, when giving the boy the helm, I stepped forward to where the Moor was, and making as if I stooped for something behind him, I took him by surprise with my arm under his legs, and tossed him clear overboard into the sea. He rose immediately, for he swam like a cork, and calling to me, begged to be taken in: told me he would go all over the world with me. He swam so strong after the boat that he nearly caught up with me. My boat was slow as there was no wind. I stepped into the cabin, and fetching one of the fowling – pieces, I presented it at him, and told him I had done him no hurt, and if he would be quiet I would do him none: "but," said I, "you swim well enough to reach the shore, and the sea is calm; make the best of your way to shore, and I will do you no harm, but if you come near the boat I'll shoot you through the head; for I am resolved to have my liberty." So he turned himself about and swam for the shore, and I made no doubt but that he reached it with ease, for he was an excellent swimmer.

I could have been content to have taken this Moor with me, and have drowned the boy, but there was no venturing to trust him. When he was gone I turned to the boy, who they called Xury, and said to him, "Xury, if

航了。当我拿到舵柄，我一口气使船开出一海里远，做出要钓鱼的样子，当把舵柄交给那个摩尔男孩时，我朝那个年轻人走过去，装出我要俯身在他后面寻找东西，我用胳膊一掀他的大脚下方，猛地把他扔进海里。他立刻浮出水面，就像一只海鸟一样，喊叫着，乞求我把他拽上去，并告诉我他将忠实于我，永远追随我。他在船后拼命地游着，眼看就要追上我，这时没一丝风，船走得很慢，我走进船舱，取了一把鸟枪，瞄准他，并告诉他我并没有伤害他的意思。如果他停止追赶，我不会伤害他的。我说，"既然你游得这么棒，你完全可以安全到岸，这会儿海上风平浪静，尽你最大能力往岸上游，我不会伤害你。但如果你接近这艘船，我将射穿你的头颅，因为我已决定去寻找我的自由了。"于是他转过身向岸上游去，我毫不怀疑他能轻快地游到岸上去，因为他是一名出色的游泳能手。

要是带上那个年轻人，而不是这个小男孩，我会更满足的，我完全可以淹死这个小男孩，但没有必要去冒信赖那个年轻人的险。当那个年轻人消失之后，我转向这个男孩，他叫埃瑟利，我

you will be faithful to me I'll make you a great man; but if you will not stroke your face to be true to me, I must throw you into the sea too;" the boy smiled in my face, and spoke so innocently that I could not mistrust him; and swore to be faithful to me, and go all over the world with me.

While I was in view of the Moor that was swimming, I stood directly to sea with the boat, rather stretching to windward: that they might think me gone towards the Straits' mouth, for who would have supposed we sailed on to the southward to the truly Barbarian coast, where whole nations of Negroes were sure to surround us with their canoes, and destroy us; where we could never once go on shore but we should be devoured by savage beasts, or more merciless savages of human kind?

Chapter 4　Escape and Rescue

As soon as it grew dusk in the evening, I changed my course, and steered directly south, bending my course a little toward the east. We saw no people.

Yet such was the fright and the dreadful apprehensions I had of falling into the hands of Moors. I would not stop, or go on shore, or come to an anchor. The wind

对他说："埃瑟利，如果你忠实于我，我可以把你造就成有头有脸的人，但如果你背叛我，我也会把你扔进海里，像那个人一样。"这个男孩笑了笑，笑得是那样纯真无邪，我不能不信任他了，他发誓要对我忠实，并跟随我到天涯海角。

站在船艏，看着那个青年拼命向岸边游去。我迎着清风伸了伸腰。他们也许认为我正朝海峡角行驶，因为他们认为我们朝南行驶时，一定会到达巴巴利湾，在那里所有的黑人肯定会用他们的独木舟把我们团团包围，然后把我们消灭，在那里我们将永远上不了岸，且会被凶猛的野兽所生吞，或被最残酷的野人所活咽。

第四章　九死一生

夜幕刚一降临，我即改变航道，径直向南驶去，然后稍稍偏东。前面看不到一个人影。

不过最令我恐惧和担心的莫过于落到摩尔人手里。我不敢停留、上岸或停泊，只能一直向前。

continued fair till I had sailed in that manner five days, and the wind shifted to the southward, I concluded also that if any of their vessels were in chase of me, they also would now give over; so I ventured to make the coast, and come to an anchor in the mouth of a little river. The principal thing I wanted was fresh water. We came into a creek in the evening, resolving to swim on shore as soon as it was dark. At dusk, we heard such dreadful noises of the barking, roaring, and howling of wild creatures, that the poor boy was ready to die with fear, and begged me not to go on shore till day. But we might see men by day, who would be as bad to us as those beasts. They made such hideous howlings and yellings that I never indeed heard the like.

Xury was dreadfully frightened, and indeed me too; but we were both more frightened when we heard one of these mighty creatures come swimming towards our boat. We could not see him, but we might hear him by his blowing to be a monstrous huge and furious beast. Poor Xury cried to me to weigh the anchor and row away. "No," says I, "Xury, we can slip our cable with a buoy to it and go off to sea; they cannot follow us far." I had no sooner said so, but I perceived the creature within two oars' length. However I immediately stepped to the cabin – door, and taking up my gun fired at him, upon

这样航行了五天后，风仍然轻轻地吹着，但已转南。我断定如果有船只在追我，那这些船也一定早就放弃了追踪。我大胆地靠近一个海岸，并在一个小河口处停泊下来。现在我最需要的是淡水。傍晚时分，我们驶入一条小溪，决意天一黑便游到岸上去取水。夜幕降临后，我们却听到了野兽的此起彼伏的狂吠声、咆哮声和嚎叫声，令人毛骨悚然。可怜的男孩怕得要死，请求我等到天亮再上岸去。但白天我们又可能遇上人，他们会像野兽一样对我们构成威胁，并发出我从未听到过的可怖的喊叫声。

埃瑟利害怕极了，我也确实如此，当听到一只巨兽游向我们的船只时，我俩就更害怕了。我们虽然看不见它，但从呼吸中能听得出那是一只凶猛的巨兽。可怜的埃瑟利哭喊着让我起锚将船划走。我回答说："不行！我们可以将缆绳系上浮标扔到海里，然后将船划到大海深处。那些野兽游不了那么远。"我话音刚落，就觉察到那家伙游到了离船两桨远的地方。我飞速跨入船舱的门，

which he immediately turned about and swam towards the shore again.

But it is impossible to describe the horrible noises, and hideous cries and howlings, that were raised. This convinced me that there was no going on shore for us in the night upon that coast, and how to venture on shore in the day was another question too; for to have fallen into the hands of any of the savages, had been as bad as to have fallen into the hands of lions and tigers.

Be that as it would, we were obliged to go on shore somewhere or other for water. Xury offered to go and I was greatly moved. I asked him why he would go. The boy answered with so much affection that made me love him ever after. Says he, "If wild men come, they eat me, you go away." "Well, Xury," said I, "we will both go, and if the wild men come, we will kill them: they shall eat neither of us."

So we started off to look for water. The boy saw a low place about a mile off and rambled to it, and by and by I saw him come running towards me. I thought he was pursued by some savage, or frightened by some wild beast, so I ran forward to help him; but when I came nearer to him, I saw something hanging over his shoulders, which was a creature that he had shot, like a hare, but different in color, with longer legs. But the great joy

操起枪朝它射击。它立刻掉转头，又向着岸边游了回去。

四周是难以描述的可怕的嚎叫声，这声音越来越大。这让我确信黑夜里是不能沿着这条海岸走了。而白天如何上岸也是个问题。因为落入野人之手如同落入狮子和老虎之口一样糟糕。

虽然如此，我们还是必须上岸找水。埃瑟利提出要去，这让我很是感动，我问他为什么要去，他充满关爱的回答让我从此喜欢上了他。他说："如果野人来了，让他们吃我好了，你跑掉就是了。"我说："如果野人来了，我们都跑，假如他们撵上来，我们就杀死他们。他们休想吃掉我们任何一个。"

就这样我们启程去找水。埃瑟利在大约一英里远的地方看到一处低洼之地，他便朝着那里走去。不一会儿，我便看到他向我跑来。我猜想一定是野人在追赶他或是野兽吓坏了他，就跑过去帮助他。当我走近他时，却看到他肩上扛着什么东西。原来是他刚捕杀的猎物，看上去像一只野兔，而颜色却与野兔不同，腿也较野兔长些。埃

that poor Xury came with, was that he had found good water, and no wild men.

As I had been one voyage to this coast before, I knew very well that the islands of the Canaries, and the Cape de Verde lay not far off the coast. But as I had no instruments I did not know what latitude we were in. Otherwise I might now easily have found some of these islands. By the best of my calculation, that place lies waste, and uninhabited, except by wild beasts. The Negroes had abandoned it, and gone farther south for fear of the Moors; and the Moors did not think it worth inhabiting, by reason of its barrenness; and indeed both forsook it because of the prodigious number of tigers, lions, leopards, and other furious creatures which harbor there; and indeed for near a hundred miles together upon this coast, we saw nothing but a waste uninhabited country by day; and heard nothing but howlings and roarings of wild beasts by night.

Several times I was obliged to land for fresh water after we had left this place; and once in particular. One day early in the morning, Xury saw a dreadful monster on the side of a hillock fast asleep. It was a terrible great lion that lay on the side of the shore, under the shade of the hill. "Xury," says I, "go on shore and kill him." Xury looked frightened, and said, "Me kill! He eats me

瑟利带来的最令人欣喜的消息是他找到了水而没遇上野人。

由于我过去航海时曾经来过这个海岸，因此我非常清楚，卡那利的岛屿以及佛得角就位于距离海岸不远的地方。由于我们没有任何仪器，因此无法得知我们所处的纬度。要不然我会毫不费力地找到一些这里的岛屿。我能测算到的是，我们处于一个荒无人烟，只有野兽栖息的地方。黑人曾放弃了此地，他们因惧怕摩尔人而向南深入。而摩尔人看到这寸草不生之地也认为不值一住。不过此地被两度放弃的真正原因是隐藏于此的大群老虎、狮子、豹子及其他猛兽。确实，在沿岸总共近百英里内，白天看到的只是一片荒芜的土地，夜晚听到的只是野兽的咆哮。

离开此地后，几次我不得不上岸找水。有一次，一大清早，埃瑟利看到一个可怕的庞然大物正躺在山边熟睡。那是一只奇大无比的狮子正躺在岸边山的背阴处。我说："埃瑟利，上岸去杀死它。"埃瑟利满脸恐惧地说："什么？我杀它？它

at one mouth." I said no more to the boy, but bade him lie still; and took our biggest gun, and loaded it with a good charge of powder, and with two slugs, and laid it down; then I loaded another gun with two bullets; and the third, for we had three pieces, I loaded with five smaller bullets. I took the best aim I could with the first piece, to have shot him into the head, but he lay so with his leg raised a little above his nose, that the slugs hit his leg about the knee, and broke the bone. He started up growling at first, but finding his leg broke, fell down again, and then got up upon three legs, and gave the most hideous roar that ever I heard. I was a little surprised that I had not hit him on the head; however, I took up the second piece immediately, and though he began to move off, fired again, and shot him into the head, and had the pleasure to see him drop, and make but little noise, but lay struggling for life.

This was game indeed to us, but this was no food: and I was very sorry to lose three charges of powder and shot upon a creature that was good for nothing to us. However, Xury said he would have some of him; so he went on board, and took the hatchet. He could not cut off his head, but he cut off a foot, and brought it with him, and it was a monstrous great one.

I bethought myself, however, that perhaps the skin

一口就能把我吞掉。"我没再说别的，只吩咐他躺着别动。我拿出最大的一支枪，将火药装满，又装入两颗子弹后放好，接着又给另一支枪装入两颗子弹，然后又装第三支枪。我们只有三支枪，我给第三支枪装入五粒较小的子弹，我用第一支枪瞄准目标，想击中它的头部，结果却击伤了腿骨，它卧着的时候把腿抬得高高的，护着鼻子。起初它怒吼着想起身站立起来，但有条腿坏了，随即就倒了下去。很快它又用三条腿支撑着站了起来，发出一阵我从未听到过的最为骇人的咆哮声。未能击中它的头部让我有点紧张，但我迅速举起了第二支枪，虽然看到它在移动，想溜掉，我还是再次开了火。这次打中了它的头。我很得意地看着它倒了下去，发出一阵阵微弱的呻吟，垂死挣扎着。

这家伙对我们来说确是一只猎物，但却不能食用。我很懊恼损失了三发火药，却打死一个毫无用处的东西。埃瑟利说他要取一些部位来。他上船去拿了斧头，想砍下狮子头却没有成功，但他砍下一只爪子带了回来，那真是一只极其硕大的狮爪哪。

我暗自思忖，这家伙的一张皮或许能对我们

of him might one way or other be of some value to us; and I resolved to take off his skin, if I could. Xury was much the better workman at it, for I knew very ill how to do it. Indeed it took us up both the whole day but at last we got the hide off him, and spreading it on the top of our cabin, the sun effectually dried it in two days' time, and it afterwards served me to lie upon.

After this stop, we made on to the southward continually for ten or twelve days, living very sparing on our provisions, which began to abate very much, and going no oftener into the shore than we were obliged to for fresh water: my design in this was, to make the river Gambia or Senegal, where I was in hope to meet with some European ship; and if I did not, I knew not what course I had to take, but to seek for the Islands, or perish there among the Negroes. I knew that all the ships from Europe, which sailed either to the coast of Guinea or to Brazil, or to the East Indies, made this Cape, or those Islands; and, in a word, I put the whole of my fortune upon this single point, either that I must meet with some ship or must perish.

When I had pursued this resolution about ten days longer, I began to see that the land was inhabited. We saw people stand upon the shore to look at us; we could also perceive they were quite black, and stark naked. I

有些用处，我决定如能办到的话就将它的皮剥下来。埃瑟利干这活儿比我在行多了，我真不知该如何下手。我们俩花了整整一天的工夫最终将皮剥了下来，把它摊开晾在我们的木屋顶上。两天后即被太阳晒干了，后来这张皮供我睡觉时享用。

这次停留后，我们在以后的十几天继续南行，省吃俭用。因为我们的东西在很快减少，而且除了必须去找水外已很少上岸。之所以如此是希望赶到赞比亚或塞内加尔河，指望在那儿能遇到欧洲的船只。如果遇不上，我就不知该走哪条航道了，而只能去寻找那些群岛，或在那里死于黑人之手。这些来自欧洲的船只，它们或驶往几内亚海岸，或驶往巴西或东印度群岛，都要经过这个海角或这些群岛。用一句话来说就是：我将自己的整个命运都押在这上面：要么遇上渡船，要么葬身海底。

在我下定这个决心的十天后，我终于看见一个有人烟的地方。我们看到那里的人们站在岸上注视着我们，可以看见他们皮肤很黑，身体赤裸

observed they had no weapons in their hands except one, who had a long slender stick. So I at a distance talked with them by signs as well as I could; and particularly made for something to eat: they beckoned to me to stop my boat, and they would fetch me some meat; upon this I lowered the top of my sail, and two of them ran up into the country, and in less than half an hour came back, and brought with them two pieces of dry flesh and some corn, we were willing to accept it but how to come at it was our next dispute, for I was not for venturing on shore to them, and they were as much afraid of us; but they took a safe way for us all, for they brought it to the shore and laid it down, and went and stood a great way off till we fetched it on board, and then came close to us again.

We made signs of thanks to them, for we had nothing to make them amends; but an opportunity offered that very instant to oblige them wonderfully; for while we were lying by the shore, came two mighty creatures, one pursuing the other with great fury, from the mountains towards the sea: whether it was the male pursuing the female, or whether they were in sport or in rage, we could not tell, any more than we could tell whether it was usual or strange, but I believe it was the latter; because, in the first place, those ravenous creatures seldom appear but in the night; and in the second place, we found the

着。我发现他们中除有一个手握细长的棍子外，其余都没带武器。我远远地尽量用手势与他们交谈着，还特别做出要些东西吃的手势，他们示意我们停船，然后去为我们拿些肉来。于是我降下船帆。有两人向村子跑去，不到半小时即返了回来，带回两块干肉和一些玉米。我们当然想要这些东西，但如何能拿到它却成了我们的一个问题。因为我不能上岸走近他们，他们也同样害怕我们。后来他们采取了一个安全之策，即他们将吃食放到岸上后远远地走开，等到我们将东西带到船上后，他们再过来，再次向我们跟前靠拢。

我们打着手势向他们表示感谢，除此之外我们没有任何东西去回报他们，这时，一个偶然的机会使得我们很快如愿以偿。当时我们正躺在岸上，看见两只巨兽在向我们跑来。其中一只愤怒地追赶着另一只，从山那儿跑到海边来。我们不晓得是雄兽在追赶雌兽，还是它们在进行比赛，或是在盛怒中，更不知这种事情是寻常之事还是很少见到，不过我认为一定是后一种情况。首先，这些饥饿的野兽只在夜晚出现，否则很少露面。

people terribly frightened, especially the women. The man that had the lance or dart did not fly from them, but the rest did, however, as the two creatures ran directly into the water, they did not seem to offer to fall upon any of the Negroes, but plunged themselves into the sea, and swam about as if they had come for their diversion. At last one of them began to come nearer our boat than at first I expected, but I lay ready for him, for I had loaded my gun with all possible expedition. As soon as he came fairly within my reach, I fired, and shot him directly into the head and he died instantly.

It is impossible to express the astonishment of these poor creatures at the noise and the fire of my gun; some of them were even ready to die for fear, and fell down as dead with the very terror. But when they saw the creature dead, and sunk in the water, and that I made signs to them to come to the shore, they took heart and came to the shore, and began to search for the creature. I found him by his blood staining the water; and by the help of a rope, which I slung round him, and gave the Negroes to haul, they dragged him on shore, and found that it was a most curious leopard, spotted and fine to an admirable degree, and the Negroes held up their hands with admiration to think what it was I had killed him with.

再者我发现人们十分害怕，特别是妇女。除了那个持有长叉和飞镖的人之外，其余的人都飞也似的躲开了。那两个野兽径直向水里奔去，跳入海中，似乎没打算进攻那些黑人。它们一头扎入大海，在水中游来游去，好像是来消遣的。令我始料不及的是其中一个家伙越来越靠近我们的船只。我已准备好随时去对付它。我以最快的速度给枪里装上火药。它一进入射程，我即开了火。子弹直射入它的头部，那家伙很快便死了。

我无法用文字表达出那些可怜的黑人们在听到枪声以及看见枪筒里喷出的火光时的震惊程度。有些人吓得倒在地上，就像死人一样，但当看到野兽已死，沉入水里时，又看到我用手势示意他们到岸边来，他们这才振作精神来到岸边，开始寻找那只野兽的尸体。我看见海水都被血染红了，随即发现了那只野兽，用一根绳子将它捆上，然后把绳头交给几个黑人，让他们将尸体拉上岸。那是一只最奇特的豹子，漂亮的花斑令人赞叹。那些黑人举起手向我表示称赞，好像在想我是用什么将它打死的。

The other creature, frightened with the flash of fire and the noise of the gun, swam on shore, and ran up directly to the mountains from whence they came. I found quickly the Negroes were for eating the flesh of this creature, so I was willing to have them take it as a favor from me. Though they had no knife, yet with a sharpened piece of wood they took off his skin as readily. They offered me some of the flesh, which I declined, but I made signs for the skin, which they gave me very freely, then I held out one of my jars to them, turning it bottom upward, to show that it was empty and that I wanted to have it filled. They called immediately to some of their friends, and filled them all three.

I was now furnished with roots and corn and water; and leaving my friendly Negroes, I made forward for about eleven days more, without offering to go near the shore, till I saw plainly land; then I concluded that this was the Cape de Verde. It was at a great distance and I could not tell what I had best do, for if I should be taken with a fresh of wind I might not reach it.

In this dilemma, as I was very pensive, I stepped into the cabin and set me down. Xury was having the helm, when suddenly the boy cried out, "Master, master, a ship with a sail!" and the foolish boy was frightened out of his wits, thinking it must be some of his

另一只野兽，被火光和枪声吓坏了，很快游上岸，径直跑回到山上去了。我很快发觉黑人们想要吃这家伙的肉，我很情愿让他们拿去作为我的一点心意。虽然他们没有刀子，但他们用一块削好的木片很快将豹皮剥了下来。他们给我一些肉但我没有要。我示意要豹皮，他们很乐意地给了我。我拿出一个罐子，将罐口朝下，示意它是空的，我想将它装满。他们很快叫来一些朋友，将三个罐子全部装满了水。

现在我有了植物的根、玉米和水，离开了友好的黑人们。我又航行了大约有十一天，直到清楚地看到平地才敢靠岸。我估计这大概就是佛得角了。但距离我们还很遥远，我也不知道该怎么办才好。因为要是一阵风将我们吹走，我们就无法到达那里了。

我进退维谷，愁眉不展，走进船舱坐了下来。埃瑟利在掌舵。这时突然听到他的喊声："主人，主人，我看见一艘带帆的船。"这个笨家伙被吓得神经有点错乱，他认为是他主人派的船来追我们

master's ships sent to pursue us, when I knew we were far enough out of their reach. I jumped out of the cabin, and immediately saw that it was a Portuguese ship bound for the coast of Guinea for Negroes. But when I observed the course she steered, I was soon convinced they were bound some other way, and did not design to come any nearer to the shore; upon which I stretched out to sea as much as I could, resolving to speak with them if possible.

With all the sail I could make, I found I should not be able to come in their way, but they would be gone by before I could make any signal to them. I made a waft of my patron's flag to them for a signal of distress, and fired a gun. They saw the smoke, though they did not hear the gun, so upon these signals they shortened sail and lay by for me, and in about three hours' time I came up with them.

They asked me what I was, in Portuguese, and in Spanish, and in French; but I understood none of them. At last a Scottish sailor on board, called to me, and I answered him, and told him I was an Englishman, that I had made my escape out of slavery from the Moors at Sallee. Then they bade me come on board, and very kindly took me in, and all my goods.

的。当时我知道我们早已到了他永远都追不上的地方了。我跳出船舱，起先认为那是一艘驶往几内亚海岸去运黑奴的葡萄牙船，但当我仔细观察它远行的航道时，我才知道是去其他地方的，根本就没打算靠近海岸。我用力将船离岸驶入海中，决心可能的话就与他们搭上话。

我满帆航行，却发现我无法截住他们，他们会在我作出示意前消失在我的视野之中。我扬起一面主人用过的信号旗向他们发出求救信号，并放了一枪。他们虽然没听到枪响，但却看见了硝烟。他们对这些信号做出反应，放下船帆，停下来等我们。三小时后，我赶上了他们。

他们问我是谁，先用葡萄牙语，然后用西班牙语，后又用法语，但我都听不懂。最后一个苏格兰水手冲我喊，我答应他，告诉他我是英国人，我不愿做奴隶，从萨利的摩尔人手中逃出。他们招呼我上船，好心地将我以及我的东西都一同载上。

Chapter 5　My Plantation

It was inexpressible joy to me that I was thus delivered from such a miserable and almost hopeless condition and immediately offered all I had to the captain of the ship, as a return for my deliverance; but he generously told me he would take nothing from me.

My boat was a very good one and he told me he would buy it. I told him he had been so generous to me in everything that I could not offer to make any price of the boat, but left it entirely to him, but he offered me some money for my boy Xury. He said that he would set him free in ten years, if he turned Christian. We had a very good voyage to Brazil, and arrived in All – Saints – Bay, in about twenty – two days after. And now I was once more delivered from the most miserable of all conditions of life, and what to do next with myself I was now to consider. What I was willing to sell he bought, such as the case of bottles, two of my guns, and a piece of the lump of bees – wax, the leopard's and the lion's skin and made a lot of money all my cargo, and with this stock I went on shore in Brazil.

I had not been long here, but was recommended to the house of a good honest man who had a plantation and

第五章　觅食果腹

我从那样一个痛苦得几乎令人绝望的境地中被解救出来，心里别提多高兴了。我立即将我所有的东西都送给船长，作为回报。但他豪爽地对我说什么都不要。

我那条船很不错，船长说他要买下来。我对他说他一直待我那样慷慨，事事照料我，我的船就不要钱白送他了，把船留给他使用。不过他付钱买下了埃瑟利，并说如果他信奉了基督教，十年后就还他自由。我们顺利地航行至巴西，二十四天后到达奥森茨海湾。现在我又一次从生活中最悲苦的境况中解脱出来，下一步自己该怎么办是我当前考虑的问题。他买下了我想卖的东西，有一箱瓶子，两支枪，一块蜂蜡，豹子和狮子的毛皮。这些货还卖了不少钱。带着这些钱，我在巴西上了岸。

我已好久没有到过这里了，我被引见给一个好心厚道的人。他有一个种植园及一个制糖作坊，

a sugar house; I lived with him some time, and acquainted myself by that means with the manner of their planting and making of sugar; and seeing how well the planters lived, and how they grew rich suddenly, I resolved, if I could get license to settle there, I would turn planter among them, resolving in the mean time to find out some way to get my money, which I had left in London, remitted to me. To this purpose, getting a kind of a letter of naturalization, I purchased as much land as my money would reach, and formed a plan for my plantation and settlement.

I had a neighbor whose name was Wells, and in much such circumstances as I was, I call him neighbor, because his plantation lay next to mine, and we went on very sociably together. My stock was but low, as well as his; and we rather planted for food, than anything else, for about two years. However, we began to increase, and our land began to come into order; so that the third year we planted some tobacco, and made each of us a large piece of ground ready for planting canes in the year to come; but we both wanted help. I had done wrong in parting with my boy Xury.

But alas! For me to do wrong was no great wonder: I had no remedy but to go on. I got into an employment quite remote to my genius, and directly contrary to the

我与他住了一段时间，通过向他们学习种植和制糖与他们混熟了。我目睹了他们优裕的生活，也知道了他们是如何暴富的。我决定如果能拿到这里的居住许可证，就成为他们中的一员，同时设法把放在伦敦的钱让他们汇过来。为此，在收到允许入籍的信后，我用所有的钱置了地，制订了我种植和定居的计划。

我有个邻居名叫威尔斯。他和我情形差不多。之所以称他为邻居是因为他的种植园与我的紧邻。我俩相处不错。我的粮食不多，他也如此。因此我们在今后的两年选择种植些能吃的东西。随后我们又增加种植，我们的土地开始变得肥沃。所以第三年我们就种植了烟草，并每人留出一大块地准备明年种植甜菜用。我们都很需要帮手，我本不该让埃瑟利走的。

唉！对我来说做错事情已不足为怪了。我除了继续走下去别无他途。我所做之事与我具有的才智相去甚远，与我喜欢的生活大相径庭。为了

life I delighted in, and for which I forsook my father's house, and broke through all his good advice; nay, I was coming into the very middle station, or upper degree of low life, which my father advised me to before; and which if I resolved to go on with, I might as well have stayed at home, and never have fatigued myself in the world as I had done.

In this manner I used to look up my condition with the utmost regret. I had nobody to converse with, but now and then this neighbor: no work to be done, but by the labor of my hands; and I used to say, I lived just like a man cast away upon some desolate island, that had nobody there but himself.

I was in some degree settled on the plantation, before my kind friend, the captain went back; for the ship remained there, proving his loading and preparing for his voyage, near three months. When I told him what little stock I had left behind me in London, he gave me this friendly and sincere advice: "If you will give me letters, and a procuration here in form to me, with orders to the person who has your money in London, to send your effects to Lisbon. But since human affairs are all subject to changes and disasters, I could have you give orders but for one hundred pounds sterling, which you say is half your stock, and let the hazard be run for the first; so

这种生活，我背弃了家庭，违背了父母的良言规劝。唉！我正进入下等生活的中游或上游。我父亲曾教导我去过这样的生活。而如果我决定继续这样生活，我或许当初应呆在家中，也用不着像这样在世界上疲于奔命了。

我曾怀着深深的懊悔审视自己的处境。除了偶尔这个邻居与我搭几句话外，无人与我交谈。除了双手劳作外，别无他事。我曾这样说过：我在过着一个漂流到荒无人烟的孤岛上的人的生活。

在我基本上已安心从事种植的时候，我的好朋友船长回到了我这里。他的船近三个月来一直在那里，装载着货物，准备航行。当我告诉他我在伦敦还有少许积蓄，他给我提了一个友好而诚挚的建议：你给伦敦那个拿着你钱的人写封信，让他将这些信及发送到里斯本的委托书交给我，由我来代你办理。不过，世事难料，吉凶无法卜算，我只能让你要回一百英镑，也就是你一半的钱，其他部分也只好听天由命啦。如果这些钱平

that if it came safe, you may order the rest same way; and if it miscarry, you may have the other half to have recourse to it for your supply."

This was so wholesome advice, and looked so friendly, that I could not but be convinced it was the best course I could take; so I accordingly prepared letters to the gentle – woman with whom I had left my money, and a procuration to the Portuguese captain, as he desired.

I wrote the English captain's widow a full account of all my adventures, my slavery, escape, and how I had met with the Portugal captain at sea; the humanity of his behavior, and what condition I was now in, with all other necessary directions for my supply; and when this honest captain came to Lisbon, he found means, by some of the English merchants there, to send over, not the order only, but a full account of my story, to a merchant at London, who represented it effectually to her; whereupon, she not only delivered the money, but out of her own pocket sent the Portugal captain a very handsome present for his humanity and charity to me.

The merchant in London vesting this hundred pounds in English goods, such as the captain had written for, sent them directly to him at Lisbon, and he brought them all safe to me; among which, without my direc-

安到达的话，你再以同样的方式要剩下的一半，如果出了岔子，你还有另一半能用，购买你所需要的东西。

这真是一条良策，是那样诚挚友好。我不得不承认这是条万全之策，于是我按他说的准备了写给持有我钱那个女士的信件，以及委托葡萄牙船长的委托书，这些都是他事先要求的。

在信中我向那个英国船长的遗孀详细叙述了我的冒险经历，我如何沦为奴隶，如何逃出，以及我如何在海上幸遇葡萄牙船长，并讲述了他的人道之举。我向她讲了自己目前的境况，并且添了一些所必须说的话，意在求她提供帮助。待到这位为人实在的船长到了里斯本后，他设法让一些在那里的英国商人将信件发给了一个伦敦商人，并详细叙述了我的经历。这位商人全权代表船长把东西交给了那位遗孀。她看到信后，不仅把钱寄给了我，而且还自己掏腰包，送给葡萄牙船长一件十分精美的礼物，作为对他菩萨心肠仁爱之举的报答。

那个伦敦商人用这一百镑照船长信中的要求买了些英国货，将他们直接寄给在里斯本的葡萄牙船长，然后船长如数带给了我。其中有我在信

tions, he had taken care to have all sorts of tools, iron –
work, and utensils necessary for my plantation, and
which were of great use to me.

When this cargo arrived I thought my fortune made,
for I was surprised with joy and my good captain had laid
out the five pounds which my friend had sent him for a
present for himself, to purchase, and bring me over a
servant under bond for six years' service, and would not
accept of any consideration, except a little tobacco,
which I would have him accept, being of my own produce.

Neither was this all; but my goods being all England manufactures, such as cloth, stuffs, baize, andth-
ings particularly valuable and desirable in the country. I
found means to sell them to a very great advantage, so
that I had more than four times the value of my first cargo, and was now infinitely beyond my poor neighbor in
the advancement of my plantation. I went on the next
year with great success in my plantation; I raised fifty
great rolls of tobacco on my own ground. And now, increasing in business and in wealth, my head began to be
full of projects and undertakings beyond my reach; such
as are indeed often the ruin of the best heads in business.

As I had done thus in breaking away from my par-

中没有提到而他却为我想到的各种工具、铁制品和我种植能用上的各种工具。这些东西对我非常有用。

货物到达后我想我是时来运转了。因为我惊喜地发现那位葡萄牙船长用我朋友送给他的五英镑给我买了一个奴仆，给我送了来，订的契约是为我干六年的活。他也不接受我的任何回报，但我让他收下了一些烟草。我执意要让他收下，因为那是我自己种的。

除了这些外，我的这些东西全是英国货，如布匹、材料、毛呢，还有其他在农村特别珍贵和实用的东西，我设法以较高的利润将它们卖了出去，得到了较原来四倍的价值。在发展我的种植园方面我远远地超过我的邻居。第二年，我的种植继续获得极大的成功。在我自己的地里种了五十行烟草。现在，随着生意的成功和财富的增长，我的心中充满了许多不切实际的宏伟构想，渴望创造业绩。而这往往是那些最善做生意之人的大敌。

由于我是以远离家庭为代价而做这一切的，

ents, so I could not be content now, but I must go and leave the happy view I had of being a rich and thriving man in my new plantation, only to pursue a rash and immoderate desire of rising faster than the nature of the thing admitted; and thus I cast myself down again into the deepest gulf of human misery that ever man fell into, or perhaps could be consistent with life and a state of health in the world.

Having now lived almost four years in Brazil, and beginning to thrive and prosper very well upon my plantation, I had not only learned the language, but had contracted acquaintance and friendship among my fellow planters, as well as among the merchants at St. Salvadore, which was our port; and that in my discourse among them I had frequently given them an account of my two voyages to the coast of Guinea, the manner of trading with the Negroes there, and how easy it was to purchase upon the coast, for trifles, such as beads, toys, knives, scissors, hatchets, bits of glass, and the like, not only gold dust, Guinea grains, elephants' teeth, but Negroes for the service of Brazil, in great numbers.

They listened always very attentively to my discourses, especially to that part which related to the buying Negroes. It happened that three of them came to me

所以我不能满足于此。我必须抛开满足于做一个富有而得志的种植园主的想法，去追求一种能超越事物本性而迅速发迹的狂妄构想。于是我将自己重新抛入人类最悲苦的深渊，或许也是世界上人类仅能维持生存苟延残喘的深渊。

在巴西我已住了将近四年，我的种植园方兴未艾，出现了欣欣向荣的景象。在这里我不仅学会了当地的语，同时也与种植园主以及圣·桑维多利的商人们混熟了，还交了朋友。圣·桑维多利是我们的一个港口。在我与他们的谈话中，我多次向他们讲述我到几内亚海岸的两次航行。在那儿与黑人搞交易以及在沿岸购买东西多么容易。用一些小东西诸如珠子、玩具、刀子、剪子、斧子、玻璃片，去换取金粉、几内亚粮食、象牙，还能买到大量的奴隶到巴西来劳作。

他们总是全神贯注地听我讲着，特别是讲到有关购买奴隶的部分。第二天上午他们当中有三

the next morning, and told me they had been musing very much upon what I had discoursed with them of the last night, and they came to make a secret proposal to me; and after enjoining me in secrecy, they told me that they had a mind to fit out a ship to go to Guinea; that they had all plantations as well as I, and were straitened for nothing so much as servants; that as this was a trade that could not be carried on, because they could not publicly sell the Negroes when they came home: so they desired to make but one voyage, to bring the Negroes on shore privately, and divide them among their own plantations; and in a word, the question was, whether I would go as their supercargo in the ship, to manage the trading part upon the coast of Guinea: and they offered me that I should have my equal share of the Negroes, without providing any part of the stock.

This was a fair proposal, it must be confessed, had it been made to any one that had not had a settlement and plantation of his own to look after, which was in a fair way of becoming very considerable, and with a good stock upon it. But for me, that was thus entered and established, and had nothing to do but go on as I had begun, for three or four years more, and to have sent for the other hundred pounds from England, and who in that time, and with that little addition, could scarce have

位来找我，说他们一直在思考着我昨晚讲过的话，过来向我提个秘密建议。悄悄对我说了以后，又告诉我他们想装备一艘开往几内亚的船，因为他们拥有和我一样好的种植园，别的不当紧，最需要的是劳力。而这又不是一件可以公开进行的交易，因为他们回来时不能明目张胆地贩卖黑人。因此他们想出一次海，将黑人悄悄带到岸上，然后将他们分到自己各个种植园。一句话，就是问我是否能作为他们的商业事务负责人乘船出海，在几内亚海岸由我去完成这种交易。然后他们说我本人不必提供任何资本，便可以免费得到与他们一样多的黑人。

如果这个建议是向一个没有安定下来，也没有已投入大量资金的、很有发展前景的种植园可经营的人提出的，那么坦白地说这是个好主意。但对我来说，这些都已着手奠定下来，而且在今后的三四年左右只能继续下去，我可以让他们将我在伦敦的另外一百英镑寄来，这笔钱在当时绝

failed of being worth three or four thousand pounds sterling, and that increasing too; for me to think of such a voyage was the most preposterous thing that ever man in such circumstances could be guilty of.

But I, that was born to be my own destroyer, could no more resist the offer, than I could restrain my first rambling designs, when my father's good counsel was lost upon me. In a word, I told them I would go with all my heart, if they would undertake to look after my plantation in my absence, and would dispose of it to such as I should direct if I miscarried. This they all engaged to do, and entered into writings or covenants to do so; and I made a formal will, disposing of my plantation and effects, in case of my death, making the captain of the ship that saved my life, as before, my universal heir, but obliging him to dispose of my effects as I had directed in my will, one half of the produce being to himself, and the other to be shipped to England.

In short, I took all possible caution to preserve my effects, and keep up my plantation. Had I used half as much prudence to have looked into my own interest, and have made a judgment of what I ought to have done and not to have done, I had certainly never gone away from so prosperous an undertaking, leaving all the probable views of a thriving circumstance, and gone upon a voyage

对能增值到三四百英镑。对于我来说，想到这样的一次航行真是荒谬至极，任何处在我这样位置上的人都会感到是荒唐的。

而我这个天生的叛逆者，注定要毁掉自己，所以无法抵御这诱惑。正如当初父亲的建议未能使我收敛自己的奇思妙想，去浪迹天涯一样。总之，我心诚意坚，满口答应跑这一趟，但在我出去时他们得看管我的种植园，并在万一有个闪失的情况下按我的吩咐去处置种植园。他们都答应了，并且立下书面条文。我立下一个遗嘱，处理我的种植园和财产，万一我死了，像从前一样，救过我生命的船长将为继承人，但要让他按遗嘱处理我的财产。其中一半归他所有，另一半发往英国。

简言之，我尽可能地想到一切措施来保存我的财产，维持我的种植园。如果当初我用这一半精明来察究自己的利益，决定自己的行为，看哪些事该干，哪些事不能干，那我就绝对不会离开正值兴旺的事业，放弃充满光明的远景，而伴着

to sea, attended with all its common hazards; to say nothing of the reasons I had to expect particular misfortunes to myself.

But I was hurried on, and obeyed blindly the dictates of my fancy rather than my reason; and, accordingly, the ship being fitted out, and the cargo furnished, and all things done as by agreement by my partners in the voyage, I went on board in an evil hour, the 1st of September, 1659—being the same day eight years that I went from my father and mother at Hull, in order to act the rebel to their authority, and the fool to my own interest.

Chapter 6　A Shipwreck

Our ship was about 120 tons burden, carried 6 guns, and 14 men. We had on board no large cargo of goods, except of such toys as were fit for our trade with the Negroes, such as beads, bits of glass, shells, and odd trifles, especially little looking – glasses, knives, scissors, hatchets, and the like.

When we set sail, we had very good weather, only excessive hot, all the way upon our own coast till we came to the height of Cape St. Augustino. In this course a violent hurricane took us quite out of our knowledge. It

各种可能的危险去出海航行，更不用说还应该考虑到我个人可能遭遇到的特殊不幸。

但我还是匆匆地继续进行着准备，盲目地照我的幻想行事而没有多想。就这样，船已备好，货物已备齐，所有的事情都按照协议由我的旅伴处置停当。我在一六五九年九月一日那个不祥的时辰登上了航船，这正是我八年前为反抗父母的权威，在赫尔逃离家庭而自讨苦吃的那个日子。

第六章　船舶残骸

我们的船载重一百二十吨，装有六门炮，共十四人。也没什么大件的货物，只是一些适合与黑人交易的小玩意儿，像珠子、玻璃片和贝壳，还有一些新奇的琐碎物品，特别是小望远镜啦，刀子、剪子、斧头啦之类。

刚启航时，还晴空万里，太阳晒得人全身发热，我们沿着海岸一直驶到奥古斯丁角那块高地，可就在这时，风暴骤起，气势汹汹地向我们袭来，

began from the south – east, came about to the north – west, and then settled into the north – east, from whence it blew in such a terrible manner, that for twelve days together we could do nothing but drive, and scudding away before it, let it carry us whither ever fate and the fury of the winds directed; and during these twelve days I need not say that I expected every day to be swallowed up, not indeed did any in the ship expect to save their lives.

In this distress, we had, besides the terror of the storm, one of our men died of fever, and one man and the boy washed overboard. About the twelfth day, the weather abating a little, the master made an observation as well as he could, and found he was gotten upon the coast of Guinea, or the north part of Brazil, beyond the river Amazons, toward the river Oronoque, commonly called the Great River. He began to consult with me what course he should take, for the ship was leaky and very much disabled, and he was going directly back to the coast of Brazil.

I was positively against that; and looking over the charts of the sea – coast of America with him, we concluded there was no inhabited country for us to have course to, till we came within the circle of the Caribbee Islands, and therefore resolved to stand away for Barbados, and avoid the in – draught of gulf of Mexico.

它从东南方向转到西北，又向东北刮去。肆虐的飓风仿佛要将一切席卷而去，整整十二天，我们被刮向远洋，无能为力，不知命运和狂风会将我们带向何方。不必说，这十二天里，我时时刻刻都在担心永沉海底，我的伙伴们也早已放弃了生还的希望。

死亡就在眼前，风暴已让我们魂不附体，而此时一个同伴又死于热病，另一人和一个小男孩被恶浪刹那间卷得无影无踪。第十二天时，风浪稍有平息，船长尽力观察了船的位置，发现我们已在圭亚那海岸或巴西北部，驶过了亚马逊河，快到那条被称为"大河"的俄利诺科河了。船长认为船已渗漏而且损坏严重，因此应直接开回巴西海岸，并就此征询了我的意见。

我一听便强烈反对，并和他一起查看了美洲沿岸的航海图，最后得出的结论是：除非我们驶到加勒比群岛，否则就找不到有人烟的地方求援，因此，我们决定避开墨西哥湾的逆流，驶向巴巴多斯群岛。

With this design we changed our course in order to reach some of our English islands, where I hoped for relief; but a second storm came upon us, which carried us away with the same impetuosity westward, and drove us so out of the very way of all human commerce. In this distress, the wind was still blowing very hard, and one of our men early in the morning cried out, "Land!" and we had no sooner run out of the cabin to look out, in hopes of seeing whereabouts in the world we were, but stuck upon a sand, and in a moment, her motion being so stopped, the sea broke over her in such a manner, that we expect we should all have perished immediately.

Now though we found that the wind did a little abate, yet the ship having thus stuck upon the sand sticking too fast for us to expect her getting off, we were in a dreadful condition indeed, and had nothing to do but to think of saving our lives as well as we could. We had a boat at our stern just before the storm, but she was first staved by dashing against the ship's rudder, and in the next place she broke away, and either sunk or was driven off to sea, there was no hope from her. We had another boat on board but how to get her off into the sea was a doubtful thing; however there was no room to debate, for we fancied the ship would break in pieces every minute, and some told us she was actually broken al-

计划一定，我们便改变航向，希望能到达一个英属海岛，在那里获得救助。可是天有不测风云，第二场风暴从天而降，我们被不可抗拒地刮向西方，最后远离了人类贸易的航线，进入荒僻的远洋。在这种凄惨的境况下，风势仍没有减弱的迹象。一日清晨，有个同伴突然大喊一声："陆地！"我们刚冲出去想看看究竟身在何方，船就猛地在一片沙滩上搁浅，不能动了。而与此同时，惊涛骇浪铺天盖地直扑而来，眼看在劫难逃，我们全都完了。

风渐渐地小了，可船仍深陷沙中；我们想尽办法，也不能使它移动分毫。一场大难迫在眉睫，无论如何得尽快逃离这可怕的境地。风暴到来之前，船艉本来有一只小艇，可它撞破在大船的舵上，要么沉入大海，要么被波涛卷走，再也指望不上了。船上还有一只小艇，可没人知道怎么把它放下海，而此时刻不容缓，根本不容我们商量对策，大船随时会被疯狂的大海撕成碎片，有人甚至还不能让我们商量对策说，船实际上已经破了。

ready.

In this distress, the mate of our vessel lays hold of boat, and with the help of the rest of the men, they got her slung over the ship's side, and getting all into her, let go, and committed ourselves, being eleven in number, to God's mercy and the wild sea; for though the storm abated considerably, yet the sea went dreadful high upon the shore, and might well be called den wild zee, as the Dutch call the sea in a storm.

And now our case was very dismal indeed; for we all saw plain that the sea went so high, that the boat could not live, and that we should be inevitably drowned. However, we committed our souls to God in the most earnest manner, and the wind driving us toward the shore, we hastened our destruction with our own hands, pulling as well as we could towards land. What the shore was, whether rock or sand, whether steep or shoaly, we knew not, but as we made nearer the shore, the land looked more frightful than the sea.

All of a sudden, a raging wave, mountain – like, came rolling astern of us, and it took us with such a fury that it overset the boat at once; and gave us not time hardly to say "O God!", for we were all swallowed up in a moment. Nothing can describe the confusion when I sunk into the water; for though I swam very well, yet I

此刻已危在旦夕，我们的大副一把抓住小艇，其他的伙伴一起用力将它从轮船上放下水，眨眼间所有的人都已在小船上了，大家拼命地划了出去，把全部十一条性命都交在上帝和狂野的大海手中。风势虽然已大大减弱，可海上依然白浪滔天，难怪荷兰人称暴风雨中的大海为"疯狂的海洋"。

前景暗淡，每个人都心知肚明，在这排山倒海的浪涛中，小艇实属九死一生，最终全都要葬身鱼腹。可是现在，除了乞求上帝的怜悯之外，还有什么办法呢？我们顺着风势，没命地划向岸边，可这无疑是加速整船的灭亡。因为究竟海岸是岩石或沙洲，还是峭壁或浅滩，我们都一无所知，只是离海岸越近，就越发地心惊胆寒。陆地看上去比海洋更加狰狞。

突然，一个怒不可遏的巨浪，山一般滚滚而来，其势之猛，转瞬间便把船掀个底朝天，一刹那间天昏地暗，船上的人还来不及高喊一声"啊！上帝！"便被恶浪吞噬了。就在坠入海中的那一刻，我心中的混乱和惊惶实在无法形容。尽管我

could not deliver myself from the waves so to draw breath, but half dead with the water I took in. My business was to hold my breath, and raise myself upon the water, if I could; so by swimming to preserve my breathing, and pilot myself towards the shore, if possible.

I was now landed and safe on shore, and began to look up and thank God that my life was saved. I believe it is impossible to express to the life what the ecstasies and transports of the soul are, when it is so saved, as I may say, out of the very grave. I walked about on the shore, lifting up my hands, and my whole being, wrapped up in the contemplation of my deliverance, making a thousand gestures and motions, reflecting upon all my comrades that were drowned, and that there should not be one soul saved but myself.

I cast my eyes to the stranded vessel, when the breach and froth of the sea being so big, I could hardly see it, it lay so far off, and considered, Lord! how was it possible I could get on shore!

After I had solaced my mind with the comfortable part of my condition, I began to look around me, to see what of place I was in, and what was next to do; and I soon found my comforts abate, and that, in a word, I had a dreadful deliverance. For I was wet, had no clothes to change, nor anything either to eat or drink to

极善游泳，可在汹涌的波涛中，连浮起来呼吸一下都极为困难。我被淹了个半死，只能屏住呼吸，竭力把头露出水面，并尽可能地向岸边游去，一边游一边竭力调整着呼吸。

我终于活着上了岸。当我仰面朝天，感谢上帝给我重生的时候，真是欣喜若狂。一个人在这种险恶的境况下还能死里逃生，那种幸福与心醉神迷没有任何言语能表达得出。简直可以说，我是从坟墓里爬出来的。我高举双手，发疯一般跑来跑去，做出千百种奇怪的姿势来发泄自己的激情。此时我全身心地回想着自己获救的经过，同伴们全都葬身海底，无一幸免，惟我化险为夷，真是难以置信。

眺望无边的大海，那只搁浅了的大船在烟波迷茫中若隐若现，遥不可及。上帝啊！我是怎么上岸的呀，这简直是不可能的！

我用自己还活着的事实自我安慰了一番，就开始环顾四周，我究竟在哪里？以后该怎么办？我顿时泄了气。一句话，我虽活着，情况却再糟不过：浑身湿透，却没有衣服更换；饥渴交加，

comfort me, neither did I see any prospect before me, but that of perishing with hunger, or being devoured by wild beasts; and that which was particularly afflicting to me, was, that had no weapon either to hunt and kill any other creature that might desire to kill me. In a word, I had nothing about me but a knife, a tobacco – pipe, and a little tobacco in a box; this was all my provision, and this threw me into terrible agonies of mind, that for a while I ran about like a madman. Night coming upon me, I began with a heavy heart to consider what would be my lot if there were any ravenous beast in that country, seeing at night they always come aboard for their prey.

When I woke up it was broad day, the weather clear, and the storm abated, so that the sea did not rage and swell as before; but that which surprised me most was, that the ship was lifted off in the night from the sand by the swelling of the tide. I wished myself on board so that at least I could save some necessary things for my use.

When I came down from my apartment in the tree, I looked about me again, and the first thing I found was the boat, which lay as the wind had tossed her, up upon the land, about two miles on my right hand. I walked as far as I could upon the shore to have got to her, but found a neck or inlet of water between me and the boat,

却没有东西吃喝；除了慢慢饿死或被野兽吞食外，看不到丝毫希望。更令人苦恼的是，我没有武器，既不能为自己捕猎食物，又不能杀死想吃掉我的任何动物。总之，除了一把刀子、一只烟斗和一小匣烟叶外，我一无所有，这叫人忧心如焚。我在岸上四处狂奔了好长一段时间，无计可施。夜幕降临，我心情沉重地想到：那些贪婪的猛兽总喜欢夜里出来觅食，一旦碰上，就必死无疑，这将是我的命运。

一觉醒来，天已大亮。碧空如洗，风平浪静，千难万险已成过去，大海也不像先前那样波涛汹涌了。但更让我惊诧的是，那只搁浅了的大船夜里被潮水冲出了沙面。我想若能上得船去，就能尽管选用所需之物了。

我从树上睡觉的地方下来，四面张望，一眼就发现那只船被风抛到了陆地上，就在我右方约两英里处。我沿着海岸向它走去，却被一个大约

which was about half a mile broad; so I came back for the present, being more intent upon getting at the ship, where I hoped to find something for my present.

I swam round her twice, and the second time I spied a small piece of rope hang down by the fore – chains, with great difficulty I got hold of it, and by the help of rope got into the forecastle of the ship. Here I found that the ship was bulged, and had a great of water in her hold, but all the ship's provisions were dry and untouched by the water. I also found some rum in the great cabin, of which I took a large dram to spirit me for what was before me. Now I wanted nothing but a boat.

It was in vain to sit still and wish for what was not to be had. So I went to work, with a great deal of labor and pains, and put the spars of wood and a topmast and ropes in the form of a raft, which was now strong enough to bear any reasonable weight. My next care was what to load it with, and how to preserve what I laid upon it from the surf of the sea. When I was filling the seamen's chests with provisions, I found the tide began to flow, though very calm; and I had the mortification to see my coat, shirt, and waist – coat which I had left on shore swim away. I swam on rummaging for clothes, but took no more than I wanted for present use. I had other things which my eye was more upon—tools to work with on

半英里宽的大水湾挡住了去路，只能暂时折回。可是我登船找一些日用品的想法更加强烈了。

我绕着它游了两圈，在第二圈时发现有根很短的绳子挂在船头，我费了九牛二虎之力才抓住绳子，攀着它爬上去，进入船的前舱。在那里我看到船已损坏，舱底灌满了水，但所有的粮食却完好无损，没有被波浪打湿。在大舱里，我还找到了一些甜酒，就喝了一大杯给自己壮胆，现在惟一需要的，就是一只可以运送东西的小船。

呆坐着空想得不到的东西徒劳无益，必须着手工作。我大费一番周折，经过艰辛劳动，才用帆桅、木板和缆绳扎成一只筏子，很牢固，能承担相当的重量。接下来的问题是：装些什么东西，以及如何防止被浪打湿。就在我用粮食装满船员箱时，潮水悄无声息地涨上来了，不过无波无澜，很平静。我眼睁睁看着自己留在岸边的上衣、衬衫和马甲随水漂走，懊悔不迭。于是我开始在船上翻箱倒柜地搜寻衣服，但只挑了几件目前能穿的，因为有些东西更重要，尤其是工具。找了半

shore; and it was after long searching that I found out the carpenter's chest, which was indeed a very useful prize to me, and much more valuable than a ship – loading of gold would have been at that time.

My next care was for some ammunition and arms. I secured two pistols and a small bag of shot, and two old rusty swords. I also managed to get three barrels of powder in the ship. And now I thought myself pretty well freighted, and began to think how I should get to shore with them, having neither sail, oar, nor rudder and the last capful of wind would have overset all my navigation.

I had three encouragements: a smooth, calm sea, the tide rising and setting into the shore, and what little wind there was blew me towards the land; and thus, having found two or three broken oars belonging to the boat, and besides the tools which were in the chest, I found two saws, an axe and a hammer, and with this cargo I put to sea.

As I imagined there appeared before me a little opening of the land, and I found a strong current of the tide set into it, so I guided my raft as well as I could to keep in the middle of the stream; all my cargo had slipped off and so fallen into the water. I did my utmost, by setting my back against the chests, to keep them in their places, but could not thrust off the raft with all my

天总算找到了木工箱，这可是一大收获，对我非常有用。此时此刻，工具对我而言，比一满船的黄金更宝贵。

接着，我还必须搞到枪支和弹药，在弄到两支手枪、一小包子弹和两把生锈的旧刀后，我还想办法在船上找到了三桶火药。筏子上东西够多了，如何运上岸呢？我认真思索了一会。一没帆，二没桨，三没舵，一丁点儿风就会让我的一番心血付诸东流。

可还有三点情况令人鼓舞：首先，海面平滑如镜；其次，时值涨潮，潮水是向岸边滚动的；第三，虽有点小风，却也吹向陆地。我找到了原来船上的两三根断桨，此外，除了工具箱中的东西外，还有两把锯子，一把斧头和一只榔头，于是，满载着这些"宝物"，我向岸边进发了。

果然不出所料，不久便看到了一处小湾，水流湍急，源源不断地涌了进去。我竭尽全力把木筏保持在水的中心，可是我所有的货物朝旁边一倾斜，全都落入了水中。我别无选择，只得使劲用背顶住那些箱子，不让它们随水漂走，结果是

strength, I stood in that manner near half an hour. I at length found myself in the mouth of a little river, with land on both sides, and a strong current or tide running up. I looked on both sides for a proper place to get to shore, for I was not willing to be driven too high up the river, hoping in time to see some ship at sea, and therefore resolved to place myself as near the coast as I could.

At length I spied a little cove on the right shore of the creek, to which, with great pain and difficulty, I could thrust her directly in. The shore was lying pretty steep, there was no place to land. All that I could do was wait till the tide was at the highest, keeping the raft with my oar like an anchor to hold the side of it fast to the shore, near a flat piece of ground, which I expected the water would flow over; and so it did. As soon as I found water enough I thrust her on upon that flat piece of ground and there fastened or moored her by sticking my two broken oars into the ground, and thus I lay till the water ebbed away, and left my raft and all my cargo safe on shore.

Chapter 7   My Fortress

My next work was to view the country, and seek a proper place for my habitation, and where to stow my

竟无法撑开木筏，足足坚持了快半个钟头，好不容易进入河口。这里两岸峭壁林立，两边是陆地，激流上涨。我东张西望，想找块合适的地方登岸。我不想让潮水将我的木筏冲到河的上游去。我只想呆在靠海最近的地方，以便能看到过往的船只。因此，得找一个合适的地点停靠。

最后，我发现有一个小湾在河的右岸，我费尽艰辛才把木筏撑了进去。河沿陡如斧削，无法停靠。我只有用桨做锚，把木筏的一边固定在岸边一小块平地上，直等到潮水涨高，漫过沙滩，才把木筏划了过去，然后用两只断桨插进地里固定住，这样单等潮水退去，我的木筏和货物就可以安然无恙地留在岸上了。

第七章　固守掩蔽

接下来我得观察一下周围的地形，以便找个合适的地方安顿自己，并贮藏物品，以防意外。

goods to secure them from whatever might happen. I took out one of the pistols, and an horn of powder, and thus armed. After I had with great labor and difficulty got to the top, I saw my fate to my great affliction that I was in an island environed every way with the sea.

I found also that this island was barren and uninhabited, I saw none of the wild beats, but abundance of fowls, but knew not their kinds. At my coming back, I shot at a great bird. I took it to be a kind of hawk, its color and beak resembling it, but had no claws; its flesh was carrion and fit for nothing.

Contented with this discovery, I came back to my raft, and fell to work to bring my cargo on shore. I now began to consider that I might yet get a great many things out of the ship which would be useful to me; and particularly some of the rigging and sails, and I resolve to make another voyage on board the vessel, if possible. I got on board the ship, as before, and prepared a second raft, and having had experience of the first, I neither made this so unwieldy, nor loaded so hard; but yet I brought away several things very useful to me. Besides, I took all the men's clothes that I could find, and a spare foretop – sail, hammock, and some bedding; and with this I loaded my second raft, and brought them all safe on shore, to my very great comfort.

我用一支枪和一角筒火药把自己武装起来，使尽力气爬上山顶，却悲伤地发现这里四面环海，是个孤岛。这种灾难是我命中注定的。

我还发现此地荒无人烟，看不到任何动物，只有许多不知名的飞鸟。回来的路上，我开枪打死了一只大鸟，从毛色和嘴来看，像是一种鹰，但没有钩爪。它的肉腐臭难吃，简直毫无用处。

我觉得对岛上的环境了解得差不多了，便回到木筏旁，动手把物品都搬上岸来。我现在才想到，船上有许多东西都大有用处，尤其是那些绳索和帆布，因此我决定尽可能地再上船一次。我后来上了船，又做了一个木筏，有了上次的经验，我不再把木筏做得那么笨重，也不再装太多的东西，但还是运回了大量极有用的物品，除此之外，我还带走了能搜集到的所有的男人衣服，一个备用樯帆，一个吊床和一些被褥，并把它们都装上船，平安抵岸，这使我大为欣慰。

I was under some apprehensions during my absence from the land, that at least my provisions might be devoured on shore; but when I came back I found no sign of any visitor, only there sat a creature like a wild cat upon one of the chests, which, when I came towards it, ran away a little distance, and then stood still. She sat very composed and unconcerned, and looked full in my face, as if she had a mind to be acquainted with me. I presented my gun at her, but as she did not understand it, she was perfectly unconcerned at it, nor did she offer to stir away; upon which I tossed her a bit of biscuit, though by the way I was not very free of it, for my store was not great. However, I spared her a bit, and she went to it, smelled it, ate it, and looked as pleased, for more; but I thanked her, and could spare no more, so she marched off.

Having got my second cargo on shore, though I was fain to open the barrels of powder, and bring them by parcels, I went to work to make me a little tent with the sail and some poles which I cut for that purpose; and into this tent I brought everything that I knew would spoil, either with rain or sun, and I piled all the empty chests and casks up in a circle round the tent, to fortify it from any sudden attempt, either from man or beast.

When I had done this, I blocked up the door of the

我离岸期间，曾担心岸上的粮食会被什么动物吃掉，可回来后一切正常，没发现动物的踪影，只有一只野猫似的不速之客卧在箱子上，我刚走近，它便跑开了几步，然后又站住不动。这小东西若无其事地盯着我的脸，一点儿也不害怕，好像要跟我交个朋友。我用枪指了指它，可它不明白枪是一种什么样的东西，所以满不在乎，根本就没有跑掉的意思。见到这种状况，我丢给它一小块饼干，虽然我的存粮不多，可还是分了与它。那小东西走过去闻了闻，便津津有味地吃了下去，表现出一种高兴的样子，接着还想要，可我实在所剩无几，没办法再给它，那小东西便大模大样地走开了。

第二批货上岸后，虽然我很想赶快打开火药桶，把火药分成小包藏起来，可还是先用帆布和砍好的支柱做了顶帐篷，然后把凡是经不起风吹日晒的物品都搬进去，又把那些空箱子放在帐篷周围绕成一圈，进行加固，以防人或野兽的突然袭击。

干完了这些，我又用几块木板把帐篷门从里

tent with some boards within, and an empty chest set up on end; and spreading one of the beds on the ground, laying my two pistols just at my head, and my gun at length by me, I went to bed for the first time, and slept very quietly all night, for I was very weary and heavy.

What comforted me more still was that after I had made five or six such voyages as these, and thought I had nothing more to expect from the ship that was worth my mending with; however, I found a great hogshead of bread, and three large runlets, and a box of sugar, and a barrel of fine flour. This was surprising to me, because I had given up expecting any more provisions.

I had been now thirteen days on shore, and had been eleven times on board the ship, in which time I had brought away all that one pair of hands could be well supposed capable to bring; though I believe verily, had the calm weather held, I should have brought away the whole ship, piece by piece. But preparing the twelfth time to go on board, I found the wind begin to rise; however, at low water I went on board, and though I thought I had rummaged the cabin so effectually that nothing more could be found, yet I discovered a locker with drawers in it, in one of which I found two or three razors, and one pair of large scissors, with some ten or a dozen of good knives and forks; in another I found thirty

面堵住，再竖上一只空箱。铺好了床，在床头放两支手枪，床旁再备上一支长枪，总算能第一次上床睡觉了。我早已筋疲力尽，肢体沉重，整晚睡得很香。

最令我高兴的是，在这样跑了五六趟后，还以为船上已没什么东西值得我搜寻了，不料又找到一大桶面包，三桶甜酒，一箱砂糖，和一桶上好的面粉。这真是一个惊喜，因为我想船上已没什么可吃之物了。

已上岸十三天了，到船上却去了十一次，我把凡是两只手能搬得动的东西全拿走了，尽管如此，我还相信，要是天气好的话，我会把整艘船都拆成木片运走。可就在我准备第十二次航行时，开始刮起了大风。然而我还是趁退潮上了船。虽然已搜遍了全船，应该不会有什么有用的东西剩下了，我还是发现了一个有抽屉的柜子。在一个抽屉里找出了两三把剃刀，一把大剪子和十几副

– six pounds value in money.

I smiled to myself at the sight of this money and all the additional objects. I began to think of making another raft; but while I was preparing this, I found the sky overcast, and the wind began to rise, and in a quarter of an hour it blew a fresh gale from the shore. It presently occurred to me that it was in vain to make a raft with the wind off shore, and that it was my business to be gone before the tide flood began, otherwise I might not be able to reach the shore at all: accordingly I let myself down into the water, and swam across the channel, which lay between the ship and the sands, and even that with difficulty enough, partly with the weight of things I had about me, and partly the roughness of the water; for the wind rose very hastily, and before it was quite high water it blew a storm.

But I had gotten home to my little tent, where I lay with all my wealth about me very secure. It blew very hard that night; and in the morning when I looked out, behold no more ship was to be seen. I was a little surprised, but recovered myself with this satisfactory reflection that I had lost no time, nor abated any diligence, to get everything out of the ship.

I soon found the place I was in was not for my settlement, particularly because it was upon a low moorish

相当好的刀叉，另一个抽屉里还有三十六镑现金。

当我看到这些钱以及意想不到的东西时，高兴地笑了出来。我考虑再做一只木筏，可正做的时候，天空乌云密布，风也愈刮愈紧，不到一刻钟，变成一股强风暴从岸上刮来。我马上意识到，风从岸上来，木筏就没用了。还不如趁潮水未到，赶快离开，否则就根本上不了岸了。我立刻跳下水，游过船和沙滩之间那片水湾。这一次困难重重，是由于带的东西太重，浪头大，风势又急。潮水上涨不久，海面已起了风暴。

但我已回到了自己的家——那个小帐篷。当我躺下休息时，想到身边全是我的财富，心中又安稳又踏实。狂风刮了一夜，第二天早上我向外一望，那只船已不复存在。我有点惊讶，可想到我没有浪费时间，也没有偷懒，不失时机地把船上一切有用之物都搬空了，不禁感到心安理得。

我很快就发现，这个地方不适合我住。此处离海太近，地势低潮，不利于健康，而且附近没

ground near the sea, and I believed would not be wholesome, and more particularly because there was no fresh water near it, so I resolved to find a more healthy and more convenient spot of ground.

I consulted several things in my situation which I found would be proper for me. Health, and fresh water, shelter from the heat of the sun; security from ravenous creatures, whether man or beast; a view to the sea, that if God sent any ship in sight, I might not lose any advantage for my deliverance.

In search of a place proper for this, I found a little plain on the side of a rising hill, I resolved to pitch my tent. Before I set up my tent, I drew a half circle before the hollow place. In this half circle I pitched two rows of strong stakes, driving them into the ground till they stood very firm, like piles. Then I took the pieces of cable which I had cut in the ship, and laid them in rows one upon another, within the circle between these two rows of stakes, up to the top, placing other stakes in the inside, leaning against them, about two foot and a half high, like a spur to a post; and this fence was so strong, that neither man nor beast could get into it or over it. This cost me a great deal of time and labor, especially to cut the piles in the woods, bring them to the place, and drive them into the earth.

有淡水，于是决定找一个比较卫生、方便的地方，作为栖身之处。

根据现状判断，我的住所必须符合以下条件：一要卫生，并有淡水；二是遮阴，避开炎热的阳光；三要安全，不受人或兽的侵扰；四要能看到大海。这样万一上帝让什么船经过，我就不会痛失脱险的良机。

在我找合适的居住地方时，发现了山坡旁的一小片平地，决定就在那里搭个帐篷。我在一块凹陷的山壁前画了一个半圆，钉上两排结实的木桩，深入泥土，非常牢靠，然后又用从船上截下来的缆绳一层一层堆在两排木桩之间，直堆到顶部，再用一些大约两英尺半的木桩插在里面支撑住，仿佛柱子上的横梁。这篱笆非常坚固，无论人或野兽也没法冲进或翻越。这项工程费时费力，尤其是从树林里砍木桩再运回来打进地里。

The entrance into this place I made to be not by a door, but by a short ladder to go over at the top; when I was in, I lifted the ladder over aftert me; and so I was completely fenced in and fortified, as I thought, from all the world, and consequently slept secure in night.

Into this fortress I carried all my riches, all my provisions, ammunition, and stores, and I made me a large tent to preserve me from the rains. And now I lay no more for a white in the bed which I had brought on shore, but in a hammock.

When I had done this, I began to work my way into the rock; and bringing all the earth and stones that I dug down through my tent, I laid them up within my fence in the nature of a terrace, that so it raised the ground within about a foot and a half; and thus I made me a cave just behind my tent, which served me like a cellar to my house.

In the interval of time while I was doing this, I went out once at least everyday with my gun, as well as to divert myself as to see if I could kill anything fit for food. The first time I went out I presently discovered that there were goats in the island, but that they were so shy, so subtle, and swift of foot, that it was the most difficult thing in the world to come at them. But I was not dis-

至于住所的入口，我没有做门，而是用一架短梯架在篱笆旁，从篱笆顶上翻过，待我进入后，即把梯子撤掉。正如所料，我完全被篱笆保护起来，夜里可以高枕无忧了。

我把所有的财产、粮食、武器弹药和补给都搬进我的堡垒，又给自己搭一顶大大的帐篷防雨。从此再也不必睡在搬上岸的那张床上——而是可以睡在一张吊床上了。

以上工作做完后，我又开始在岩壁上打洞，把挖出来的泥土和石块都通过帐篷运到外面，再沿着篱笆堆成一个平台，约一英尺半高，就这样，我在帐篷后挖了一个洞作为地窖。

在建立新家的这些日子里，我每天至少带枪出门一次，一来散心，二来想猎点什么吃的。第一次外出我便发现岛上有好多山羊，但它们胆小又狡黠，而且跑得飞一般快，要靠近它们难于登

couraged at this. After I had found their haunts a little, I laid wait this manner for them. The first shot I made among these creatures I killed a she – goat, which had a little kid by her, which she gave suck to. This grieved me heartily; but when the old one fell, the kid stood stock still by her till I came and took her up; and not only so, but when I carried the old one with me upon my shoulders, the kid followed me quite to my enclosures, upon which I laid the dam, and took the kid in my arms and carried it over my pale, in hopes to have bred it up tame, but it would not eat, so I was forced to kill it and eat it myself. These two supplied me with flesh a great while, for I ate sparingly, and saved my provisions as much as possible.

After I had been there about ten or twelve days, it came into my thoughts that I should lose my reckoning of time for want of books, and pen and ink, and should even forget the Sabbath days from the working days; but to prevent this, I cut it with my knife upon a large post in capital letters, and making it into a great cross, I set it up on the shore where I first landed. I came here on the 30th of Sept. 1659. Upon the sides of this square post I cut every day a notch with my knife, and every seventh notch was as long again as the rest, and every first day of the month as long again as that long one; and

天。但我没有灰心，在找到山羊经常出没之地后，便埋伏起来对付它们。第一回打死了一只正给小羊哺乳的母羊，不由得心里一阵难过。老羊倒下后，小羊还傻呆呆地站在那里，看着我走过去收取猎物。不但如此，我背起母羊往回走时，小羊竟跟着我一直走到篱笆外。于是我放下母羊后，又把小羊抱进去想驯养长大，可小羊不管怎样就是不吃东西，我无可奈何，只得把它也杀了吃掉。这两只羊我吃了好长一段时间，因为要尽量节约粮食，我吃得很省。

上岛后约十一二天，我忽然想到没有本子、笔和墨水，就一定会忘记计算时间，也会忘记安息日和工作日。为了防止这种情况发生，我拿刀在一根柱子上用大写字母刻上：我于一六五九年九月三十日上岸。并把柱子做成一个大十字架，竖立在我第一次上岸的地方。在这个柱子的四边，我每天用刀刻一个凹痕，每第七天刻得长一倍，而每月的第一天刻得比第七天的再长一倍，这样

thus I kept my calendar, or weekly, monthly, and yearly reckoning of time.

I have already described my habitation , which was a tent under the side of a rock, surrounded with a strong pale of posts and cables, but I might now rather call it a wall, for I raised a kind of wall up against it of turfs, about two feet thick on the outside, and after some time, I think it was a year and a half, I raised rafters from it, leaning to the rock, and thatched or covered it with boughs of trees, and such things as I could get to keep out the rain, which I found at some times of the year very violent.

I had to make things sometimes myself, but I had never handled a tool in my life, and yet in time by labor, application, and contrivance, I found at last that I wanted nothing but I could have made it, especially if I had had tools; however, I made abundance of things, even without tools, and some with no more tools than an adze and a hatchet, which, perhaps, were never made that way before.

However, I made me a table and a chair in the first place, and this I did out of the short pieces of boards which I brought on my raft from the ship; but when I had wrought out some boards, I made large shelves, of the breath of a foot and a half, one over another, all along

我便有了日历，可以按照周、月和年计算日期了。

　　前面我已描述过自己的住所，是一个搭在山岩下的帐篷，并用木桩和缆索做成坚固的栅栏四面环绕。但现在我可以叫它作围墙了，因为我在栅栏外用草皮堆成了一道两英尺厚的墙，还在大约一年半的时间里，搭起屋椽靠着岩壁，并用茅草和树枝覆盖起来遮雨，因为我发现这里一年中总有段日子大雨如注。

　　我不得不自己制造一些用品，虽然我这辈子从未用过任何工具，可久而久之，以我的劳动、勤勉和创意，我终于知道，只要有适当的工具，没有什么东西是不能做的。然而，就算没有工具，我也做成了大量东西，有些是仅用一把斧头和砍刀做成的，尽管也许从未有人以这种方法做过它们。

　　我先用船上运回的几块短木板做了一张桌子和一把椅子，又用一英尺半宽的木板沿着墙壁一层层搭成一个大架子，分门别类地把钉子和铁器

one side of my cave, to lay all my tools, nails, and iron
- work, and in a word, to separate everything at large
in their places, that I might come easily at them. I
knocked pieces into the wall of the rock to hang my guns
and all things that would hang up.

Chapter 8 My Exploration

The rainy season, and the dry season, began now
to appear regular to me, and I learned to divide them so
as to provide for them accordingly. But I bought all my
experience before I had it; and this was one of the most
discouraging experiments that I made at all. I had saved
a few ears of barley and rice which I had so surprisingly
found spring up, as I thought, of themselves, and believe there were about thirty stalks of rice, and about
twenty of barley; and now I thought it a proper time to
sow it after the rains.

Accordingly I dug up a piece of ground with my
wooden spade, I sowed my grain; but as I was sowing,
it casually occurred to my thought, that I should not sow
it all at first, because I did not know when was the proper time for it; so I sowed about two thirds of the seeds,
leaving about a handful of each. It was a great comfort to
me afterwards that I did so, for not one grain of that I

放在上面，以便取用。然后又在洞壁上钉上小木钉，挂枪和其他可以挂起来的东西。

第八章　荒岛探奇

　　我逐渐掌握了雨季、旱季的规律，学会了划分它们，这样便于为它们的到来提前做些准备。为了掌握这个规律，我付出了很大的代价，而且这是最令人气馁的一个尝试。当初我意外的发现地里长出一些稻子、大麦苗——大概三十棵水稻、二十棵大麦——等到成熟后，我把穗子存了下来。现在雨季刚过，我想应该是播种的时候了。

　　随后我用木锹翻了一片地，并撒下种子。但是我播种时，脑中不时闪现出这样的念头：刚开始不能把所有的种子都种上吧，因为我自己并不清楚播种的最佳季节。于是，我只撒了三分之二的种子，每样都留下一些。我真庆幸自己这样做了，因为这次我撒的种子没有一粒发芽的。播种

sowed this time came to anything; for the months following, the earth having had no rain after the seed was
sown, it had no moisture to assist its growth, and never
came up at all, till the wet season had come again, and
then it grew as if it had been newly sown.

Finding my first seed did not grow, I sought for a
moister piece of ground to make another trial in; and I
dug up a piece of ground near my new bower, and sowed
the rest of my seed in February, a little before the vernal
equinox; and this, having the rainy months of March and
April to water it, sprung up very pleasantly, and yielded
a very good crop; but having part of the seed left only,
and not daring to sow all that I had yet, I had but a
small quantity at last, my whole crop not amounting to
above half a peck of each kind.

But by this experience I was made master of my
business, and knew exactly when the proper season was
to sow; and that I might expect two seed – times, and
two harvests every year.

While this corn was growing, I made a little discovery. The circle or double hedge that I had made, was
not only firm and entire, but the stakes which I had cut
off of some trees that grew thereabouts, all shot out, and
gew with long branches, as much as a willow – tree usually shoots the first year after lopping its head. I could

后的几个月内一直干旱，没有雨水，种子得不到滋润，所以也就没有发芽，一直埋在土里。直到下一个雨季来临，种子才发芽，好像刚种下似的。

当我发觉第一次播下的种子没有发芽，就又找了一块比较湿润的地再次进行试验。我在新茅屋附近又翻了一片地，二月，春分前几天，我又将剩下的种子播下去。随着三、四月份雨季的来临，这片庄稼得到充分滋润，长势非常不错，最终获得了好收成。但是因为种子本来就剩得不多，又没敢全部种下去，所以收获甚微，每样大概只收了一加仑（约四升半）。

不过这次经历使我成为这方面的专家。我已经准确掌握了什么时候是最佳播种季节，而且我估计一年可以种两季，那么也就可以一年收获两次了。

在庄稼生长这段时间，我有了一个小发现：我原来围起来的那道双层篱笆墙不但坚固完整，而且我在附近树上砍下的那些木桩都发了芽，长出长长的枝条，就像前一年刚修剪过的柳树。我也不知道那些都是什么树，我只顾一味地砍木桩。

not tell what tree to call it that these stakes were cut from. I was surprised, and yet very well pleased, to see the young trees grow; and I pruned them, and led them grow as much alike as I could, and it is scarce credible, how beautiful a figure they grew into in three years; so that though the hedge made a circle of about twenty – five yards in diameter, yet the trees soon covered it; and it was a complete shade, sufficient to lodge under all the dry season.

This made me resolve to cut some more stakes, and make me a hedge like this in a semicircle round my wall, I mean that of my first dwelling, which I did; and placing the trees or stakes in a double row, at about eight yards' distance from my first fence, they grew presently, and were at first a fine cover to my habitation, and afterwards served for a defense also.

The rainy season sometimes held longer or shorter, as the winds happened to blow; but this was the general observation I made. After I had found, by experience, the ill consequences of being abroad in the rain, I took care to furnish myself with provisions beforehand, that I might not be obliged to go out; and I sat within doors as much as possible during the wet months.

In this time I found much employment, for I found great occasion for many things which I had no way to fur

我惊喜地看着这些小树成长，心里有说不出的高兴，我不断地给它们修剪枝叶，让它们按照我的意愿成长，最好长得一样。三年后，它们居然长得婀娜多姿，真是让人无法相信。虽然我的篱笆墙圈出了一个直径达二十五码（约二十三米）的场地，但是这些树很快把它完全覆盖起来了，形成很大的阴凉，旱季住在那里非常地凉爽。

有了这个发现，我决定再去砍些木桩，在我的墙外——我的第一个住所的墙外再围一道半圆形的篱笆墙。说干就干。我把那些树和木桩排成两排，离我的旧篱笆墙大概八码（约七米）。不久，它们长成了一道很好的荫蔽墙，后来还成为我的防御工事。

根据我的大致观察：雨季有时长，有时短，那要看有没有风。凭经验，我已经知道下雨时不宜外出，外出只能是凶多吉少。所以就留心提前备足粮食，这样下雨时就不用出去了。阴雨连绵的日子，我尽量足不出户，呆在屋里。

这段期间我很忙，做了许多许多事情，我发现这是一个好时机——努力工作，不断实验，制

nish myself with, but by hard labor and constant application. Particularly, I tried many ways to make myself a
basket; but all the twigs I could get for the purpose
proved so brittle that they would do nothing. It proved of
excellent advantage to me now, that when I was a boy, I
used to take great delight in standing at a basket – maker's in the town where my father lived, to see them
make their wicker ware. I wanted nothing but the materials; the twigs of that tree from whence I cut my stakes
might possibly be as tough as the willows in England,
and I resolved to try.

Accordingly, the next day I went to my country
house, as I called it, and cutting some of the smaller
twigs, I found them to my purpose as much as I could
desire; whereupon I came the next time prepared with a
hatchet to cut down a quantity which I soon found, for
there was a great plenty of them. These I set up to dry
within my circle of hedges; and when they were fit for
use, I carried them to my cave; and here, during the
next season, I employed myself in making a great many
baskets, both carry earth, or to carry or lay up anything,
as I had occasion; and though I did not finish them very
handsomely, yet I made them sufficiently serviceable for
my purpose; and thus afterwards I took care never to be
without them; and as my wicker ware decayed, I made

作要添置的东西。特别值得一提的是，我试了好多方法编织篮子，但是我所能找到编织篮子的树枝一弄就断，根本用不上。但是有件事情还是让我沾了不少光。小的时候，我最喜欢到父亲居住的镇上的柳器店，站在工匠旁边看他们编东西。我现在就是手头没材料。我猛然想起做木桩的那种树的枝条可能和英国的柳条一样坚韧，于是决定试一试。

于是，第二天，我就到我的别墅去了——我总是这样称呼我的住所——砍了些小树枝，它们正是我想要的材料。第二次再去的时候我带了一把斧头，那里有好多这样的枝条，我就要多砍一些。我把树枝晒到别墅的篱笆墙上，待到能用时再把它们运回山洞。在接下来的雨季里，我编了许多篮子，既可以用来运土，又可以在必要时装运其他东西，这主要取决于我要用它做什么。尽管我编得不太漂亮，但足以满足各种需要了。从此以后，我的生活就再也离不开这类东西用。篮子烂了，我就再编织一些。尤其后来我的粮食渐

more; especially I made strong, deep baskets to place my corn in, instead of sacks, when I should come to have any quantity of it.

I mentioned before, that I had a great mind to see the whole island, and that I traveled up the crook, and soon to where I built my bower, and where I had an opening quite to the sea, on the other side of the island. I now resolved to travel quite across the sea – shore on that side; so taking my gun, and hatchet, and my dog, and a large quantity of powder and shot more than usual, with two biscuit cakes, and a great bunch of raisins in my pouch, for my store, I began my journey. When I had passed the vale where my bower stood, as above, I came within view of the sea, to the west; and it being a very clear day, I fairly descried land, whether an island or continent I could not tell; but it lay very high at a very great distance; by my guess it could not be less than fifteen or twenty leagues off.

I could not tell what part of the world this might be, otherwise than that I knew it must be part of America; and, as I concluded by all my observations, must be near the Spanish dominions, and perhaps was all inhabited by savages, where, if I should have landed, I would have been in a worse condition than I was now; and therefore I acquiesced in the dispositions of Providence,

渐多了起来，我又编了一些又深又结实的篮子当做布袋装粮食。

前面我已讲过，我很想看看整个小岛。我沿着小溪不一会儿就走到我的别墅，那里有一条路通向岛的另一端的大海。我决定到那边走一走，看一看，于是带上枪、斧子和狗，还比平时多带了些弹药，再带上两大块饼干及一大串葡萄干，我把这些东西准备好后，便踏上了旅程。我穿过茅屋所在的山谷，向西眺望，就看到了大海。那天天气非常好，我可以清楚地望见大海对面的陆地，不知道那里是一个岛屿还是一片陆地，只知道它的地势很高，且离我这里很远，估计离我这儿至少十五到二十海里。

我说不上来那是什么地方，不过根据我的观察，不应该是别的什么地方，应该是美洲的一部分，靠近西班牙领地，说不定上面住的全是野人。如果我在那里登陆了，那我的处境一定比现在更糟。于是我默认了上帝对我的安排，并开始承认、

which I began now to own, and to believe, ordered everything for the best; I say I quieted my mind with this, and left afflicting myself with fruitless wishes of being there.

Besides, after some pause upon this affair, I considered, that if this land was the Spanish coast, I should certainly, one time or other, see some vessel pass or re – pass one way or other; but if not, then it was the savage coast between the Spanish country and Brazil, which is inhabited by the worst of savages; for they are cannibals, or man – eaters, and fail not to murder and devour all the human bodies that fall into their hands.

With these considerations I walked very leisurely forward. I found that side of the island where I now was, much pleasanter than mine, the open or savanna fields sweet, adorned with flowers and grass, and full of very fine woods. I saw abundance of parrots, and fain would I have caught one, if possible, to keep it to be tame, and taught it to speak to me. I did, after some pains taken, catch a young parrot, for I knocked it down with a stick and, having received it, I brought it home, but it was some years before I could make him speak. However, at last I taught him to call me by my name, very familiarly; but the accident that followed, though it be a trifle, will be very diverting in its place.

I was exceedingly diverted with this journey. I

相信这种安排是最好的。这样想着，我的心态平静了许多，不再自寻烦恼，妄想着到对面的陆地上去看看。

此外，对这件事的一番思考后，我想，如果那片陆地接近西班牙海岸，我迟早会看到船只在此穿梭经过；如果不是，那就是位于西班牙海岸和巴西之间的荒蛮之地，上面住着最野蛮的土人。他们都是野人，吃人的野人，任何人只要落入他们手中，就别想活了，都会被杀死和吃掉。

我一边想着这个问题，一边十分悠闲地向前踱着。我发现岛的那边比我住的那里要宜人得多。开阔芳香的土地上鲜花缤纷，绿草茵茵，处处是郁郁葱葱的树丛。我还看到许多鹦鹉，如果有可能，真想抓上一只，训化它，教它和我说话。费了一番力气，我总算捉了一只小鹦鹉。我是用一根树枝把它从树上打下来的，我捉住它，然后带回家。但是教会它说话却是几年以后的事情了。尽管如此，它最终还是能够亲昵地叫出我的名字。后来这件事还引出点儿意外，虽说小事一桩，但颇有趣味。

这次旅行玩得非常愉快，我在低地发现了野

found in the low grounds, hares, foxes, goats, pigeons, and turtles. Though my case was deplorable enough, yet I had great cause for thankfulness, that I was not driven to any extremities for food; but rather plenty, even to dainties.

I never traveled in this journey above two miles outright in a day, or there-about; but I took so many turns and returns, to see what discoveries I could make, that I came weary enough to the place where I resolved to sit down for all night; and then either reposed myself in a tree, or surrounded myself with a row of stakes set upright in the ground, either from one tree or another, or so as no wild creature could come at me without waking me.

As soon as I came to the sea-shore, I was surprised to see that I had taken up my lot the worst side of the island, for here indeed the shore was covered with innumerable turtles, whereas on the other side I found but three in a year and a half. Here was also an infinite number of fowls of many kinds, some of which I had not seen before, and many of them very good meat; but such as I knew not the names of, except those called penguins.

I could have shot as many as I pleased, but was very sparing of my powder and shot; and therefore had

兔、狐狸、山羊、鸽子和海龟。虽然我的境况够惨的，我仍有非常好的理由感谢上苍，感谢上苍没有让我为填饱肚子来回奔波。我有的是吃的，甚至还有美味。

在这次旅行中，我每天行程从不超过两、三英里，因为我总是绕来绕去的，看看能否发现什么。所以每到一处，晚上准备睡觉时，我都疲倦得很，要么在树上睡觉，要么在两棵树之间的空地上打上一圈木桩，睡到里面。这样如果有野兽侵袭，我总是能被惊醒。

当我走到大海边时，我惊讶地发现我住的那边称得上是岛上最差的地方。因为这边海滩上，海龟多得不计其数；而我住的那边，一年半只看到三只。这里还有数不尽的禽类，品种繁多，有些我以前从未见过，其中有不少还是口中美味。除了企鹅，其他的我都叫不上名字。

只要我愿意，我可以打很多飞禽，但是我想节约着用弹药。如果可能的话，我此时最想捕杀

more mind to kill a she – goat, if I could, which I could better feed on; and though there were many more goats here than on the other side of the island, yet it was, with much more difficulty that I could come near them, the country being flat and even, so that they saw me much sooner than when I was on the hills.

I confess this side of the country was much pleasanter than mine, but yet I had not the least inclination to remove; for, as I was fixed in my habitation, it became natural to me; and I seemed all the while was here to be, as it were, upon a journey, and from home. However, I traveled along the shore of the sea toward the east, I suppose about twelve miles; and then setting up a great pole upon the shore for a mark, I concluded I would go home again; and the next journey I took should be on the other side of the island, east from my dwelling.

I took another way to come back than that I went, thinking I could easily keep all the island so much in my view, that I could not miss finding my first dwelling by viewing the country; but I found myself mistaken; for having come about two or three miles, I found myself descended into a very large valley, but so surrounded with hills covered with woods, that I could not see which was my way by any direction but that of the sun.

It happened, to my farther misfortune, that the

一只母山羊，这样就可以美美的吃上一大顿。这里的山羊虽然比我住的那边多，但是想靠近它们却是非常困难的。因为这里地势平坦，它们比我站在山上时更容易发现我。

我承认这边比我那边要宜人得多，但我却丝毫没有搬家的念头。因为我在那边已经安定下来了，也习惯了。我在这边总是感觉自己是在旅行，而不是在家里。然而我沿着海岸向东走，大约走了十二英里，然后立了一根杆子作标记。我决定先回家再说，下次再出来时从相反方向出发，也就是从我的住处向东走。

回家时我另选了一条路走。我认为自己能够把全岛看个一清二楚并轻易地掌握全岛的情况，这样，只要我看看周围的地形，我就能回到自己的住处，但是我错了。刚走了两三英里，我发现自己进入一个大山谷中，四周群山环绕，满山树丛。除非看见太阳，否则很难分清东南西北。

更为倒霉的是，来到山谷中三四天，天空总

weather proved hazy for three or four days while I was in this valley; and not being able to see the sun, I wandered about very uncomfortably, and at last was obliged to find out the sea-side, look for my post, and come back the same way I went; and then by easy journeys I turned homeward.

In this journey my dog surprised a young goat, and seized upon it; and I, running to take hold of it, and saved it alive from the dog. I had a great mind to bring home, for I had often been musing whether it might not be possible to get a kid or two, and so raise a breed of tame goats, which might supply me when my powder and shot should be spent.

I made a collar for this little creature; and with a string I led him along, though with some difficulty, till I came to my bower, and there I enclosed him, for I was very impatient to be at home, from whence I had been absent above a month.

I cannot express what a satisfaction it was to me to come into my old hutch and lie down in my hammock-bed: this little wandering journey, without a settled abode, had been so unpleasant to me, that my own house was a perfect settlement to me, compared to that; and it rendered everything about me so comfortable, that I resolved that I would never go a great way from it

是阴霾的，连太阳都看不见。我心里很不安，胡乱地走着。最后只能再回到海边，找到那根做标记的杆子，沿原路返回，然后我才轻松地踏上回家的路。

这次旅行中，我的狗发现了一只小山羊，便冲了上去咬住它。我连忙奔上前去把它救了下来。幸亏它没有被狗咬死，我决定把它带回去。因为我常想，如果能抓一两只小山羊驯养，再繁殖成群，这样弹药用尽后，我也能吃上羊肉了。

我给小山羊做了一个项圈，用绳子牵着它走。费了不少劲儿才把它领回家，我把它圈起来。我在外面游荡了一个多月，早就归心似箭了。

我不知道该怎么形容回到家躺在吊床上的那份满足。这趟小小的旅行，居无定所，我感觉特别不舒服，像个夜游神，相比之下，我的房子简直是一个完美的住处。家里的一切都让我觉得非常舒服惬意，我决定再也不离家出远门了。我命

again, while it should be my lot stay on the island.

Chapter 9   Celebration

I reposed myself there a week, to rest and regale after my long journey; during which, most of the time was taken up in the weighty affair of making a cage for my Poll, who began now to be a mere domestic, and to be mighty well acquainted with me. Then I began to think of the poor kid, which I had pent in within my little circle, and resolved to go and fetch it home, and give it some food: accordingly I went, and found it where I left it; for indeed it could not get out, but was almost starved for want of food. I went and cut boughs of trees and branches of such shrubs as I could find, and threw over to it; and having fed it, I tied it as I did before to lead it away; but it was so tame with being hungry, that I had no need to have tied it; for it followed me like a dog; and as I continually fed it, the creature became so loving, so gentle, and so fond, that it became from that time one of my domestics also, and would never leave me afterwards.

The rainy season of the autumnal equinox now came, and I kept the 30th of September in the same solemn manner as before, being the anniversary of my land-

中注定要呆在这个岛上。

第九章　喜筵庆贺

在经历了长长的一段旅行之后，我在岛上休息、恢复了一个星期，在此期间，我把大部分的时间都花在为鹦鹉波尔做鸟笼子这件大事上。经过了一段时间的磨合之后，它现在看起来很是听话，而且也渐渐开始和我熟悉了。然后我又想到了那只被我圈起来的小山羊，决定将它带到家里喂些吃的。找到了圈它之处，发现它还乖乖地呆在那里，由于出不来，都快饿死了。于是我去砍了些树枝和灌木丢给它吃。喂完之后我还像以前那样把它拴起来。但这小山羊由于饥饿已变得非常温顺，或许根本没必要把它拴起来，因为它就像小狗一样跟在我的身后。结果我发现它越喂越听话越可爱。所以在那之后，它便加入了我的"家畜"行列，而且从未离开过我。

秋分姗姗来临了，不时夹着一些淅沥的小雨，我还像往常那样记录着日子——九月三十日，即

ing on the island, having now been there two years, and no more prospect of being delivered than the first day I came there. I spent the whole day in humble and thankful acknowledgments of the many wonderful mercies, which my solitary conduction was attended with, and without which it might have been infinitely more miserable. I gave humble and hearty thanks, that God had been pleased to discover in me, even that it was possible I might be more happy in this solitary condition, than I should have been in society, and in all the pleasures of the world: that he could fully make up to me deficiencies of my solitary state and the want of human society, by his presence, and the communications of his grace to my soul, supporting, comforting, and encouraging me to depend upon his providence here, and hope for his eternal presence hereafter.

Before, as I walked about, either on my hunting, or for viewing country, the anguish of my soul in my condition would break upon me on a sudden, and my very heart would die within me, to think of the woods, the mountains, the deserts I was in; and how I was a prisoner, locked up with the eternal bolts and bars of the ocean, in an uninhabited wilderness, without redemption. In the greatest of my mind, this would break out upon me like a storm, and make me wring my handsaw,

我来到这个小岛的纪念日，对日子的记录我是严肃认真，一丝不苟的。我来到该岛都已经整整两年了。从第一天来到这里我便没有什么对未来的憧憬了。但是我很珍惜自己在这里所度过的每一天，感谢上苍对我的恩赐，感谢上帝对我的仁慈。如果没有这些恩赐，如果没有这些仁慈，一切想必都是无止境的痛苦，我将永远生活在孤独无援的境况中。衷心地感谢上天让我来到这里，在这里生活也许会很孤独，但是总要比现实社会快乐多了，没有什么别的地方比这里更快乐了，它可以弥补我现实生活中的不足及对生活的看法，这些在现实生活中都是不可能感悟到的。是上天美化了我的灵魂，是上帝显灵，他支持鼓励着我对未来不断的向往，他让我不断祈祷，福祉总会降临于我。

之前，我经常漫步游走，要么是寻觅猎物，要么是环顾旷野的美景，可是一种莫名的痛苦常常会萦绕在心头。一想到那茂密的树林，连绵的山脉和一望无垠的沙漠，我整个人都要崩溃了，我就好像囚犯一样没有自由，难道我注定要永远地被困在这个"大海的牢笼"里吗？这里荒无人烟，没有任何希望，这一切的一切好似暴风雨一样袭入我的脑海，使我无法呼吸，有时甚至潸然

and weep like a child. Sometimes it would take me in the middle of my work, and I would immediately sit down and sigh, and look down upon the ground for an hour or two together; and this was still worse to me; for if I could burst out into tears, or vent myself by words, it would go off, and the grief, having exhausted itself, would abate.

But now I began to exercise myself new thoughts; I daily read the word of God, and applied all the comforts of it into my present state. One morning, being very sad, I opened the Bible upon these words, "I will never, never leave thee, nor forsake thee!" Immediately it occurred, that these words were to me, why else should they be directed in such a manner, just at the moment when I was mourning over my condition, as one forsaken of God and man? Well then, said I, if God does not forsake me, or what matters it, though the world should all forsake me: seeing on the other hand, if I had all the world, and should lose the favor and blessing of God, there would be no comparison in the loss.

My very soul within me blessed God for directing my friend in England, without any order of mine, to pack the Bible among my goods; and for assisting me afterwards to save it out of the wreck of the ship.

In this disposition of mind, I began my third year.

泪下，经常在干活干到一半的时候，这种可怕的经历便涌上心头，使我不得不停下来，叹叹气，凝视着地面，一看便是一两个小时。这一切对我来说简直就是一种痛苦和煎熬，或许只有通过言语或放声痛哭的方式才能彻底地解脱自己，不过物极必反，也许在彻底地痛过之后就不会再那么难过了。

现在我慢慢想开了，我天天都读着上帝的话，将这些安抚之词运用在我目前的情形中。一天早晨，我怀着莫名的悲哀打开《圣经》，"我不会，永远不会离开你！"这样一行文字映入眼帘，我突然感到这不正是对我所说的吗？为什么其他人没有得到这样的教诲，而恰恰在我悲叹自己是上帝和人类的弃儿时看到了这句话，于是我对自己说，如果上帝不遗弃我的话，即使整个世界都将我抛弃，那又有什么关系呢？从另一方面看，如果我失去了上帝的恩宠和祝福，那么即使我拥有整个世界，那我的损失将更是无可比拟的。

我真诚地感谢上帝指引我英格兰的朋友将《圣经》装在了我的行囊里，其实我并没有要求他这么做，又让我后来有幸将"它"从海难中解救出来。

就在这种思想状态下，我开始了在荒岛上的

In general, I was very seldom idle; having regularly divided my time, according to the several daily employments that were before me, such as first, my duty to God, and reading the Scriptures, which I constantly set apart some time for, thrice every day. Secondly, the going abroad with my gun for food, which generally took me up three hours every morning when it did not rain. Thirdly the ordering, curing, preserving, and cooking what I had killed or caught for my supply. These took up a great part of the day. Also it is to be considered, that in the middle of the day, the violence of the heat was too great to stir out; so that about four in the evening was all the time I could be supposed to work in; with this exception, that sometimes I changed my hours of hunting and working, and went to work in the morning, and abroad with my gun in the afternoon.

I was now in the months of November and December, expecting my crop of barley and rice. The ground I had manured or dug up for them was not great; for, as I observed, my seed of each was not above the quantity of half a peck; for I had lost one whole crop by sowing in the dry season; but now my crop promised very well, when on a sudden I found I was in danger of losing it all again to enemies of several sorts, with it was scare possible to keep from it; at first, the goats, and wild crea-

第三个年头。但总的来说，我并没有虚度时光，有规律地根据我的工作划分了时间，比如：首先要爱上帝，必须读《圣经》，我可是花了不少时间读《圣经》，一天至少读三次。其次，如果早上不下雨的话，我就会带上枪去找食物，通常在早间进行，一般要花三个小时的时间。再次，把自己杀死的动物或是弄来的蔬菜，洗呀，储藏呀，烹调呀等等，这些往往就要花掉我一天大部分的时间。另外我要提到的便是中午的时候，中午这里天气热得要死，所以下午四点左右便成了我的干活时间，除非有时我调换一下打猎和干活的时间，上午干活，下午带着枪出去打猎。

一转眼到了十一、十二月了，我期待着大麦和稻谷庄稼的丰收。这次播种的面积不是很大，我没有好好施肥，也管理不善，上次由于干旱，庄稼全遭殃了，连芽都没有发，根本没有苗，所以剩下的种子也不多了。令人欣慰的是这次庄稼长得不错，但是我很担心这次又会因那些无法对付的天敌而颗粒无收，像什么山羊、野兔之类的

tures which I called hares, which, tasting the sweetness of blade, lay in it night and day, as soon as it came up, and ate it so close, that it could get no time to shoot into stalks.

This I saw no remedy for, but my making an enclosure about it with a hedge, which I did with a great deal of toil; and the more, because it required a great deal of speed; the creatures daily spoiling my corn. However, as my arable land was but small, suited to my crop, I got it totally well fenced in about three weeks' time; and shooting some of the creatures in the day-time, I set my dog to guard it in the night, tying him up to a stake at the gate, where he would stand and bark all night long: so in a little time the enemies forsook the place, and the corn grew very strong and well, and began to ripen apace.

But as the beasts ruined me before, while my corn was in the blade, so the birds were as like to ruin me now, when it was in the ear; for going along by place to see how it throve, I saw my little crop surrounded with fowls of I know not how many sorts, which stood watching till I should be gone. I immediately let fly among them. I had no sooner shot, but there arose up a little cloud of fowls, which I had not seen at all, from among the corn itself.

动物，它们靠吃麦叶为生，并在庄稼里睡觉，只要庄稼长出嫩芽，兔子和山羊就会啃食掉。恐怕这庄稼还没长成秆呢，就被它们全干光了。

怎么办呢，总得想个办法补救吧！于是我想做一个能围得住庄稼的篱笆。虽然费劲，也得做。而且不但得做，还得快动手，以防它们来搞破坏。幸好田地还不是很大，我只用了三周的时间就把所有的篱笆都插好了。白天我拿着枪"站岗"，晚上让猎狗去"值班"，我把它拴在大门口的柱子上，它便守护着大门，一有情况便"汪汪"大叫，那些该死的小动物见事不妙便望风而逃了，所以庄稼长得又高又大，慢慢开始成熟了。

以前是在庄稼长叶时野兽来搞破坏，到抽穗时野鸟又来侵扰，原打算去看看庄稼长得怎么样了，可是定睛一看，一大群野鸟都落在我辛勤耕作的庄稼的周围，大大小小熙熙攘攘的一片，眼睛瞅着我，等我一走便向庄稼进攻。真是不计其数，且都叫不上名字。我正准备开枪扫射呢，只见一片鸟刹时间"轰"地一下全飞跑了。

This touched me sensibly, for I foresaw, that in a few days they would devour all my hopes; that I should be starved, and never be able to raise a crop at all; and what to do I could not tell; however, I resolved not to lose my corn, if possible, though I should watch it night and day. In the first place, I went among it to see what damage was already done, and found they had spoiled a good deal of it; but that, as it was yet too green for them, the loss was not so great, but the remainder was like to be a good crop, if it could be saved.

I stayed by it to load my gun, and then coming away, I could easily see the thieves sitting upon all the trees about me, as if they only waited till I was gone away, and the event proved it to be so; for as I walked off, as if I was gone, I was no sooner out of their sight, but they dropped down one by one into the corn again. I was so provoked, that I could not have patience to stay till more came on, knowing that every grain that they ate now was, as it might be said, a peck loaf to me in the consequence. But coming up to the hedge, I fired again, and killed three of them. This was what I wished for; so I took them up, and served them, as we serve notorious thieves in England, that is, hanged them in chains, for a terror to others. It is almost impossible to imagine, that this should have such an effect as it had, for the

这种景象让我警觉起来，我估计再不想办法，这些东西会使我的美梦化为乌有，那还不得饿死，而且再也不能种庄稼了。但是至于怎么办，我暂时还未想好。然而我决定要保住我辛勤耕种的庄稼，哪怕是昼夜都去站岗。不过，我得先去看看损失有多大！结果发现那些可恶的家伙对庄稼的破坏还不小啊，幸亏这些庄稼还没怎么熟，损失不算太大，所以剩下的，如果精心保护的话，收成应该还是不错的。

我站在地边给枪里装上了火药，躲了起来，一眼便能看到那些落在树上想不劳而获的鸟，这些鸟真贼，想必它们就在等着我离开之后去偷袭庄稼，结果果然不出我所料，事实就是这样。因为我刚走了几步，假装走开，刚准备从它们眼前消失时，那些家伙便一哄而上冲到庄稼上了，天啊，我都要气疯了，简直是已经忍无可忍了，因为它们吃的那些东西对我来说以后可是我的"口粮"啊。我马上冲向前去，向它们开枪，打中三只。哈哈，正合我意，我把它们捡起来，决定好好"款待"它们，就像英格兰"对付"那帮臭名昭著的恶贼一样，我用绳子把它们绑成一串吊起来，吓唬它们那些可恶的"伙伴"，不过，真是不可思议，没想到这一招儿还真灵，打那之后，

fowls would not only not come at the corn, but in short they forsook all that part of the island, and I could never see a bird near the place as long as my scarecrows hung there. This I was very glad of, you may be sure, and about the latter end of December, which was our second harvest of the year, I reaped my corn.

Chapter 10   Farming Operations

I was sadly put to it for a scythe or a sickle to cut it down, and all I could do was to make one as well as I could, out of one of the broadswords, or cutlass, which I saved among the arms out of the ship. However, as my crop was but small, I had no great difficulty to cut it down; in short, I reaped it my way, for I cut nothing off but the ears, and carried it away in a great basket which I had made, and so rubbed it out with my hands. And at the end of all my harvesting I found, that out of my half peck of seed, I had near two bushels of rice, and above two bushels and a half of barley.

However, this was a great encouragement to me, and I foresaw that in time it would please God to supply me with bread; and yet here I was perplexed again, for I neither knew how to grind or make meal of my corn, or indeed how to clean it and part it; nor, if made into

它们再也没来捣乱了，好像从这个岛上消失了。只要稻草人挂在那儿，没有一只鸟敢来骚扰我的庄稼。可以猜想到，这令我非常高兴。十二月下旬是第二次收获期，我准备收割庄稼。我怀着满心的欢喜迎来了那年第二次庄稼的丰收。

第十章 庄园生涯

看着成熟的庄稼，我又发愁了，因为没有收割庄稼的镰刀。我只能把从船上武器堆中找来的一把弯刀改做成镰刀。幸运的是，我的庄稼不多，收割起来也没太大的困难。我用自己的方式收庄稼——只割穗子，然后用自己做的筐子把它们运回去，再用双手把谷粒搓出来。收完庄稼后，我发现除了投入的一加仑的种子，我收获了近十六加仑的稻谷和二十多加仑的大麦。

然而，这对我已经是一个很大的鼓励了。我早就知道上帝迟早会让我吃上面包的。可是，现在难题又摆在面前了。我既不知道如何把麦粒磨成面粉，也不知道如何脱谷、筛谷；即使磨成面

meal, how to make bread of it; and if how to make it, yet I knew not how to bake it. These things being added to my desire of having a good quantity for store, and to secure a constant supply, I resolved not to taste any of this crop, but to preserve it all for seed against the next season, and in the meantime to employ all my study and hours of working to accomplish this great work of proving myself with corn and bread.

First, I had no plough to turn the earth, no spade or shovel to dig it. Well, this I conquered by making a wooden spade, as I observed before, but this did my work in but a wooden manner; and though it cost me a great many days to make it, yet, for want of iron, it not only wore out the sooner, but made my work the harder, and made it be performed much worse.

However, this I bore with too, and was content to work it out with patience, and bear with the badness of the performance. When the corn was sowed, I had no harrow, but was forced to go over it myself, and drag a heavy bough of a tree over it, to scratch the earth, as it may be called, rather than rake or harrow it.

But I was to prepare more land, for I had now seed enough to sow above an acre of ground. Before I did this, I had a week's work at least to make me a spade, which, when it was done, was a very sorry one indeed,

粉，也不知如何把面粉做成面包，即使做成了面包，我也不知道如何焙制。我还想多有一些粮食，以保证日后供应。于是，这些因素促使我决定不吃这次收获的庄稼了，而把它们全部留做种子，为下一季播种做准备。我还决定用全部时间和精力来研究这谷物制作面包这一伟大的工作。

首先，我没有犁犁地，没有铁锹或铁铲翻地。前面我已说过，我曾经做了一个木锹，克服了这个困难。但是这把锹并不好使，尽管它花了我不少日子才得以做成。我手头没有铁，木锹很容易坏，这使得我的工作更加困难了，而且很难再做下去。

所有这些我都忍着，耐着性子凑合着用这把木锹，尽管用它翻出的地显得乱七八糟。播完种，没有耙子，我还得自己来耙。我让自己拖着一根很重的大树枝把地耙了一遍又一遍。与其说我在耙地，还不如说在给地挠痒，如果可以这样说的话。

我得预先准备更多的耕地，我现在的种子是够种一英亩以上的土地了。在我播种前，我花了一星期的时间做成了一把锹。做成后，它确实很

and very heavy, and required double to work with it; however, I went through that, and sowed my seeds in two large flat pieces of ground, as near my house as I could find them to my mind, and fenced them in with a good hedge, so that in one year's time I knew I should have a quick or living hedge, that would want but little repair. This work was not so little as to take me up less than three months; because a great part of that time was in the wet season, when I could not go abroad.

Within – door, that is, when it rained, and I could not go out, I found employment on the following occasion, always observing, that all the while I was at work, I diverted myself with talking to my parrot, and teaching him to speak; and I quickly taught him to know his own name; at least to speak it out pretty loud, Poll; which was the word I ever heard spoken in the island by any mouth but my own. This therefore, was not my work, but an assistant to my work; for now, as I said, I had a great employment upon my hands, as follows; I had long studied, by some means or other, to make myself some earthen vessels, which indeed I wanted sorely, but knew not where to come at them; however, considering the heat of the climate, I did not doubt, but if I could find out any such clay, I might botch up some such pot as might, being dried by the sun, be hard enough, and

难看，而且很笨重，用它干活需要花两倍的力气。尽管如此，我总算过了这一关，把种子播到两大块平整的田地里。这两块地离我的房子很近，我很满意。我在地的四周围起了一圈牢固的篱笆墙。我知道，要不了一年的时间，这些木桩就能很快长成一圈郁郁葱葱的篱笆墙，而且不需要什么整修。我花了将近三个月才完成这项不算太小的工程。这期间大部分时间是雨季，因此我也出不了门。

出不了门时，也就是下雨不能出门的时候，我也找些事做，就是我一直提到的一边干活，一边找时间，寻开心和我的鹦鹉说话，教它学舌，权当是消磨时间。很快，我教会它说自己的名字。最起码它能响亮清晰地叫出"波儿"。不管怎么说，这是我落难荒岛以来除自己以外，从其他的生物嘴中听到的第一句话。当然，这不是我的工作，只是对我的工作的一种调剂。目前，我很忙，我正着手做一件很重要的事情，就是下面说到的，我早就打算设法给自己做些陶罐用。我确实非常需要这些东西，但是不知道怎么做。不过，想到这里炎热的气候，我肯定如果我能找到陶土，就能大概捏出些盆盆罐罐来，然后在太阳下晒干，等到足够坚硬、足够结实的程度，它肯定能够经

strong enough, to bear handling, and to hold anything that was dry, and required to be kept so; and as this was necessary in preparing corn, meal, I resolved to make some as large as I could, and fit only to stand like jars to hold what should be put into them.

I took many awkward ways to raise the paste. The reader may laugh at me if I told you what odd, misshapen, ugly things I made, how many of them fell in, and how many fell out, the clay not being stiff enough to bear its own weight; how many cracked by the over violent heat of the sun, being set out too hastily; and how many fell to pieces with only removing, as well before as after they were dried; and, in a word, how, after having labored hard to find the clay, to dig it, to temper it, to bring it home, and work it, I could not make above two large earthen ugly things, I cannot call them jars, in about two months' labor.

However, as the sun baked these two very dry and hard, I lifted them very gently up, and set them down again in two greater wicker baskets, that I had made on purpose for them, that they might not break, as between the pot and the basket there was a little room to spare, I stuffed it full of the rice and barley straw; and these two pots being to stand always dry, I thought it would hold my dry corn, and perhaps the meal when the corn was

得起使用，能够装一些需要保存的干东西。这对于我当前正在进行的加工粮食和磨面粉的工作是必要的。我要把它们做得尽可能的大，放在地上像缸那样，里面能放很多东西。

我也不知道用了多少笨办法和陶泥。如果我告诉你我做了好多奇形怪状的难看的东西，可能你会嘲笑我。不知道有多少因陶泥太软，盛受不住自身重量而陷进去或凸出来；也不知道有多少因仓促摆出来，被强烈的太阳晒爆；更不知道有多少在晒干前后，轻轻动一下就碎成残片了。总之一句话，我费了好大的劲儿找陶土，然后挖出来，和好陶泥，运回去，然后想方设法做器皿，结果花了差不多两个月的时间，做出了两个简直不能称之为缸的特别难看的大罐子。

最后，太阳终于把这两个罐子晒得又干又硬。我把它们轻轻地搬起来，放到两只预先编好的，专门放它们的大柳条筐中，以防它们破裂。我还在陶罐和筐的空隙中塞满稻草和麦秆，这样，它们就不会受潮了，永远都是干燥的。我想这下可以放干燥的粮食和磨出的面粉了吧。

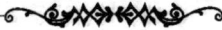

bruised.

Though I miscarried so much in my design for large pots, yet I made several smaller things with better success, such as little round pots, flat dishes, and pitchers, and anything my hand turned to, and heat of the sun baked them strangely hard.

But all this would not answer my end, which was to get an earthen pot to hold what was liquid, and bear the fire, which none of these could do. It happened after some time, making a pretty large fire for cooking my meat, when I went to put it out after I had done with it, I found a broken piece of one of my earthen ware vessels in the fire, burnt as hard as a stone, and red as a tile. I was agreeably surprised to see it, and said to myself, that certainly they might be made to burn whole, if they would burn broken.

This set me to study how to order my fire, so as to make it burn me some pots. I had no notion of a kiln, such as the potters burn in, or of glazing them with lead, though I had some lead to do it with; but I placed two or three pots, in a pile one upon another, and placed my firewood all round it, with a great heap of embers under them; I plied the fire with fresh fuel round the outside, and upon the top, till I saw the pots in the inside red – hot quite through, and observed that they

虽说我做大缸的计划大多破产了，但我做的一些小东西却比较成功，比如说小圆罐、碟子、带柄的罐及其他顺手做成的东西。太阳把它们晒得非常的坚硬。

但是这些东西并没有达到我的目的，我想要的是一个可以装水并能够在火上烧的泥锅，它们没一个符合我的要求。又过了些日子，我生了一堆很旺的火烤肉吃，烤完肉后要把火灭掉的时候，忽然在火里看到一块泥制器皿的碎片，已被火烧得同石头一样硬，像瓦一样红了。我一见之下异常惊喜，然后我对自己说，碎片的能烧，那整个陶器皿当然也能烧了。

我开始研究怎样控制我的火力来烧制几只罐子。我不会搭那些制陶工人烧陶用的窑，也不知道怎样用铅去涂釉，虽然我还有一点儿铅可用。我把两三只泥罐一个搭一个地堆起来，在四周放满干柴，干柴下放上一大堆炭火，然后从四周和顶上点起火来，一直烧到罐子红透为止，而且当

did not crack at all; when I saw them clear red, I let them stand in that heat about five or six hours, till I found one of them, though it did not crack, did melt or run. For the sand which was mixed with the clay, melted by the violence of the heat, and would have run into glass, if I had gone on; so I slacked my fire gradually, till the pots began to abate of the red color, and watching them all night that I might not let the fire abate too fast, in the morning I had three very good, I will not say handsome earthen pots.

After this experiment, I need not say that I wanted no sort of earthen ware for my use, but the shapes of them, they were very indifferent, as any one may suppose, when I had no way of making them, but as the children make dirt pies, or as a woman would make pies that had never learnt to raise paste. No joy at a thing of so mean a nature was ever equal to mine, when I found I had made an earthen pot that would bear the fire; and I had hardly patience to stay till they were cold, before I set one upon the fire again, with some water in it, to boil me some meat, which it did admirably well; and with a piece of a kid I made some very good broth, though I wanted oatmeal, and several other ingredients requisite to make it so good as I would have had it.

My next concern was to get me a stone mortar to

心不让它们炸裂。我看见它们已经红透后，又让它们那样保持了五六小时的热度，直到我发现有一只虽然没裂，但已经熔化了。因为陶土里所含的沙子已被过大的火烧溶了，再烧下去就成玻璃了。于是我慢慢将火熄灭，让那些罐子的红色渐渐退下去，而且守了整夜，不让火熄得太快。到了第二天早晨，我烧出了三只很不错的瓦罐，虽然它们算不上美观。

经过这次试验，不用说，我不缺什么陶器用了，但它们的形状太难看了，简直不太像样，这个大家可以想象得到，因为我实在没有别的办法去制做一些像样的器皿，只好像小孩做泥饼，或一个没学过和面的女人做馅饼那样去做。当我发现自己制成了一只耐火的陶罐时，我对这件微不足道的小事感到了无可比拟的快乐。我来不及等到它们冷透，便给其中一只加了点儿水，重新放到火上，煮了一点肉，效果很不错。我用一块小山羊肉，煮了一碗很好的肉汤，虽然我缺少燕麦粉和一些别的配料，否则我会把它做得香美可口，合乎我的理想。

我想做的第二件事，是想做一个石臼来舂粮

stamp or beat some corn in; for as to the mill, there was no thought of arriving to that perfection of art with one pair of hands. To supply this want, I was at a great loss; for of all trades in the world I was as perfectly unqualified for a stonecutter, as for any whatever; neither had I any tools to go about it with. I spent many a day to find out a great stone big enough to cut hollow, and make fit for a mortar, and could find none at all, except what was in the solid rock, and which I had no way to dig or cut out; nor indeed were the rocks in the island of hardness sufficient, but were all of a sandy crumbling stone, which would neither bear weight of a heavy pestle, nor would break the corn without filling it with sand; so, after great deal of time lost in searching for a stone, I gave it up, and resolved to look out for a great block of hard wood, which I found indeed much easier; and getting one as big as I had strength to stir, I rounded it, and formed it on the outside with my axe and hatchet; and then, with the help of fire and infinite labor, made a hollow place in it, as the Indians in Brazil make their canoes. After this, I made a great heavy pestle or beater, of the wood called the ironwood.

My next difficulty was to make a sieve, to dress my meal and part it from the bran and the husk, without which I did not see it possible I could have any bread.

食，或用来捣碎食物，因为我明白，仅靠我的一双手是无法达到这一目的的。对如何满足这一需要，我一点儿头绪也没有，因为在世上所有的行当中，我对石匠手艺比对别的手艺更外行，而且我也没有工具来进行此项工作。我花了几天时间，想找一块足够大的，但中间挖空的石头，做一个石臼，但除了那些无法挖凿的岩石之外，就找不到别的石料了。这岛上的岩石也不够坚硬，都是沙石，既经不住重杵的重量，也捣不碎粮食，而且还会给粮食里搀些沙子。所以，在花了很长时间还找不到一块硬料后，我放弃了这一努力，决定去找一大块硬木头，这果然容易一些；我找到一块勉强可以搬得动的大木头，把它砍得圆圆的，拿大小斧头把它修得初具外形，然后用火力和无限的劳力，在它上面做了一个槽，就像巴西的印第安人做独木舟那样，做好之后，我又用一种叫铁树的木头做了一只又大又重的杵。

我的下一个困难，就是要做一个筛子来筛面粉，把它和糠皮麸皮分开；没有筛子，我看我是没有任何办法做面包的。这是最困难的一件事，

This was a most difficult thing, for I had nothing like the necessary things to make it with; I mean fine thin canvas, or stuff, to sift the meal through. And here I was at a full stop for many months; nor did really know what to do: linen I had left but was mere rags; I had goat's hair, but neither knew I how to weave or spin it; and had I known how, here were no tools to work it with. All the remedy that I found for this, was some muslin; and with some pieces of these I made three small sieves, but proper enough for the work.

The baking part was the next thing to be considered, and how I should make bread when I came to have corn; for, first, I had no yeast. As to that part, there was no supplying the want, so I did not concern myself much about it. But for an oven I was indeed in great pain. At length I found out an experiment for that also, which was this: I made some earthen vessels very broad, but not deep; about two feet in diameter, and not above nine inches deep; these I burnt in the fire, as I had done the other, and laid them by; and when I wanted to bake, I made a great fire upon the hearth, which I paved with some square tiles of my own making and burning also; but I should not call them square. When the firewood was burnt pretty much into embers, or live coals, I drew them forward upon this hearth, so as to

因为我实在没有做筛子的必要材料，就是那种可以使面粉漏出去的网眼布之类的东西。这使我彻底停工了几个月，真不知道怎样去做。我仅剩的亚麻布几乎成了破布条，山羊毛倒是有，但我不知怎样去纺织它，把它织成线。而且就算我知道，也没有工具去做。我所能做的补救，就是找到一些细薄棉布，我用其中几块做了三面很小的筛子，不过总算能凑合着用。

接下来我便要考虑焙烘的问题，以及等我有了粮食后怎么做面包的问题。因为，第一我没有酵粉，这一方面我无论如何是没有办法的，所以我也不太在意。但有关炉子的问题，却让我大费脑筋。后来我居然想出一个试验办法，就是我先做一些宽而不深的陶器，直径约二尺，深不过九寸，我像烧别的陶器那样放在火中烧过，放在一边；到烘面包的时候，我先在我的炉子里生起一堆旺火来；炉子是用我自己烧制的方瓦砌成的，但是这瓦并不能说是很方整。当木柴烧透变成炽炭时，我把它们放在炉膛里并盖好，让它们把炉子烧得非常热后再通通扫去。我把我的面包放在

cover it all over; and there I let them lie, till the hearth was very hot: then sweeping away all the embers, I set down my loaves; and whelming down the earthen pot upon them, drew the embers all round the outside of the pot, to keep in, and add to the heat: and thus, I baked my barley – loaves, and became in a little time a pastry – cook into the bargain, for I made myself several cakes of the rice, and puddings.

Chapter 11 Hopes of Escape

All the while these things were doing, I fancied seeing the main-land, and an inhabited country, I might find some way or other to convey myself farther, and perhaps at last find some means of escape.

But I feared that I might fall into the hands of savages, and perhaps I might have reason to think far worse than the lions and tigers of Africa. That if I once came into their power, I should run a hazard more than a thousand to one of being killed, and perhaps of being eaten; for I had heard that the people of Caribbean coat were cannibals.

Now I wished for my boy Xury, and the long boat which had sailed above a thousand miles along the coast of Africa; but this was in vain. Then I thought I would

里面，用瓦盆把它们扣住，再把瓦盆外面盖满热炭，以便保持和增高温度。这样，我把我的大麦面包烘得非常好，而且在很短时间内我变成一位很好的面包师，因为我自己又用大米做了一些蛋糕和布丁。

第十一章　生还之光

我在做这些事情的时候，一直幻想着在找到大陆和有人烟的城市之后，我一定会发现继续生存的办法，说不定最后还能找到逃生的途径。

但我非常害怕会落到野人手里，而且我也有理由相信野人比非洲的狮子和老虎还要恶劣，凶残得多，如果有一天我落到他们手里，我就要冒九死一生的危险，也许还会被他们吃掉；因为我听说加勒比海岸的人都是食人族。

现在我又怀念起我的小仆人埃瑟利和载着我在非洲海岸航行了一千多英里的长艇了，但这都是无济于事的。后来我又想去看看我们那只船的

go and look on our ship's boat. She lay almost where she did at first, but not quite; and was turned by the force of the waves, and the winds, almost bottom upwards, against the high ridge of a beachy rough sand, but no water about her as before.

Had I had hands to have refitted her, and have launched her into the water, the boat would have done well enough, but I might have easily foreseen that I could no more turn her, and set her upright upon her bottom, than I could remove the island. However, I went to the wood, and cut levels and rollers, and brought them to the boat, resolving to try what I could do; suggesting to myself, that if I could but turn her down, I might easily repair the damage she had received, and she would be a very good boat, and I might go to sea in her very easily.

I spared no pains indeed in this piece of fruitless toil, and spent, I think, three or four weeks about it. At last, finding it impossible to heave it up with my little strength, I fell to digging away the sand to undermine it, and so to make it fall down, setting pieces of wood to thrust and guide it right in the fall.

But when I had done this, I was unable to stir it up again, or to get under it, much less to move it forwards towards the water; so I was forced to give it over: and

小艇，它差不多还是躺在原来的位置，但有些许的移动，且被风浪掀翻了，底朝上，被搁浅在一堆很高的沙石堆上，不过同以前一样，四面没有水。

如果我有帮手把它修理一下，再把它放到水里，这船一定很好用，但显而易见，我不可能把它翻转过来，让它底朝下，就像我无法搬动这个小岛一样。尽管如此，我还是去树林里砍了一些杠杆滚木之类的东西，把它们运到小艇旁，决定尽力试一下，看能不能把它翻过来，然后推到水里。我想，只要把它翻转过来，我就可以轻而易举地把它所受的伤修好，那样它又可以成为一只很棒的船，我不难乘着它去航海。

我不辞劳苦去干这件没有结果的事，费了三四个星期，最后发现凭我微薄的力量是不可能把它抬起来的。我开始去挖它下面的沙石使它倾斜倒下，并用一些木头在下面支着它，想趁它落下来的时候把它翻转过来。

但做到这一步时，我再也移动不了它，也不能插手到船底去，更别说把它拖到水里去了，所以我只好放弃了这个想法。但是，我虽然对小艇

yet, though I gave over hopes of the boat, my desire to venture over for the main land increased, rather than decreased, as the means for it seemed impossible.

I went to make my own boat the most like a fool. I pleased myself with the design, without determining whether I was ever able to undertake it; not but that the difficulty of launching my boat came often into my head; but I put a stop to my own inquires into it by this foolish answer which I gave myself: Let me first make it, I will warrant I will find some way or other to get it along when it is done.

When I had gone through this work, I was extremely delighted with it: the boat was really much bigger than I ever saw a canoe in my life. Many a weary stroke it had cost, for there remained nothing but to get it into the water.

Then I measured the distance of ground, and resolved to cut a dock, or canal, to bring the water up to the canoe, seeing I could not bring the canoe down to the water. Well, I began this work, and when I began to enter into it, and calculated how deep it was to be dug, how broad, how the stuff to be thrown out, I found that by the number of hands I had, being none but my own, it must have been ten or twelve years before I should have gone through with it; for the shore lay high, so that

放弃了希望，而我要到大陆上去的愿望不但没有因为无法实现而减退，反而较前更强烈了。

我就像一个傻瓜一样开始了自己造船的工作。我对这计划很满意，根本不再去想我是否能做到。其实我并不是没想到过下水的困难，但我总是用自以为是的愚蠢回答来阻止自己的疑问：让我先把它做成再说，我想做成之后，我肯定能想出什么办法把它拖进水里的。

我完成这工程之后，对它非常满意：这只小船真是比我平生所见的任何独木舟都要大。我已经被它搞得筋疲力尽了，现在船已造成，惟一可做的就是想法把它推下水。

之后，我大概估算了一下这块地距离水有多远，决定凿一个船埠或是运河出来，既然我没有办法将船拖到水里，那么我可以将水引到船这边来。然后我便开始工作了，在我准备挖的时候，我先得计算出得挖多深多宽才行，还有怎样把这些泥土沙石都铲出去，但是我发觉单凭我的双手的力量，恐怕得花上十年或十二个年头的时间，才能干完，因为海滨非常高，所以最深处至少需

at the upper end it must have been at least twenty feet deep; so at length, though with great reluctance, I gave this attempt over also.

This grieved me heartily; and now I saw, though too late, the folly of beginning a work before we count the cost, and before we judge rightly of our own strength to go through with it.

In the first place, I was removed from all the wickedness of the world here: I had neither the lust of the flesh, the lust of the eye, or the pride of life: I had nothing to covet, for I had all I was now capable of enjoying. I was lord of the manor; or, if I pleased, I might call myself king or emperor over the whole country, there were no rivals; I had no competitor, none to dispute sovereignty or command with me. I might have raised ship – loadings of corn, but I had no use for it; so I let as little grow as I thought enough for my occasion; I had tortoises, or turtles enough; but now and then one was as much as I could put to any use: I had timber enough to have built a fleet of ships; I had grapes enough to have made wine, or to have cured into raisins.

I had now been here so long, that many things which I brought on shore for my help, were either quite gone, or very much wasted, and near spent. My ink, as I observed, had been gone for some time, all but a very

要挖二十英呎才行，尽管我非常想这样做，但最终还是不得不放弃这个想法。

这一切令我非常难过；虽然已经太迟了，但是我终于意识到了自己的愚蠢，因为我在这之前根本没有计算过想做好这一切要付出多大的代价，也未曾考虑过凭自己的能力是否能做好它。

在这个地方，我首先避开了一切凡尘的庸俗与罪恶，没有肉欲，没有目欲，也没有人生的虚荣。我毫无所求，因为我可以自由地享受我现有的一切。我是这片土地的主人，如果觉得还不够过瘾，我还可以将自己称之为统治整个"国家"的"国王"或是"皇帝"。在这里，没有敌人，也没有竞争对手和我争夺主权或领导权。我可以生产一整船的谷物，但是太多了对我来说根本就没用，所以一般情况只要种得够吃就可以了。我还有很多乌龟和海龟，也足够我"享用"了。但是有些东西是需要多准备一些的，因为它们可能在很多地方派上用场，譬如说：我有充分的木料，可以建造一支船队，我有足够的葡萄，可以酿酒和制葡萄干。

我来这里已经很长时间了，当初带到海滨上的好多东西要么是耗尽了，要么就是浪费掉了或是差不多用完了。就拿墨水来说吧，有一段时间已经差不多用完了。可能还剩那么一点点，于

little, which I eked out with water a little and a little, till it was so pale it scarce left any appearance of black upon the paper. As long as it lasted, I made use of it to minute down the days of the month on which any remarkable thing happened to me, and first, by casting up times past, I remembered that there was a strange concurrence of days, in the various providences which befell me, and which, if I had been superstitiously inclined to observe days as fatal or fortunate, I might have had reason to have looked upon with a great deal of curiosity.

First, I had observed, that the same day that I broke away from my father and my friends, and ran away to Hull in order to go to sea, the same day afterwards I was taken by the Sallee man-of-war, and made a slave.

The same day of the year that I escaped out of the wreck of that ship in Yarmouth Roads, that same day of the year afterwards I made my escape from Sallee in the boat.

The same day of the year I was born on, namely, the 30th of September, the same day I had my life so miraculously saved 26 years after, when I was cast on shore in this island; so that my wicked life, and solitary life, both began on a day.

The next thing to my ink being wasted was that of my bread, I mean the biscuit, which I brought out of the

是我便给它一点儿一点儿地加水以便延长它的"寿命"，但是到了最后它淡到了在纸上留不下任何一点儿黑色的痕迹的地步了。不过只要它还能写得出来，我会把在岛上对我来说很有意义的点点滴滴都记录下来，开始的时候总是喜欢回忆一些往事，可是后来有段时间，我开始了幻想，我幻想种种假设发生在我身上的事情，比如假如有一天我遇上了什么生死攸关或是大喜临头的事，在那个时候我会带着一种什么样的眼光去看待，这真的很有趣。

首先，我想，就在我离开父母和朋友的那天，我跑到赫尔，打算去航海，但是后来也就是在同一天却被萨利人抓去当了俘虏，做了奴隶。

我幸免于海难逃脱亚摩斯船舶残骸的那一天，也是我一年后乘船逃脱萨利人追捕我的那一天。

我出生的那一天——九月三十号，正好是二十六年后生命得救的那一天，也就是我被"抛"在小岛上的那一天，也就在同一天，我过起了痛苦而孤立的生活。

我不仅浪费了墨水，也浪费了"口粮"，这使我很难受。我指的是饼干，是我从船上带来的，

ship. This I had husbanded to the last degree, allowing myself but one cake of bread a day for above a year, and yet I was quite without bread for near a year before I got any corn of my own; and great reason I had to be thankful that I had any at all, the getting it being, as has been already observed, next to miraculous.

My clothes too began to decay mightily: as to linen, I had had none a good while, except some checkered shirts which I found in the chests of the other seamen, and which I carefully preserved, because many times I could bear no other clothes on but a shirt; and it was a very great help to me, that I had among all the men's clothes of the ship almost three dozen of shirts. There were also several thick watch – coats of the seamen's, but they were too hot to wear; and though it is true, that the weather was so violent hot that there was no need of clothes, yet I could not go quite naked.

One reason why I could not go quite naked was that the very heat frequently blistered my skin; whereas, with a shirt on, the air itself made some motion, and whistling under the shirt, was twofold cooler than without it. No more could I ever bring myself to go out in the heat of the sun without a cap; the heat of the sun beating with such violence as it does in that place, would give me the headache presently, by darting so directly on my head,

我费尽心思地想把它节省到最后一刻，我只允许自己每天只吃一块饼干，这种状况一直延续了一年。其实在我没有收获谷物之前，已经差不多有一年没吃到它了。庆幸地是，它竟然安然无恙地还保存在那里，这简直是一个奇迹。

我的衣服也开始受到腐蚀了，至于白麻衣，已经没一件好的了，除了一些各式各样的花格衬衫，那是我在别的海员箱子里找到的，我保存得很好，因为在好些时候我除了衬衣就没有别的衣服可以穿了，它们确实很有用，我从船上的男士衣服中几乎找到了三四十件衬衣，还有几件厚厚的海员瞭望时穿的衣服，但是天太热了根本就不能穿，天真的是非常炙热，其实根本就用不着衣服，但我总不能赤裸着身子出去吧。

其实，我不能赤裸身体的一个原因是炙热的阳光常常会把我的皮肤晒出泡，但是穿上衬衣就会比不穿凉爽得多，空气隔着衬衫也不会那么曝晒了，而且空气在衣服里的流通也会使皮肤感到凉爽。在这么热的天气下，我不戴帽子是不会出去的，这个鬼地方灼热的阳光强烈地直晒着我的头，要是不戴帽子的话，头一定疼得受不了的。

without a cap on, so that I could not bear it; whereas if I put on my cap, it would presently go away.

Upon these views, I began to consider about putting the few rags I had, which I called clothes, into some order. I had worn out all the waistcoats I had, and my business was now to try if I could not make jackets out of the great watch – coats which I had by me, and with such other materials as I had; so I set to work—tailoring, or rather indeed botching; for I made most piteous work of it. However, I made shift to make two or three waist – coats, which I hoped would serve me a great while; as for breeches or drawers, I made but a very sorry shift indeed, till afterwards.

Then I made for my head a great cap of these skins of all the creatures that I killed with the hair on the outside to shoot off the rain, and this I performed so well, that after this I made a suit of clothes wholly of those skins; that is to say, a waistcoat, and breeches open at the knees, and both loose; for they were rather wanted to keep me cool than to keep me warm. I must not omit to acknowledge that they were wretchedly made; for if I was a bad carpenter, I was a worse tailor. However, when I was abroad, if it happened to rain, the hair of the waistcoat and cap being outmost, I was kept very dry. After this I spent a deal of time and pains to make

可是一戴帽子，就没事了，头也不疼了，也不感到曝晒了。

想了想之后，我开始把这些仅有的破衣烂衫，当然是我所谓的"衣服"整理了一番，我已经把所有的背心都穿破了，我现在在想我是否能将我手头现有的一些衣服，比如说瞭望员的衣服或是其他衣料改一改，做成夹克。这样我便开始了裁剪缝纫工作。与其说开始了裁剪工作，还不如说是笨手笨脚瞎捣腾，因为我做的这些东西真的是"丑不可观"。然而，我还是凑合着改好了两三件马甲，我想这已经足够了，够我穿一阵子了。至于裤子和内裤，最终也没改好，但能应付着穿。

然后我把射杀的小动物的皮用来做帽子，毛在外可以防雨，我干得很好，然后用那些毛皮做了一套衣服，也就是说，做了个马甲，还有长度打到膝盖上的裤子，都是松松散散的，与其说它们是为了保暖，不如说它们令我更"凉爽"。我始终不能忘记它们的做工是多么差劲，假如我要是一个笨木匠的话，那我将会是一个更糟糕的裁缝。可是当我外出时，每逢遇到下雨，马甲和帽子上的毛总是为我遮风避雨。在这之后，我花了好一

me an umbrella. I was indeed in great want of one. At last, I made one to answer. I covered it with skins, the hair upwards, so that it cast off the rain like a penthouse, and kept off the sun so effectually, that I could walk out in the hottest of the weather, with greater advantage than I could before in the coolest; and when I had no need of it, I could close it, and carry it under my arm.

Thus I lived mighty comfortably for another five years, in the same course, in the same posture and place, just as before. I had one labor to make me a canoe, which at last I finished: so that by digging a canal to it six feet wide, and four feet deep, I brought it into the creek, almost half a mile. Now I had a boat, I thought of nothing but sailing round the island.

Having fitted my mast and sail, and tried the boat, I found she would sail very well. Then I made little lockers and boxes at each end of my boat, to put provisions, necessaries, and ammunition into, to be kept dry, either from rain, or the spray of the sea; and a little long hollow place I cut in the inside of the boat, where I could lay my gun, making a flap to hang down over it to keep it dry.

I fixed my umbrella also in a step at the stern, like a mast, to stand over my head, and thus I every now and

阵子工夫做雨伞，我确实很需要它。最后，我终于做出了一把，然后用毛皮子盖上，毛朝外，这样它就可以像一个有屋顶的房间一样遮风避雨了，就算我在炎热的夏天行走，也不用害怕太阳的照射了，再也不用像以前那样了，我可以凉爽地度过夏天。在我不需要的时候，我还可以把它合上，夹在胳膊底下，非常方便。

这样，我又舒心地生活了五年。就在同一个地方，以一种同样的心态经历着同样的过程，一切依旧。经过我不懈的努力，船终于造好了，这样我便可以挖一个宽六英尺，深四英尺的运河，将它引入小溪，大约在半英里之外吧，现在我有了小船，我只想绕着小岛航行而已。

在修好了帆柱和帆之后，我试了试船，发觉还不错，肯定能航行。然后在船的两端做了些橱和盒子，放一些必需品，包括生活用品和一些弹药，以免它们受到雨或浪花的冲噬而受潮，我还在船里凿出一个长长的、空空的小槽，这样就可以将枪放在里面，上面还吊着一块遮盖物，是用来防潮的。

我把雨伞固定在船尾的台子上，就好像一个船桅一样，耸立在我的头上方，这样我可以随时

then took a little voyage upon the sea, but never went far out, or far from the little creek. But at last, being eager to view the circumference of my little kingdom, I resolved upon my tour, and accordingly I victual my ship for the voyage; putting in two dozen of my loaves of barley bread; an earthen pot full of parched rice, a food I ate a great deal of; a little bottle of rum, half a goat, and powder with shot for killing more, and two large watch – coats, of those which, as I mentioned before, I had saved out of the seamen's chests; these I took, one to lie upon, and the other to cover me in the night.

It was the sixth of November, in the sixth year of my reign, or my captivity, which you please, that I set out on this voyage, and I found it much longer than I expected; for though the island itself was not very large, yet when I came to the east side of it, I found a great ledge of rocks lie out about two leagues into the sea, some above water, some under it; and beyond this a shoal of sand, lying dry half a league more; so that I was obliged to go a great way out to sea to double that point.

Having secured my boat, I took my gun, and went on shore, climbing up a hill, saw the full extent of it, and resolved to venture. In my viewing the sea from that hill where I stood, I perceived a strong, and indeed a most furious current, which ran to the east, and even

出海，但是不能走得太远，离小溪太远的地方就不可以去了。一切安排好后，我决定进行一次旅行，因为我好想看看我的小"王国"到底是个什么样子。于是我开始准备一些航行用的东西了，先装了两打大麦面包，一陶壶干米和一些我经常吃的东西，还有一瓶酒，半只羊，一些用来捕猎用的，再加上两件大衣，我说的当然是从海员的箱子里拿来的那些，我带着它们，一件用来铺，另一件用来晚上盖。

那是我独立生活或是被困的——怎么说都可以——第六年的十一月六号吧，我开始了那一次航行，它比我想象的要漫长得多。尽管岛屿本身不是很大，但是当我来到了岛屿的东边，我发现岛屿中布满了许多凸凹的岩石，大概绵延了有两个多海里，有些在水上，有些在水下，然后是一浅滩沙子，大概有半海里的距离，所以我得走两倍的路程才能进入大海。

系好船之后，我便拿着枪上岸了，爬上山顶放眼望去，整个小岛一览无余，于是我打算去探险，从我站的地方望海，明显地感觉到了一股强烈的急流直向我袭来，方向好像是从西往东流，

came close to the point; and I took the more notice of it, because I saw there might be some danger, that when I came into it, I might be carried out to sea by the strength of it, and not be able to make the island again.

I lay here, however, two days; because the wind blowing pretty fresh made a great breach of the sea upon the point; so that it was not safe for me to keep too close to the shore for the breach, nor to go too far off because of the stream.

The third day in the morning, the wind having abated overnight, the sea was calm, and I ventured; but I was again all rash and ignorant; for no sooner did I come to the point, I found myself in a great depth of water, and a current like the sluice of a mill. It carried my boat along with it with such violence, that all I could do could not keep her so much as on the edge of it; but I found it hurried me farther and farther out from the eddy, which was on the left hand. There was no wind stirring to help me, and all that I could do with my paddles signified nothing. And now I began to give myself over for lost; for, as the current was on both sides of the island, I knew in a few leagues' distance they must join again, and then I was irrecoverably gone; nor did I see any possibility of avoiding: so that I had no prospect before me but of perishing; not by the sea, for that was

好像马上就要波及到这里，我看了又看，想着我要是下去了会不会有危险，我意识到，凭着它的力量，一旦我走近它，我一定会被卷进大海的，再也回不到岛上了。

于是我就在那儿躺了两天，因为风势越刮越大，海浪也更加凶猛，我不敢离开海岸一步，更不敢靠近海岸边，惟恐被海浪卷走。

第三天的早上，刮了一夜的强风，风力渐渐减弱了，海面也平静了，我又开始了冒险。但我太仓促了，太无知了，太缺乏常识了。因为不一会儿，我发现水流湍急，威力无比猛烈，它狂打着我的船，我被置于水浪之中，根本就不能靠岸。我使出浑身力气，用力划着，试图靠近岸边，但这一切都无济于事。我被冲得越来越远了，海浪似小山一般劈头盖脑地打来，左边是一巨大的漩涡，起风或许可以帮得上忙，但是现在连一丝风都没有，此时用桨划船似乎一点儿用都没有。我想这回惨了，因此也就放弃了求生的欲望。在几海里之外我就知道了，小岛的两股气流会合成一股，到那时候，我就彻底的完了，根本没有生还的希望，我也看不到任何逃脱的希望。所以我除了祈求之外，无计可施，只好听天由命吧。现在的问题并不是我会不会被海浪吞噬，因为它已经

calm enough, but of starving for hunger. I had indeed found a tortoise on the shore, as big almost as I could lift, and had tossed it into the boat; and I had a great jar of fresh water. But what was all this to being driven into the vast ocean, where, to be sure, there was no shore, no mainland or island, for a thousand leagues at least!

Now I looked back upon my desolate, solitary island, as the most pleasant place in the world, and that all the happiness my heart could wish for, was to be there again. I stretched out my hands to it with eager wishes. O happy desert, said I, I shall never see thee more! O miserable creature! said I, whither am I going? It is scarce possible to imagine the consternation I was now in, being driven from my beloved island into the wild ocean. However, I worked hard, till indeed my strength was almost exhausted, and kept my boat as much to the northward I could; when about noon, as the sun passed the meridian, I thought I felt a little breeze of wind in my face. This cheered my heart a little, and especially when in about half an hour more, it blew a pretty small gentle gale. By this time I had gotten at a frightful distance from the island; and, had the least cloud or hazy weather intervened, I would have been undone another way too; for I had no compass on board, and

够静了，而是怎么渡过饥饿的难关——我会被饿死的。我在海滨上找到一个大得我快拿不动了的海龟，且将它抛到了船上，还灌了一大罐淡水。但是这所有一切都将"落入"大海，当然，至少在一千多海里内，肯定没有海滨、没有大陆，也不会有岛屿。

现在回想一下我那个荒凉孤寂的小岛，真的可以称得上是世界上最安逸舒适的地方了，在那里我可以重拾以往所有期盼已久的幸福和快乐。我伸出双手真诚祈盼能重归它的怀抱。我是多么地思念我的小岛。噢，快乐的荒岛，我自言自语道，我再也无法与你重逢了。噢，可怜的家伙，我说道，你到底会飘向何方？我当时的惊慌处境是人们根本无法想象的。我就这样和我挚爱的小岛分别了，而现在所面临的却是被抛向无情的汪洋大海。可是，尽管在我已经筋疲力尽、无能为力的时候，我仍然尽我所能地将船向北方划动。就在正午，太阳偏离了子午线的时候，一阵微风轻拂着我的脸颊，我非常的高兴，尤其在接下来的半个小时中，风开始渐渐变强了。可这时，我发觉现处位置和小岛的距离远得可怕。天气也不是很晴朗，灰蒙蒙的，我也不可能走另一条路，因为我没把指南针装在船上，所以根本不知道怎

should never have known how to have steered towards the island, if I had but once lost sight of it. But the weather continuing clear, I applied myself to get up my mast again, and spread my sail, standing away to the north as much as possible, to get out of the current.

Just as I had set my mast and sail, and the boat began to stretch away, I saw even by the clearness of the water, some alteration of the current was near; for where the current was so strong, the water was foul. But perceiving the water clear, I found the current abate, and presently I found to the east, at about half a mile, a breach of the sea upon some rocks. These rocks, I found, caused the current to part again; and as the main stress of it ran away more southernly, leaving the rocks to the northeast, so the other returned by the repulse of the rock, and made a strong eddy, which ran back to the northwest with a very sharp stream.

This eddy carried me about a league in my way back again directly towards the island, but about two leagues more towards the northwards than the current lay, which carried me away at first; so that when I came near the island I found myself open to the northern shore of it, opposite to that which I went out from. About four o'clock in the evening, being then within about a league of the island, I stretched across this eddy, slanting

样才能驶向小岛的方向，除非我可以看到它。天气越变越晴了，我再次将帆樯立起，开始我的航行，当然尽我所能向北方驶去，以便脱离急流。

就在我立好帆柱和帆的同时，船开始缓缓移动了，尽管水清了许多，但是我仍然可以看得出来水流的改变一触即发，因为那里水流湍急，且浑浊不堪。但是看到水较以前清了许多，我知道水流一定是减弱了。我还发现在东面大概半里的地方有一片海水，那里有很多的岩石块，我发现，这些岩石致使激流再次分开，有一大股冲向南去，将岩石甩在了东北方向，另一股由于岩石的阻力向回拍打着，形成一个汹涌的漩涡，带着一股巨大的激流向西北方向涌去。

多亏这股逆流，它将我顺着回小岛的方向推进了大概有一个海里的距离，再加上我先前被推的那一次，我已经向北"行进"了大约两个海里了，所以当我靠近小岛时才发觉，我现在处于小岛的北岸，和原来的出发地正好是相对的。大概晚上四点钟的时候，我离小岛大概还有一个海里的距离，我开始穿越这股微偏西北的逆流，大约

northwest, and in about an hour came within about a mile of the shore; it being smooth water, I soon got to land.

When I was on shore. I fell on my knees, and gave God thanks for my deliverance, resolving to lay aside all thoughts of my deliverance by my boat; and refreshing myself with such things as I had. I brought my boat close to the shore in a little cove that had been espied under some trees, and laid me down to sleep, being quite spent with the labor and fatigue of the voyage.

Chapter 12　Hard Times

I was now at a great loss which way to get home with my boat. I had run so much hazard, and knew too much the case, to think of attempting it by the way I went out, and what might be at the other side I knew not, nor had I any mind to run any more ventures; so I only resolved in the morning to make my way westward along the shore, and to see if there was no creek where I might lay up my frigate in safety, so as to have her again if I wanted her. In about three miles, I came to a brook, where I found a convenient harbor for my boat, and where she lay as if she had been in a little dock made on purpose for her. Here I put in, and having stowed my

一个小时后，距离海滨还有约一英里。在这里可以看到平静的水面，不久，我终于到家了。

我一上岸，便跪在地上感谢上帝赐予我生还之光，我要将这所有的一切宝贵经历永远地封存在我的记忆中，并且重新振作起来，继续我未竟的事业。我将船停泊在一个树木遮蔽的小海湾的岸边，然后带着一身旅途的辛劳与疲惫，进入了梦乡。

第十二章　度日如年

现在我根本不知道该怎样才能驾船回家。我遇到这么多危险，所以很了解这种状况，知道照原路返回是十分危险的，而另一边的情况我一无所知，然而更不想再去冒险。所以，我决定第二天早晨沿海岸西行，看看能不能找到一条小河安全地停泊我的小船，以便我需要它的时候可以再来找到它。我驾船行驶了约三英里，找到了一条小河。这对于我的小船倒是一个进出方便的港口，你别说，就仿佛这个港口是专门为它建立的小船坞似的。我把小船停放妥当后，便上岸了。我环

boat very safe, I went on shore to look about me and see where I was. I soon found I had but a little passed by the place where I had been before when I traveled on foot to that shore; so taking nothing out of my boat but my gun and my umbrella, for it was exceeding hot, I began my march. The way was comfortable enough after such a voyage as I had been upon, and I reached my old bower in the evening, where I found everything standing as I left it; for I always kept it in good order.

I got over the fence, and laid me down in the shade to rest my limbs, for I was very weary, and fell asleep. What a surprise I must be in, when I was awaked out of my sleep by a voice calling me by my name several times, "Robin, poor Robin Crusoe!" "Where are you, Robin?" "Where have you been?"

I was so dead asleep at first, being fatigued with rowing and walking that I did not awake thoroughly; and dozing between sleeping and waking, thought I dreamed that somebody spoke to me; but as the voice continued to repeat "Robin Crusoe, Robin Crusoe," at last I began to awake more perfectly, and was first dreadfully frightened, and started up in the utmost consternation. But no sooner were my eyes open, but I saw my Poll sitting on the top hedge, and immediately knew that this was he that spoke to me; for just in such bemoaning language I

顾四周，看看这里到底是什么地方。我很快发现，这儿离我上次徒步旅行所到过的地方不远。因为这里天气很热，所以我什么都没有拿，除了从船上拿了枪和伞就出发了。经过这次危险的航行之后，我感到在陆上行走十分舒服。傍晚时分，我就回到了自己的小屋，屋里一切如旧，因为我总是把一切收拾得整整齐齐。

我翻过栅栏，躺在树阴下歇歇脚。我太累了，所以很快就睡着了。但是出乎意料的是，我被惊醒了，仿佛有一个声音在呼唤着我的名字："鲁宾逊，可怜的鲁宾逊·克鲁索！""你在哪儿？""你去哪儿啦，鲁宾逊？"

开始我睡得很熟，因为划船和步行使我疲惫不堪，我睡得昏昏沉沉的，所以还不大清醒，只是处于半睡半醒之间。刚开始我还以为是梦中有人在同我说话，但是当我听到那声音不断地叫着："鲁宾逊·克鲁索！鲁宾逊·克鲁索！"终于使我完全清醒过来。这一醒，把我吓了一大跳，一骨碌从地上爬起来。睁眼一看，我的那只鹦鹉正站在篱笆上面，原来是它在和我说话。它之所以能说出这些令人伤心的话语，正是我当初教它这么

had used to talk him, and teach him.

However, even though I knew it was the parrot, I was amazed how the creature got thither, and then how he should just keep about the place, and nowhere else: but as I was well satisfied it could be nobody but honest Poll, I got it over; and holding out my hand, calling him by his name, Poll, the sociable creature came to me, and sat upon my thumb, and continued talking to me.

I had enough of rambling to sea for some time, and enough to do for many days to sit still, and reflect upon the danger I had been in. In this government of my temper I remained near a year, lived a very sedate, retired life, and my thoughts being very much composed as to my condition, and fully comforted in resigning myself to the dispensations of Providence, I thought I lived really very happily in all things expect that society.

I improved myself, in this time, in all the mechanic exercises which my necessaries put me upon applying myself to; and I could have made a very good carpenter, especially considering how few tools I had.

I arrived at an unexpected perfection in my earthen ware, and contrived well enough to make them with a wheel, because I made things round and shapeable, which before were filthy. Things indeed began to look

说的。

可是，尽管我明知刚才说话的是一只鹦鹉，我还是感到奇怪，这只小鸟怎么会飞到这儿来？并且它为什么老守在这儿，不到别处去？在我弄清与我说话的不是别人而是我那忠实的鹦鹉后，心就定了下来。我向它伸出手，叫着它的名字，这只小鸟便很听话地飞过来，落在我的大拇指上，然后接连不断地和我说话。

我在海上漂流了那么长时间，现在也该好好地安安静静地休息几天，细细回味一下我所经历过的危险。差不多有一年的工夫，我克制着自己的性子，过着恬静悠闲的生活。我安于自己的现状，安于上天对我命运的安排。我感到我的生活十分幸福，惟一不足的就是没有人可以交往，因为我离开了社会这个大环境。

在这段时间，为了应付生活的需要，我得尝试各种各样的活儿，当然经过了一段时间的锻炼，也有了很大进步。我必须得成为一个手艺出色的木匠，尤其是在工具缺乏的条件下。

令人难以意料的是，我的制陶技术也达到了一个非常完美的"境界"，我是用一只轮盘来制造陶器的，这些陶器不仅容易制做而且式样好看。我过去做出来的东西很丑陋，现在情况有很大的

on. In my wicker ware I also improved much, and made abundance of necessary baskets as well as my inventions showed me, though not very handsome, yet convenient for my laying things up in, or fetching things home in.

I began now to perceive my powder abated considerably; and this was a want which it was impossible for me to supply; then I began seriously to consider what I must do when I should have no more powder. I had, as I observed, in the third year of my being here, kept a young kid and bred her tame. I was in hopes of getting a he – kid, but I could not by any means bring it to pass, till my kid grew an old goat; and I could never find in my heart to kill her, till she died at last of mere age.

But being now in the eleventh year of my residence, and, as I have said, my ammunition grew low, I set myself to study some art to trap and snare the goats, to see whether I could not catch some of them alive; and particularly I wanted a she-goat with her young. To this purpose I made snares to hamper them; and believe they were more than once taken in them; but my tackle was not good, for I had no wire, and always found them broken, and my bail devoured. At length I resolved to try a pit-fall; I dug several large pits in the earth, in places where I had observed the goats used to feed, and over these pits I placed hurdles of my own making too, with a

改变。在藤皮编织方面，我也有不少进步，编了不少自己需要的筐子，虽然样子不好看，却也方便实用，可以用来放东西或是用来搬运东西回家。

我现在开始发现我的火药已经远远满足不了我的需要了，我已用去许多，而且我必须得想办法弥补这个不足，因为这对我来说是非常重要的，是必不可少的物品。我开始认真考虑没有弹药我该怎么办。如前所述，在我落难荒岛后的第三年，我捉到了一只雌小山羊，经过驯养它已长大了。我一直想再捉一只雄山羊与它配对，可是想尽办法也没能捉到。最后，小山羊变成了老山羊，我不忍心杀它，直到它老死。

现在我已经在岛上生活了十一年。前面也已说过，我的弹药越来越少了。于是我开始研究如何利用陷阱或夹子捕捉山羊，看看能否活捉一两只。我特别希望能捉到一只怀孕的母山羊。为了达到这一目的，我做了几只夹子来捕捉山羊。我确信有好几次山羊曾被夹子夹住了。但是，由于没有铁丝之类的金属线，夹子做得不理想，结果发现它们总是吃掉诱饵弄坏夹子逃之夭夭。后来，我决定挖陷阱试试看。于是我就在山羊经常吃草的地方掘了几个大陷坑，在坑上盖几块自制的木

great weight upon them; and several times I put ears of barley, and dry rice, without setting the trap; and I could easily perceive that the goats had gone in. At length, I set three traps in one night, and going the next morning, I found them all standing, and yet the bait eaten and gone. This was very discouraging; however, I altered my trap; going one morning to see my traps, I found in one of them a large old he-goat; and, in one of the others, three kids, a male and two females.

As to the old one, I knew not what to do with him; he was so fierce I durst not go into the pit to him; to bring him away alive, which was what I wanted; I could have killed him, but that was not my business, nor would it answer my end; so I let him out, and he ran away as if he had been frightened out of his wits.

It was a good while before the kids would feed; but throwing them some sweet corn, it tempted them, and they began to be tame; and now I found that if I expected to supply myself with goat's flesh, when I had no powder or shot left, breeding some up tame was my only way, when perhaps I might have them about my house like a flock of sheep. But then it presently occurred to me that I must keep the tame from the wild, or else they would always run wild when grew up; and the only way for this was to have some enclosed pieces of ground, well

条格子，再在上面压一些很重的东西。开始几次我在覆盖好的坑上面放了一些大麦穗子和干米，但故意未装上机关，我一看就知道，山羊曾走过去吃过谷物，所以，有一天晚上我在每个陷阱里都安了机关。可是第二天当我跑去一看，只见食饵都给吃掉了，可三个机关都没有动，这真使人丧气，于是我改装了机关。等到有一天早上我再去看，发现在一个陷阱里有一只老公羊，另一个陷阱里有三只小羊，一只公羊，还有两只母羊。

对那只老公羊我不知道如何处理掉它，它凶猛异常，我不敢下坑去捉它。我想抓活的，我真是这么想的。我也可以把它杀死，但我不想那么做，那不是我的意愿，所以我把它放走了。老山羊像吓掉魂一样一溜烟逃跑了。

小山羊很久都不肯吃东西，但是当我扔给它们一些谷粒时，它们很喜欢吃，这样它们慢慢就驯顺起来。现在我知道，如果弹药用尽之后还想吃山羊肉，惟一的办法就是驯养一些小山羊。将来也许有一天会在我屋子周围有一大群山羊呢！但是我突然想到，我必须把驯养的山羊与野山羊隔离开。否则，驯养的小山羊一长大，就会跑掉又变成野山羊。而惟一的办法是找一块空地，用

fenced either with hedge or pale, to keep them in so effectually that those within might not break out, or these without break in.

My hedge was begun and carried on, and I resolved to enclose a piece of about 150 yards in length, and 100 yards in breadth, as my flock increased, I could add more ground to my enclosure.

This was acting with some prudence, and I went to work with courage. I was about three months hedging in the first piece; and till I had done it, I tethered the three kids in the best part of it, and used them to feed as near me as possible, to make them familiar; and very often I went and carried them some ears of barley, or a handful of rice, and fed them out of my hand; so that after my enclosure was finished, and I let them loose, they would follow me up and down, bleating after me for a handful of corn. This answered my end, and in about a year and a half I had a flock of about twelve goats, kids and all; and in two years more I had forty.

But this was not all; for now I not only had goat's flesh to feed on when I pleased, but milk, too, a thing which indeed in my beginning I did not so much as think of, and which, when it came into thoughts, was really an agreeable surprise; for now I set up my dairy, and had sometimes a gallon or two of milk in a day. After a

坚固的篱笆或栅栏把它们圈起来。这样，里面驯养的出不来，外面野生的也进不去。

于是我开始动手修筑篱笆。我决定先圈一块长约一百五十码，宽约一百码的地方。等羊群增加了，我可以进一步扩大圈地。

干这个活儿可是需要谨慎小心，我鼓起勇气大胆动手干起来。第一块圈地用了差不多三个月时间才完成。在完工之前，我一直把三只小羊拴在最好的地方，并让它们尽可能地和我保持近距离，以便我好喂养并使它们与我混熟。我还经常用大麦穗子和一把把大米喂它们，让它们从我手里吃。这样，当我把篱笆修筑完成之后，即使把它们放开，它们也会跟着我转，并咩咩叫着向我讨食吃。我的目的总算实现了。不到一年半，我已连大带小有了十二只小山羊，又过了两年，我有四十只了。

这还不算，现在我不仅随时有羊肉吃，还有羊奶喝。说实话，这在开始我根本想也没想到。所以我忽然想到可以喝羊奶时，真是喜出望外。现在我有了自己的挤奶房，有时每天可产一两加

great many essays and miscarriages, I made me both butter and cheese at last.

How mercifully can our great Creator treat his creatures, even in those conditions in which they seemed to be overwhelmed in destruction! How can he sweeten the bitterest providence, and give us cause to praise him for dungeons and prisons! Where a table was here spread for me in a wilderness, where I saw nothing at first but to perish for hunger!

I had on a broad belt of goat's-skin dried, which I drew together with two thoughts of the same, instead of buckles; and in a kind of frog on either side of this; instead of a sword and dagger: hung a little saw and hatchet; I had another belt not so broad, and fastened in the same manner, which hung over my shoulder; and at the end of it, under my left arm, hung two pouches, both made of goat's-skin too; in one of which hung my powder, in the other my shot: at my back I carried my basket, on my shoulder my gun, and over my head a great clumsy goat's-skin umbrella, but which, after all, was the most necessary thing I had about me, next to my gun. My beard I had once suffered to grow till it was about a quarter of a yard long; but as had both scissors and razors sufficient, I had cut it pretty short, except what on my upper lip, which I had trimmed into a

仑的羊奶，经过多次的试验和失败，我终于做出了奶油和干酪。

造物主对待自己所创造的一切生灵是多么仁慈，甚至在他们身处逆境的时候。他能把苦难的命运变得甜蜜，即使我们因于牢狱或是身处逆境之中时也都要赞美他！当我刚来到这片荒野时，一定以为自己会饿死，而现在摆在我面前的是多么丰盛的筵席啊！

我腰间系了一条用晒干的小羊皮做的宽皮带，皮带没有搭扣，只用两根山羊皮系着。皮带子两边两个搭环，原来是水手用来挂短刀或短剑的，我挂了一把小锯和一把斧头。我还有另一条较窄的皮带，是用同一种方法系的，斜挎在我的肩膀上，也用皮条系着。在这条皮带的末端，在我左胳膊下，挂着两个山羊皮袋，一个用来装火药，一个用来装子弹。我背上背着筐子，肩上扛着枪，头上撑着一顶羊皮做的看起来很笨拙的太阳伞。除了枪之外，这把伞也是我随身不可缺少的东西。我的胡子曾给我添了不少麻烦，现在已长到四分之一码长。我有的是剪刀和剃刀，所以就把它剪短了，剪得非常短，但上嘴唇的胡子仍留着，并

large pair of whiskers, such as I had seen worn by some Turks whom I saw at Sallee.

As for my wall, made as before, with long stakes or piles, those piles grew all like trees, and had by this time grown so big, and spread so very much, that there was not the least appearance, to any one's view, of any habitation behind them.

Near this dwelling of mine, but a little farther within the land, and upon lower ground, lay my two pieces of corn-ground, which I kept duly cultivated and sowed, and which duly yielded me their harvest in its season; and wherever I had occasion for more corn, I had more land adjoining as fit as that.

Besides this, I had my country – seat, and I had now a tolerable plantation there also; for first I had my little bower, I kept the hedge which circled it in constantly fitted up to its usual height, the ladder standing always in the inside: I kept the trees, which at first were no more than my stakes, but had now grown very firm and tall. I kept them always so cut, that they might spread and grow thick and wild, and make the more agreeable shade, which they did effectually to my mind. In the middle of this I had my tent always standing, being a piece of sail spread over poles set in that purpose, and which never wanted any repair or renewing; and un-

修剪成八字胡，像我在萨利见到的土耳其人留的胡子那样。

说到那堵围墙，我当时是用高大的树桩筑成的；现在，这些树桩已长成了树，又大又密，遮天蔽日，一点都不显眼，你无论怎么看都看不出后面竟会住着人。

靠近我的住所，往外多走几步，便有一片地势较低的地方，那里有两块庄稼地。我按时耕种，按时收获。如果我需要更多的粮食，毗邻还有不少同样相宜的土地可以扩大。

此外，在我的乡间别墅那边，现在也有一座像样的庄园。首先，我有一间栖身的茅舍。我经常修剪周围的树篱，使其保持一定的高度。我的梯子也一直放在树篱里面。那些树起初只不过是一些树桩，现在却长得又粗又高了。我精心护理着这些树。我不断修剪树桩，希望它们能长得枝多叶茂，生机勃勃，绿荫成行。后来，这些树真的长得蔚然成荫，令我十分称意。树篱中央则搭着一顶帐篷。帐篷是用一块帆布做成的，由几根柱子支撑着，永远不必修理或重搭。帐篷底下我

der this I had made me a couch, with the skins of the creatures I had killed, and with other soft things, and a blanket laid on them, such as belonged to our sea – bedding, which I had saved, and a great watch – coat to cover me.

Adjoining to this I had my enclosures for my cattle, my goats; and as I had taken an inconceivable deal of pains to fence and enclose this ground, I was so uneasy to see it kept entire, let no shoulder break though, that I never left off, till infinite labor had stocked the outside of the hedge so full of small stakes, so near to one another, that it was rather a pale than a hedge, and there was scarce room to put a hand through between them, which afterwards, when those stakes grew, as they all did the next rainy season, made the enclosure strong like a wall, indeed stronger than wall.

This will testify for me that I was not idle, and that I spared no pains to bring to pass whatever appeared necessary for my comfortable support; for I considered the keeping up a breed of tame creatures thus at hand would be a living magazine of flesh, milk, butter, and cheese for me, as long as I lived in the place, if it were to be forty years; and that keeping them in my reach depended entirely upon my perfecting my enclosures to such a degree that I might be sure of keeping them together;

给自己做了一个床，是用我猎的小动物的毛皮做的，还有一些其他细软的材料，我给床上铺了一条毯子，那是水手用的。我把它捡了回来。另外，我还找了一件瞭望员值班用的大衣当被子用。

与此相邻的是我的圈地，里面养着山羊和牛。为了圈这块地，我曾历尽艰辛，颇费周折，我竭尽全力，把篱笆做得十分严密，免得圈在里面的山羊逃出去。我不遗余力辛勤劳作，在篱笆外插满小树桩，而且插得又密又多，样子不像篱墙，倒像是一个栅栏，在木桩与木桩之间，连手都插不进去。后来在下个雨季中，和以前的木桩一样，这些小木桩都成活了，且长势茂盛，成了一堵坚固的围墙，甚至比围墙还坚固。

这一切都证明我并没有偷懒，为了使生活舒适，凡是必须做的事，我都会不辞辛劳地去完成。我认为手边驯养一批牲畜，就等于替自己建立一座羊肉、羊奶、奶油和奶酪的活仓库。无论我在岛上生活多少年，哪怕是四十年，也将取之不尽，用之不竭。同时，我也认为，要想一伸手就抓到这些山羊，就得把羊圈修筑得十分严密。不能让

which, by this method, indeed, I so effectually secured that, when these little stakes began to grow, I had planted them so very thick I was forced to pull some of them out again.

In this place also I had my grapes growing, which I principally depended on for my winter store of raisins, and which I never failed to preserve very carefully as the best and most agreeable dainty of my whole diet; and indeed they were not only agreeable, but physical, wholesome, nourishing, and refreshing to last degree.

As this was also about half way between my other habitation and the place where I had laid up my boat, I generally stayed and lay here in my way thither; for I used frequently to visit my boat, and I kept all things about or belonging to her in very good order. Sometimes I went out in her to divert ever but no more hazardous voyages would I go, nor scarcely ever above a stone' scast or two from the shore, I was so apprehensive of being hurried out of my knowledge again by the currents, or winds, or other accident. But now I came to a new scene of my life.

Chapter 13　The Strange Footprint

It happened one day about noon, going towards my

它们到处乱跑。我把这个主意实施得过于彻底，结果把木桩插得太密了，等树长大后，我还得拔掉一些。

在这里，我还种了一些葡萄，我每年都贮藏大量的葡萄干，以备冬天食用。我小心保存，因为这是我现有食物中最富营养最可口的食品。葡萄干不仅好吃，而且营养丰富，香甜可口，足以提神，还可以强身健体。

我的乡间别墅正处于我泊船的地方和海边住所的中途，因此每次去泊船处我总要在这里停留一下，我常去看看那条独木舟，并把船里的东西，不管是什么东西，都整理得井井有条。有时我也驾船出去，但不敢离岸太远，惟恐无意中被急流、大风把我冲走或刮走，或由于自己的无知而发生意外事故。然而这时我的生活发生了新的变化。

第十三章　足迹之谜

一天中午，我向我的船走去，忽然惊讶地发

boat, I was exceedingly surprised with the print of a man's naked foot on the shore, which was very plain to be seen in the sand. I stood like one thunderstruck, or as if I had seen an apparition. I listened, I looked round me; I could hear nothing, nor see anything; I went up to a rising ground to look farther. I went up the shore, and down the shore, but it was all one, I could see no other impression but that one, I went to it again, to see if there were any more, and to observe if it might not be my fancy, but there was no room for that, for there was exactly the very print of a foot, toes, heel, and every part of a foot: how it came thither I knew not, nor could in the last imagine. But after innumerable fluttering thoughts, like a man perfectly confused, and out of myself, I came, not feeling, as we say, the ground I went on, but terrible to the last degree, looking behind me at every two or three steps, mistaking every bush and tree, and fancying every stump at a distance to be a man. Nor was it possible to describe how many various shapes an affrighted imagination represented things to me in; how many wild ideas were formed every moment in my fancy, and what strange unaccountable whimsies came to my thoughts by the way.

When I came to my castle, I fled into it like one pursued; whether I went over by the ladder, as first con-

现沙滩上留着清晰的五趾足印。这可把我吓坏了，犹如被雷劈中，像大白天见了鬼。我侧耳细听，环顾四周，但什么也没听到，什么也没看到，我爬上沙滩的高处向远方看了看，又到海滨，来来回回看了几遍，但脚印只有这一个，除了它我没有发现其他足印。我又跑到脚印前，看看还有没有其他足印，想知道那是否是我的幻觉。但我错了，这决非是我的幻觉，而实实在在是脚印，而且很完整，有脚趾、脚后跟，有脚的每一个部位。为何这里会出现脚印？我不知道，也猜不出。我使劲想，不停地猜，就好像一个神经错乱的人，又好像失去了自我。最后，我身不由己，沿着原路往回走。我害怕到了极点，拔腿往自己的防御工事跑去，跑得几乎感觉不到地面的存在。而且一步三回头，疑神疑鬼，甚至把远处的树丛、树木、树桩都当成了人。我无法描绘那可怕的东西在我心中幻化的无数吓人的鬼影。一路上，头脑里每时每刻都闪现着各种幻景，充满数不清的荒诞不经的想法。

我一跑到自己的城堡，就钻了进去，好像有人在后面追赶似的。至于我是按事先设想好的法

trived, or went in at the hole in the rock, which I called a door, I cannot remember; no, nor could I remember the next morning. I had no sleep that night; the farther I was from the occasion of my fright the greater my apprehensions were; which is something contrary to the nature of such things, and especially to the usual practice of all creatures in fear. But I was so embarrassed with my own frightful ideas of the thing, that I formed nothing to myself, even though I was now a great way off it.

At last I concluded that it must be some more dangerous creature; namely, that it must be some of the savages of the main – land over against me, who had wandered out to sea in their canoes, and, either driven by the currents or by contrary winds, had made the island, and had been on shore, but were going away again to sea, being as loath, perhaps to have starved in this desolate island as I would have been.

While these reflections were rolling upon my mind, I was very thankful in my thought that I was so happy as not to be thereabouts at that time, or that they did not see my boat, by which they would have concluded that some inhabitants had been in the place, and perhaps have searched farther for me. Then terrible thoughts racked my imaginations about their having found my boat, and that there were people here; and that, if so, I

子从梯子爬进去的，还是从岩洞，也就是我称之为所谓的门里钻进去的，我已记不清了，一点儿都想不起来。甚至到了第二天清早也想不起来。我彻夜未眠，时间越长，我越觉得害怕，这似乎不合乎常理，但对我却是千真万确的。这是所有受惊动物的不正常反应。我被自己种种可怕的念头困扰着，自己也说不清为什么，到头来也没有理出个头绪，完全是自己吓自己，尽管我现在离那脚印很远。

最后，我终于得出结论，那一定是某种更危险的生物，也就是说，那一定是大陆上的野人跑到此地和我作对。这些野人可能乘坐小木舟在海上闲荡，被急流冲到这个岛上，也可能被逆风刮到这里。也许他们上岸后觉得这里不理想而不愿留在这里，还会回到海上。也可能和我当初一样，他们也会饿死在这座孤零零的荒岛上。

当这些想法萦回在我的脑际时，我不禁暗自庆幸自己当时没有在他们登岸那里，也没有让他们发现我的小船，要不然，他们就会断定岛上一定有人，说不定还会来到岛上搜寻我。忽然我又转念一想，如果他们发现了我的小船，发现岛上居住着人，他们一定会来更多的人马将我生吞活

should certainly have them come again in great numbers, and devour me; that if it should happen so that they should not find me, yet they would find my enclosure, destroy all my corn, carry away all my flock of tame goats, and I should perish at last for mere want.

Thus my fear banished all my religious hope; all that former confidence in God which was found upon such wonderful experience as I had had of his goodness, now vanished; as if he that had fed me by miracle hitherto, could not preserve by his power the provision made for me by his goodness. I reproached myself with my easiness, Why I had not sown any more corn one year than would just serve me till the next season, as if no accident could intervene to prevent my enjoying the crop upon the ground. And this I thought so just a reproof, that I resolved for the future to have two or three years' corn beforehand, so that whatever might come, I might not perish for want of bread.

These thoughts took me many hours, days, I may say, weeks and months; and one particular effect of my cogitations on this occasions I cannot omit; namely, one morning early in bed and filled with thoughts about my danger from the appearance of savages, I found it discomposed me very much; upon which those words of the Scripture came into my thoughts, "Call upon me in the

吃掉，如果我碰巧没有给他们发现，他们也一定会发现我的围墙，破坏掉我所有的庄稼，掠走我那驯养好的山羊，最终我也会因饥寒而死。

就这样，恐惧驱走了我所有的宗教信仰。以前，我亲身感受到了上帝的恩惠，上帝对我的仁慈，从而建立起对他的信仰，可现在这种信仰也消失了。过去，他神奇地赐给我食物，而现在，他似乎无力保护他所赐给我的食物了，也无力保护他所创造的生灵。我开始责怪自己由于贪图安逸而不肯多种些粮食，当时我种庄稼时，只图能赶上下一季吃就行了，从来不对以后的日子做过多的打算，仿佛永远不会有意外事故来打扰我的安宁，总想着我有吃不完的粮食，有享不完的福，没想到我现在被剥夺了享用所收获粮食的满足。现在眼前所发生的这一切证明我的想法是错误的，于是我决定今后一定要事先存好两三年的食物，这样无论发生什么事情，我都不会饿死。

我不住地思索，花去了许多天、许多小时甚至几个星期、几个月。说真的，这种思索对我产生了一个特殊的、无法磨灭的影响。那就是，一天清早，我正在床上思索那群野人会给我带来什么样的危险，正感到心里恐慌的时候，忽然想起《圣经》上的一段话：“你在患难的时候呼求我，

day of trouble I will deliver thee, and thou shalt glorify me."

In the middle of these cogitations, apprehensions, and reflections, it came into my thoughts one day, that all this might be a mere chimera of my own, and that foot might be the print of my own foot when I came on shore from my boat. This cheered me up a little too, and I began to persuade myself it was all a delusion; that it was nothing else but my own foot; and why might not I come that way from the boats as well as I was going that way to the boat? Again, I considered also that I could by no means tell for certain where I had trod, and my own foot, I had played the part of those fools who strive to make stories of specters and apparitions, and then are themselves frightened at them more than anybody else.

Now I began to take courage, and to peep abroad again; for I had begun to starve for provision; for I had little of nothing within doors but some barley cakes and water. Then I knew that my goats wanted to be milked, which usually was my evening diversion; and poor creatures were in great pain and inconvenience for want of it; and indeed it almost spoiled some of them, and almost dried up their milk.

Heartening myself, therefore, with the belief that this was nothing but the print of one of my own feet, I

我就必然拯救你，而你要赞颂我。"

就在我胡思乱想，疑神疑鬼，心神不定的时候，一天，我忽然觉得所有这一切说不定只是我的幻觉，那脚印也许是我自己下船上岸时留下的。这个想法使我有了些许欢欣，我开始说服自己，使自己相信所有的这一切都是幻觉，那个脚印一定是自己的，因为既然可以从那里上船，为什么我不可以从那里下船呢？而且，我又想，我自己也不知道自己从哪里走过，都到什么地方去过，我也辨不出哪个是自己的脚印。我岂不成了那些自己编造精灵鬼怪故事，自己吓唬自己的大傻瓜了吗？

于是我鼓起勇气，开始向外偷窥。因为这时我快要断粮了，家里只剩一些大麦饼和水了。另外，我还想到该给山羊挤奶了，给山羊挤奶一直是我黄昏时的消遣。由于好久没挤奶，那些可怜的家伙一定痛苦不堪，十分难受。事实上，由于长久没有挤奶，有好几只几乎已挤不出奶而糟蹋掉了。

我开始相信那个脚印只不过是我自己的，于是觉得振奋了许多，我壮起胆子重新外出了，并

began to go abroad again, and went to my country – house to milk my flock; but to see with what fear I went forward, how often I looked behind me, how I was ready, every now then, to lay down my basket, and run for my life; it would have made any one have thought I was haunted with an evil conscience, or that I had been lately most terribly frightened; and so indeed I had.

However, as I went down thus two or three days, and having seen nothing, I began to be a little bolder, and to think there was really nothing in it but my imagination; but I could not persuade myself of this till I should go down to shore again, and see this print of a foot, and measure it by my own, and see if there was any similitude of fitness, that I might be assured it was my own foot. But when I came to the place, it appeared evidently to me, that when I laid up my boat, I could not possibly be on shore anywhere thereabouts. Secondly, when I came to measure the mark with my own foot, I found my foot not so large by a great deal. Both these things filled my head with new imaginations, and gave me the vapors again to the highest degree, so that I shook with cold like one in an ague, and I went home again, filled with the belief that some man or men had been on shore there: or, in short, that the island was inhabited, and I might be surprised before I was aware;

跑到我的乡间别墅去挤奶。可我走在路上还是感到害怕，还是一步三回头，准备随时扔掉手中的篮子去逃命，我这副模样若是被别人看见，他一定会以为我做了什么亏心事，贼头贼脑的，或者以为我最近受了什么惊吓——实际上我的确是受了惊吓。

就这样我在外面走了两三天，什么也没看见，我胆子稍大了一些，我便开始想，真的没什么，真的只是我自己的幻想。可是如果我不亲自再到海边走一趟，亲自看看那个脚印，亲自用自己的脚去量量，看看是否有相似之处，我无论如何也不能说服自己。可是当我到达海岸时，我发现，而且是显而易见的是，首先我停船时不可能在那里上岸，再者，我用自己的脚去量那个脚印时，发现那只脚印比我的脚大得多。这两个新发现又使我思绪纷乱，忐忑不安。我满脑子的幻觉，又开始胡思乱想了，就像得了瘟疫一样直打冷颤。我赶紧回家，同时深信有个人或有些个人已经上岸，总之岛上已有人居住，而且说不定哪天，我会被打个措手不及，可是我目前还不知道采取怎

and what course to take for my security I knew not.

This confusion of my thoughts kept me waking all night, but in the morning I fell asleep, tired, and my spirits by the amusement of my mind had been, as it were, tired, and my spirits exhausted, I slept very soundly, and awaked much better composed than I had ever been before. And now I began to think sedately; and, island, which was so exceeding pleasant, fruitful, and no farther from the main – land than as I had seen, was not so entirely abandoned as I might imagine. That although there were no stated inhabitants who lived on the spot, yet that there might sometimes come boats off from the shore, who either with design, or perhaps never but when were driven by cross winds, might come to this place.

That I had lived here fifteen years now and not met with the least shadow or figure of any people before; and that, if at any time they should be driven here, it was probable they went away again as soon as ever they could, seeing they had never thought fit to fix upon any to this time.

The danger I could suggest was from any such casual accidental of straggling people from the main, who, as it was likely, if they were driven hither, were here against their wills; they made no stay here, went off

样的手段以保障自身的安全。

　　我思绪混乱，辗转反侧，彻夜难眠，到早晨时，由于过度思虑，觉得疲惫不堪——我一直都在思考这个问题，并在思考中昏昏睡去。再一觉醒来，发现自己比以往任何时候都觉得安定。我的情绪也好了许多。我镇定下来后，暗自思忖着，这座岛既离大陆不远，又令人愉快，结满果实，就不会像我原先想的那样人迹罕至，孤独无援了。岛上虽没有其他居民，而对面大陆上的人有时完全可以乘坐船只，离海登岸，到这里来，无论他们是有目的而来，还是碰到逆风而迫不得已停泊船只，总之他们来到了这个荒岛上。

　　自从十五年前我住在这里到现在，我连一个人影也未见到，即使有人被风刮到这里，他们也总是尽快离开，不在此久呆，看来，到目前为止，他们仍然认为这座孤岛不适合人居住。

　　看来我最大的危险就是那些偶尔在此登陆的对面大陆上的人而已，我暗自思忖着，很有可能他们来这里并非出自本意，而是被风吹来，落难于此地，这样他们也不愿留下过夜，上岛后会尽

again with all possible, seldom speed, seldom staying one night on shore lest they should not have the help of the tides and daylight again. And that, therefore, I had nothing to do but to consider some safe retreat, in case I should see any savages land upon the spot.

Now I had dug my cave so large as to bring a door through again, which door, as I said, came out beyond where fortification joined to the rock. Upon maturely considering this, therefore, I resolved to draw me a second fortification, in the manner of a semicircle, at a distance from my wall, just where I made a double row of trees about twelve years before, of which I made mention; these trees having been planted but a few piles to be driven between them, that they should be thicker and stronger, and my wall would be finished.

So that I had now a double wall, and my outer wall was thickened with pieces of timber, old cables, and everything I could think of to make it strong; having in it seven holes about as big as I might put my arm out at. In the inside of this I thickened my wall to about ten feet thick, continually bringing earth out of my cave, patting it at the foot of the wall, and walking upon it; and through the seven holes I contrived on plant muskets, of which I took notice that I got seven in out of ship; these, I say, I planted like my cannon, and fitted them

快离开。否则潮水一退，天色一暗，他们要离岛就困难了。这样一来，我要做的只不过是想一条安全退路而已，有一条一见到野人就能躲过的退路就行了。

现在我把山洞挖得很大了，地方很宽敞，而且还在防御工事与岩石的衔接处开了一个门。经过一番深思熟虑，我决定在我的围墙外，就是那个我十二年前种两行树的地方再修建一个半圆的围墙，做防护自身安全用，我原先栽的树，中间缝隙太大、不安全，我只须在那两行树之间再打一些木桩就行了，以使它们变得更密更坚固，我的围墙就这样修好了。

现在，里外我有两个围墙了，我又用木料、旧绳子等我所能想到的一切东西来加固我的外墙，我还在外墙上挖了七个洞，洞的大小刚好能够把我手臂伸出去。我又不断地从洞里运出土倒在围墙里面，用脚踩实，以此把内墙又加宽十多英尺。通过那七个洞，我在架子上安置了七把我从船上拿来的毛瑟枪，我将这七支枪摆好，发现这七支枪摆的好像七尊大炮。我把它们用架子支牢，就

into frames that held them like carried, that so I could fire all the seven guns in two minutes' time: this I was many a weary month in finishing, and yet never though safe till it was done.

When this was done, I stuck all ground without my wall, for a great way ever, as full with stakes or sticks of the osier – like wood, which I found so apt to grow, as they could well stand: insomuch that I might set in near twenty thousand of them, leaving a pretty large space between them and my wall, that I might have room to see an enemy, and they might have no shelter from the trees, if they attempted to approach my outer wall.

Thus in two years' time I had a thick grove, and in five or six years' time I had a wood before my dwelling, grown so monstrous thick and strong that it was indeed perfectly impassable; and no man of what kind would ever imagine that there was anything beyond it, much less a habitation. As for the way I proposed myself to go in and out, it was by setting two ladders, one to a part of the rock which was low, and then broke in, and left room to place another ladder upon that; so, when the two ladders were taken down, no man living could come down to me without mischiefing himself; and if they had come down, they were still on the outside of my outer wall.

好像是行军拿着枪那样，这样，我就可以在两分钟之内连开七枪。我辛苦了好几个月才完成这一切，而且在完成之前，我一直提心吊胆，觉得不安全。

完成这项工程之后，我又在墙外密密麻麻地插上一些树枝——一种像柳树一样的树枝，好大一片。我发现这些树枝特别能长，而且直挺挺的，特别坚固结实。我插了差不多两万枝。另外，我还在树枝与围墙之间留出一条很宽的空地。这样，如果有敌人从外墙来袭击我，我就可以发现他们，因为他们无法在这个空地中隐蔽自己。

这样，不到两年我就有了一片小丛林，稠密茂盛，郁郁葱葱的，在不到五六年的时间里，我的居住地前会出现一片茂密葱郁的森林，无人能通过。谁也不会想到树林后有什么东西，更不会想到会有人居住。我还为自己设计了进出的方式，就是给自己架了两架梯子。一架梯子靠在树林侧面岩石较低的地上，岩石上有一个凹进去的地方，正好留出地方来放第二架梯子。这样，只要把两架梯子都拿走，任何一个想要靠近我的人都毫无例外会受到反击。就算他们越过森林，也进不了我的外墙。

Thus I took all the measures human prudence could suggest for my own preservation; and it will be seen at length, that they were not altogether without just reason, though I foresaw nothing at that time more than my mere suggested.

Chapter 14   New Problems

While this was doing I was not altogether careless of my other affairs; for I had a great concern upon me for my little heard of goats: they were not only a present supply to me upon every occasion, and began to be sufficient for me without the expense of powder and shot, but also abated the fatigue of my hunting after the wild ones; and I was loath to lose the advantage of them, and to have them all to nurse up over again.

Accordingly I spent some time to find out the most retired parts of the island, and I pitched upon one, for it was a little damp piece of ground in the middle of the hollow and thick woods, where I almost lost myself once before, endeavoring to come back that way from the eastern part of the island. Here I found a clear piece of land, three acres, so surrounded with woods that it was almost an enclose by nature; at least it did not want so much labor to make it so as the other piece of ground I

这样，我为了保护自己而几乎用尽了人类可能拥有的所有的智慧。而且不久以后就会看出这一切并非没有道理，尽管目前的危险仅仅只是我的猜想。

第十四章　难题再现

在做这件事的时候，我并不是对其他事情完全不理了；我最最放心不下的是我那为数不多的一群羊：它们不但在任何情况下能为我提供现成的食物，而且已经开始能满足我的需求，而不必再浪费我的任何枪枝弹药，况且能减少我捕杀野羊的疲劳；有很多好处使我不愿失去它们，也不想以后再重新驯养。

于是我花了些时间，在岛上找了几个最隐蔽的地方，我选定了其中一个地方，这是一小片比较潮湿的地方，正处在在山谷和密林的中央，我以前有一次试图经由这块地从岛东部回来时，差点迷路。在这里我找到一块三英亩左右的空地，周围被树林围得严严实实，就像大自然为我围好了一块地，至少围好它无需我再费力地大干一

had worked so hard at.

I immediately went to work with this piece of ground, and in less than a month's time I had so fenced it round that my flock or herd were well enough secured in it. So, without any farther delay, I removed ten she – goats and two he – goats to this piece. I continued to perfect the fence till I made it as secure as the other.

All this labor I had at the expense of purely apprehensions on the account of a man's foot which I had seen; for as yet I never saw any human creature come near the island, and I had now lived two years under these uneasinesses, which indeed made my life much less comfortable than it was before, as may well be imagined by any who know what it is to live in the constant snare of the fear of man.

But to go on; after I had thus secured one part of my little living stock, I went about the whole island searching for another private place to make such another deposit; when wandering more to the west point of the island than I had ever done yet, and looking out to sea, I thought I saw a boat upon the sea at great distance. I had found a perspective glass or two in one of the seamen's chests, which I saved out of our ship; but I had it not about me; and this was so remote that I could not tell what to make of it, though I looked at it till my eyes

番，不用像圈以前那几块地那样辛苦。

我立即就在这块地上干起活来，用了不到一个月的时间，我已经把那里围了起来，使我那群羊，或者叫牲畜，在里面很安全。所以我毫不耽搁，把十头母羊和两头公羊赶到这里。我继续加工围栏，把它做的和别处一样坚固。

我费力做的所有的这些工作，仅仅只是因为看到一个人的脚印所产生的忧虑；因为我还从来没有看见过任何人接近这个岛，两年来我却在不安中志忑度过，这当然使我的生活过的不如以前舒服，任何人只要知道时时刻刻担心别人算计他是一种什么感觉，就不难想象我的生活了。

但言归正传，在我把羊群的一部分安置好以后，我就在整个岛上到处寻找，想再找一个隐蔽的地方作同样安置。我在山上游逛，走得比以往任何一次都更接近岛的西端，在朝海上眺望的时候，我觉得很远的海面上好像有一条船。我以前从我们的船上曾经搬下几个海员的箱子，并在一个箱子里找到一两只望远镜，但却没有把它带在身边；现在距离实在太远，我看不清那到底是什么东西，尽管我一直看到我的眼睛不能再看了，

were not able to look any longer. Whether it was a boat or not I do not know; but as I descended from the hill I could see no more of it, so gave it over, only I resolved to go no more without a perspective glass in my pocket.

When I came down the hill to the shore, I was perfectly confounded and amazed; nor is it possible for me to express the horror of my mind at seeing the shore spread with skulls, hands, feet, and other bones of human bodies; and particularly I observed a place where there had been a fire made, and a circle dug in the earth, like a cock – pit, where it is supposed the savage wretches had sat down to their inhuman feastings upon the bodies of their fellow – creatures.

I was so astonished with the sight of these things that I entertained no notions of any danger to myself from it for a long while; all my apprehensions were buried in the thoughts of such a pitch of inhuman, hellish brutality, and the horror of the degeneracy of human nature; which, though I had heard of often, yet I had had not so near a view before; in short, I turned away my face from the horrid spectacle, my stomach grew sick, and I was just at the point of fainting, when nature discharged the disorder from my stomach, and, having vomited with an uncommon violence, I was a little relieved, but could not bear to stay in the place a moment; so I got me up

我还是没弄清那是不是一艘船；往山下走时再看不见了，我只好作罢，但决定以后出来时口袋里都要带上望远镜。

当我下山走到海边，看到海岸上到处散落的头骨、手骨和人体其他部分的骨头，我惊得魂飞魄散，无法用语言描绘当时内心恐怖的感觉；特别令我惧怕的是，我发现一个生过火的地方还挖有一个斗鸡坑似的圆穴，想来这些野蛮的家伙曾坐在这儿，进行他们惨无人道的食人盛宴，吃着同类的血肉。

眼前的这个场面使我惊呆了，竟在很长时间里让我忘记这件事对我本人所意味的危险；我的思想完全沉浸在对这种毫无人性的野蛮行为，这种另人毛骨悚然的兽行和对人性堕落的恐惧之中；虽然，我以前经常听说类似的事情，但从没有在如此近的距离亲眼目睹过；总之，我扭过头不再看这恐怖的景象，胃里直觉得阵阵恶心，就在我快要晕倒的时候，胃里的恶心却化为一阵呕吐，在翻江倒海的一阵呕吐之后，我稍微舒服了一点儿，但是在这地方我是一刻也呆不下去了，于是

the hill again with all the speed I could, and walked on towards my own habitation.

When I came a little out of that part of the island I stood still awhile as amazed; and then, recovering myself, I looked up with the utmost affection of my soul, and, with a flood of tears in my eyes, gave God thanks that had cast my first lot in a part of the world where I was distinguished from such dreadful creatures as these; and though I had esteemed my present condition very miserable, had yet given me so many comforts in it, that I had still more to give thanks for than to complain of; and this above all, that I had, even in this miserable condition, been comforted with knowledge of himself, and the hope of this blessing, which was a felicity more than sufficiently equivalent to all the misery which I had suffered or could suffer. In this frame of thankfulness I went home to my castle and began to be much easier now, as to the safety of my circumstances, than ever I was before; for I observed that these wretches never came to this island in search of what they could get; perhaps not seeking, nor wanting, or not expecting anything here; and having often, no doubt, been up in the covered woody part of it without finding anything to their purpose I knew I had here now almost eighteen years, and never saw the least footsteps of a human creature

我以最快的速度又爬上山，往自己的住处走去。

当和那个地方拉开一段距离之后，我呆呆的站了好大一会儿，回过神来以后，我心中满怀深深的敬爱，眼里充满感激的泪水，感谢上帝让我降生在世界的另一个地方，使我和这些可怕的家伙有了区别；尽管我认为自己目前的处境很不幸，但也有很多地方让我感到欣慰，所以我更多的应该是感激，而不是抱怨；最重要的是，正是在这不幸的环境里，我认识了上帝并期望他的保佑，这本身就是一种幸福，而且这足以抵消我以前受过的苦或是以后还要受的苦。我就是怀着这种感激之情，回到了我的城堡之中，对于自己处境安全与否这一问题，心里远不像以前那样紧张了；因为我发现这些家伙来这个岛上的目的，并不是寻找看能得到什么，也许他们来这里根本不是找什么，也不想，或者根本不指望能得到什么东西；当然，他们曾经常出入树木茂密的地方，但一无所获，没有找到自己想要的东西。我知道，我来这个岛上快十八年了，以前从来没有见过人的脚

there before; and might be here eighteen years more as entirely concealed as I was now, if I did not discover myself to them which I had no manner of occasion to do, it being my only business to keep myself entirely concealed where I was, unless I found a better sort of creatures than cannibals to make myself known to.

Time, however, and the satisfaction I had that I was in no danger of being discovered by these people, began to wear off my uneasiness about them; and I began to live just in the same composed manner as before, only with this difference, that I used more caution, and kept my eyes more about me than I did before, lest I should happen to be seen by any of them; and particularly, I was more cautious of firing my gun, lest any of them being on the island should happen to hear it; and it was therefore a very good providence to me, that I had furnished myself with a tame breed of goats, that I had no need to hunt any more about the woods, or shoot at them, and if I did catch any more of them after this, it was with traps and snares, as I had done before; so that for two years after this, I believe I never fired my gun once off, though I never went out without it.

But my invention ran quite another way; for night and day I could think of nothing but how I might destroy some of these monsters in their cruel bloody entertain-

印；也许再这样隐蔽地呆上十八年也没问题，只要我不把自己暴露在他们面前，我也没有理由这样暴露自己，我惟一要做的，就是在自己的地方像以前一样好好隐蔽自己，除非发现了不吃人肉的人，才可以让他知道我。

然而，时间长了，我自认为他们完全没有可能发现我，不安的心情开始渐渐淡化；于是我开始像以前那样平静地过日子，惟一不同的是，我小心谨慎多了，对周围的情况也比以前注意多了，免得不凑巧被他们哪个家伙发现；特别是在开枪方面，我更谨慎，以防他们中有人在岛上碰巧听见我的枪声；幸亏由于上天保佑，让我驯化了一群羊来供给我食物，我不必再到林子里去打猎了，也不必开枪打野羊了，我在以后确实还逮到过野羊，但都像以前一样，利用陷阱或罗网；所以在那以后两年里，虽说我每次外出都带着枪，但却一次都没放过。

但我的创造力完全在另一个方面，我日思夜想的不是别的，而是要如何在他们野蛮血腥的宴会上消灭几个吃人恶魔，而且如果有可能，救出

ment, and if possible, save the victim they should bring hither to destroy. It would take up a large volume than this whole work is intended to be to set down all the contrivances I hatched, or rather brooded upon in my thoughts, for destroying these creatures, or at least frightening them, so as to prevent their coming hither any more; but all was abortive, nothing could be possible to take effect unless I was to be there to do it myself; and what could one man do among them, when perhaps there might be twenty or thirty of them together, with their darts, or their bows and arrows, with which they could shoot as true to a mark as I could with my gun?

Sometimes I contrived to dig a hole under the place where they made their fire, and put in five or six pounds of gunpowder, which, when they kindled their fire, would consequently take fire, and blow up all that was near it; but I should be very loath to waste so much powder upon them, so I laid it aside, and then proposed that I would place myself in ambush, with my three guns double – loaded, and in the middle of their bloody ceremony let fly at them. This fancy pleased my thoughts for some weeks, and I was so full of it that I often dreamt of it, and sometimes, that I was just going to let fly at them in my sleep.

After I had thus laid the scheme for my design, and

几个被他们带来要杀害的受害者。为了要消灭这些野人，或者至少吓吓他们，使得他们不敢再来，我脑子里酝酿了许多方法许多念头，要是把这些计划写下来，这本书的篇幅会比我预计的大得多。但是所有的方案都不了了之，因为除非我亲自到现场去实行，这些方案都不可能奏效；但我一个人又有什么用？他们说不定总共有二三十人，还有带来的标枪、弓箭，而且他们投标枪、射箭的准头或许不亚于我的枪法呢？

有时候，我想在他们生火的地方挖一个洞，放五六磅炸药进去，这样只要他们一生火，炸药就会被点燃，把周围的一切全炸飞；但我不愿为他们浪费那么多火药，于是把这个计划撂在一边。又想我自己可以在灌木丛中埋伏起来，给我的三支枪都加上双倍的弹药，在他们的血腥仪式举行到一半时向他们射击。这个想法让我高兴了好几个星期，我满脑子都是这事，结果连做梦都梦见这事，有时候梦见自己正要向他们开枪呢。

我不定期地这样计划着，并准备着实施这计

in my imagination put it in practice, I continually made my tour every morning up to the hill, which was from my castle about three miles or more, to see if I could observe any boats upon the sea coming near the island, or standing over towards it: but I began to tire of this hard duty, after I had for two or three months constantly kept my watch; but came always back without any discovery, there having not in all that time been the least appearance, not only on or near glasses could reach every way.

As long as I kept up my daily tour to the hill to look out, so long also I kept up the vigor of my design, and my spirits seemed to be all the while in a suitable for so outrageous an execution as the killing twenty or thirty naked savages. But now, when I began to be weary of the fruitless excursion which I had made so long, and so far, every morning in vain; so my opinion of the action itself began to alter, and I began, with cooler and calmer thoughts, to consider what it was I was going to engage in.

When I had considered this a little, it followed necessarily that I was certainly in the wrong in it; that these people were not murderers and had done me no injury: that if they attempted me, or if I saw it necessary for my immediate preservation to fall upon them, something might be said for it; but that I was yet out of their

划，我每天都要毫不例外地爬到山上去，到距我城堡三英里远的山顶，看有没有船驶近这个岛或正在远处驶来，从来没有间断过；但两三个月下来，我对这个辛苦的差使开始厌倦了，因为尽管那段时间我一直守望，但总是一无所获地回家，而且海岸上根本看不见一个人影，即使在我目力和望远镜能所及的范围内全没有动静。

在我每天去小山上观察期间，对自己实施计划的劲头很足，似乎随时可以干出那种残忍之举，杀掉二三十个光身的野人。但现在，我每天上午这样徒劳地走一趟，距离又远，花时间也很长，终于产生了厌倦情绪；于是，对自己是否应该采取那种行动，我的观点发生了变化，我开始对自己所要干的事作冷静的考虑。

把这件事稍加考虑之后，我得出结论，对这件事我想我错了；这些家伙不是杀人犯，也没有伤害过我；如果说他们要杀我，或是我觉得有必要先袭击他们，那还有点儿道理可说；但是他们根本碰不到我一根汗毛，而且完全不知道我的存

power, and they had really no knowledge of me, and consequently no design upon me; and therefore it could not be for me to fall upon them:

These considerations really put me to a pause, and to a kind of full stop; and I began by little and little to be off my design, and to conclude I had taken a wrong measure in my resolutions to attack the savages; that it was not my business to meddle with them, unless they first attacked me, and this was my business, if possible, to prevent; but that, if I were discovered and attacked, then I knew my duty.

The thoughts of this sometimes sunk my very soul within me, and distressed my mind so much, that I could not recover it. I confess that these anxieties, these constant dangers I lived in, and the concern that now upon me put an end to all invention, and to all the contrivances that I had laid for my future accommodations and conveniences. I had the care of my safety more now upon my hands than that of my food. I cared not to drive a nail, or chop a stick of wood now, for fear the noise I should make should be heard; much less would I fire a gun, for the same reason; and above all, I was intolerably uneasy at making any fire, lest the smoke, which is visible at a great distance in the day, should betray me: and for this reason I removed that part of my business

在，也不会打我的主意；那么，若我对他们发动袭击就没有道理了。

经过这番考虑，我暂缓了实施自己的计划，也可说是完全停止了；渐渐的，我放弃了这个计划，并且认识到我攻击野人的主意是错误的；我不应该去干涉他们，除非他们先来攻击我，而我应该尽量防止这一点；但如果他们发现并攻击我，我知道自己该怎么做。

每次想到这里，我都感到心情沉重，十分难过，以致于难以排解。我承认，我所处的生活环境随时都有忧患都有危险，而我由此产生的种种不安以及对自己安全的担心，使我无暇再为改善自己的生活环境而想办法，动脑筋了；我现在做事时想到的首先是安全，而不是食物问题了。我现在不敢敲钉，也不敢劈柴，害怕有人会听到发出的声音。出于同样的理由，我更不敢放枪了；最糟糕的是，我在生火时也极端地忐忑不安，老是害怕白天别人在大老远就能看出烟柱，把我暴露出来；为此，我把需要用火的活，例如烧制陶

which required fire, such as burning of pots and pipes in my new apartment in the woods; where, after I had been some time, I found, to my unspeakable consolation, a mere natural cave in earth, which went in a vast way, and where, I dare say, no savage, had he been at the mouth of it, would be so hardy as to venture in, nor indeed would any man else, but one who, like me, wanted nothing so much as a safe retreat.

The mouth of this hollow was at the bottom of a great rock, where, by mere accident, I was cutting down some thick branches of trees to make charcoal; and before I went on, I must observe the reason of my making this charcoal, which was thus:

I was afraid of making a smoke about my habitation, as I said before; and yet I could not live there without baking my bread, cooking my meat, so I contrived to burn some wood here, as I had seen done in England, under turf, till it became dry coal; and then putting the fire out, I preserved the coal to carry home, and perform the other services which were wanting for at home, without danger of smoke.

While I was cutting down some wood here, I perceived that behind a very thick branch of low brushwood, or under – wood, there was a kind of hollow place. I was curious to look into it, and getting with difficulty into the

器和烟斗，都移到林中的新住处去做；我在里面住了段时间，欣慰地发现这个天然的洞穴很深，我敢大胆的说，即使有一个野人到了洞口，也未必有胆量进来，除了这种像我一样急需一个安全退路的人，还有谁会进来？

这个洞穴的洞口在一块巨岩的底部，我在那儿茂密的林间砍些树枝，想用来烧成炭，无意间发现了这个洞口。在我继续叙述之前，我必须把烧炭的原因交代一下，那就是：

我以前说过，我不敢在自己的住处弄出烟来；但既然生活在那儿，又不能不烤面包、不烤肉，所以我就照在英国看到的那样，把树枝放在草皮底下闷烧，直到它们变成木炭，然后灭了火，把木炭收起来带回家去，待家里要时就以炭代柴，就不会有冒烟的危险了。

话说当时我在这儿砍着树枝，看到浓密低矮的灌木丛或小树丛后面仿佛有个洞穴似的所在。我感到好奇，想进去看看，好不容易费力地进了

mouth of it, I found it was pretty large, sufficient for me to stand upright in it, and perhaps another with me, but I must confess to you, I made more haste out than I did in; when looking farther into the place, which was perfectly dark, I saw two broad shining eyes of some creature, whether devil or man I knew not, which twinkled like two stars, the dim light from the cave's mouth shinning directly in, and making the reflection.

However, after some pause, I recovered myself, and began to call myself a thousand fools, and tell myself that he that was afraid to see the devil, was not fit to live twenty years in an island all alone, and that I durst to believe there was nothing in this cave that was more frightful than myself, upon this, plucking up my courage, I took up a great firebrand, and in I rushed again, with the stick flaming in my hand. I had not gone three steps in, but I was almost as much frightened as I was before; for I heard a very loud sigh, like that of a man in some pain; and it was followed by a broken noise, as if of words half – expressed, and then a deep sigh again. I stepped back, and was indeed struck with such a surprise, that it put me into a cold sweat; and if I had had a hat on my head, I will not answer for it that my hair might not have lifted it off. But still plucking up my spirits as well as I could, and encouraging myself a little,

洞口以后，我发现里面很大，足够我在里面直站着，或许还能容下另一个人；但我得承认，我出洞时比进洞时仓促得多；因为朝里面一望，在一片漆黑之中，我发现两只亮晶晶的眼睛，不知是人是鬼还是什么动物的；从洞口直射进来的微光，照在这双眼睛上反射出来，就像两颗闪闪发光的星星。

我愣了一会儿，但是回过神来之后，我开始骂自己是个傻瓜中的傻瓜，告诉自己谁要是怕见鬼，就不配孤身一人在这荒岛上住二十年；我敢说，在那个洞里，只有我本人才是最可怕的，这样一想，我就鼓足了勇气，手里拿着一个熊熊燃烧的火把，重新钻进了洞里。我在洞里走了还不到三步，又像先前那样吓了一大跳；因为我听见一声很响的哼哼声，像一个人正处在痛苦中那样；紧接着又是几声断断续续的声音，像是含糊不清的字音，然后又是一声深深的哼哼声。我倒退了几步，并且惊得出了一身冷汗；我不知道要是头上戴着帽子，我的头发会不会竖起来把帽子顶掉。但是我还是尽量鼓起勇气，一边还给自己壮胆，

with considering that the power and presence of God was everywhere, and was able to protect me; upon this I stepped forward again, and saw lying in the ground a most monstrous frightful old he – goat, just making his will, as we say, and gasping for life, and dying indeed of mere old age.

I stirred him a little to see if I could get him out, and he essayed to get up, but was not able to raise himself: and I thought with myself, he might even lie there; for he had frightened me so, he would certainly fright any of the savages, if any of them should be so hardy as to come in there, while he had any life in him.

I was now recovered from my surprise, and began to look round me, when I found the cave was but very small; but in no manner of shape, either round or square, no hands ever having been employed in making it, but those of mere nature. I observed also, that there was a place at the farther side of it that went in farther, but was so low, that it required me to creep upon my hands and knees to go into it, and whither I went I know not; so having no candle, I gave it over for some time, but resolved to come again the next day, provided with candles and a tinderbox, which I had made of the lock of one of the muskets, with some wild – fire in the pan.

Accordingly, the next day, I came provided with

说上帝的威力与保佑无所不在，他的威力无限，肯定能保护我；就这样想着，我又向前走了几步，借着火光，我发现地上躺着一只体型巨大、丑陋无比的老公羊，它因为衰老不堪，正是奄奄待毙，用我们的话来说，正在吩咐后事呢，说不定他正在立遗嘱呢！

我踢了它几下，看能不能把它赶出洞去，它也想起身，但已经站不起来了；我一想，让它就趴在那儿，既然它把我都吓了一大跳，那万一有大胆的野人也进了这个洞，只要老公羊还有一口气，也会吓他一大跳的。

当时我定下神来，开始环视四周，发现洞穴很小；而且不方也不圆，形状完全不规则，它完全是天然的，没有经过任何人工的开凿。我还发现，在洞的尽头还有一个更深的去处，但那入口很低，以致于我要趴在地上手脚并用才能爬进去，但能爬到哪儿就不得而知了；由于没有蜡烛，我只好暂时作罢，但已打定主意明天再来，并提醒自己来时带上蜡烛和火绒盒——它是我用火枪上的保险改造的，里面放着引火的东西。

第二天，我带着自制的六根大蜡烛来了，然

six large candles of my own making; and going into this low place, I was obliged to creep upon all fours, almost ten yards; which by the way, I thought was a venture bold enough, considering that I knew not how far it might go, nor what was beyond it. When I got through the straight, I found the roof rose higher up, I believe near twenty feet; but never was such a glorious sight seen in the island, to look round the side and roof of this vault or cave. The walls reflected a hundred thousand lights to me from my two candles: what it was in the rock, whether diamonds, or any other precious stones, or gold, which I rather suppose it to be, I knew not.

The place I was in was a most delightful cavity, or grotto, of its kind, as could be expected, though perfectly dark; the floor was dry and level, and had a sort of small loose gravel upon it; so that there was no nauseous or venomous creature to be seen, neither was there any damp or wet on the sides or roof; the only difficulty in it was the entrance, however, as it was a place of security, and such a retreat as I wanted, I thought that was a convenience; so that I was really rejoiced at the discovery, and resolved, without any delay, to bring some of those things which I was most anxious about to this place; particularly, I resolved to bring hither my magazine of powder, and all my spare arms, namely, two

后进入了这个低矮的地方，我不得不四肢着地爬进去，大约有十码的距离，我觉得这是个很大胆的举动，我不知道究竟要爬多远，也不知道爬进去会遇见什么。当我通过这直直的一段，我发现洞顶升上去了，大约有二十英尺高；但向这洞穴的四周和顶部一看，那种辉煌的景象是我在这个岛上从未见过的。我手中两支蜡烛的光，经过洞壁的反射，发出万千点火光照在我身上；不知这岩壁里究竟是钻石呢，还是其他宝石或黄金，我想应该是黄金吧，我不知道。

这个洞穴尽管没有光线，非常阴暗，却是我所期望的一个非常美妙的洞府；地面干燥而平坦，上面有一层细细的碎石沙砾；所有有毒有害、令人恶心的东西一概看不见，周围石壁和洞顶也不潮湿；惟一的困难就是入口不容易进入，但是这里很安全，是我所需要的藏身之所，我觉得这里很便利，很适合我；因为我对自己的这一发现大为高兴，决定立即动手，把我最放心不下的东西转移到这里来；特别是决定要搬来我所储存的火

fowling – pieces and three muskets; so I kept at my castle only five, which stood ready mounted, like pieces of cannon, on my outmost fence, and were ready also to take out upon any expedition.

Upon this occasion of removing my ammunition, I took occasion to open the barrel of powder which I took up out of the sea, and which had been wet; and I found that the water had penetrated about three or four inches into the powder on every side, which, caking and growing hard, had preserved the inside like a kernel in a shell; so that I had near sixty pounds of very good powder in the center of the cask; and this was an agreeable discovery to me at that time; so I carried all away thither, never keeping above two or three pounds of powder with me in my castle, for fear of a surprise of any kind. I also carried thither all the lead I had left for bullets.

I fancied myself now like one of the ancient giants, which are said to live in caves and holes in the rocks, where none could come at them; for I persuaded myself while I was here, if five hundred savages were to hunt me, they could never find me out; or if they did, they would not venture to attack me here.

The old goat, whom I found expiring, died in the mouth of the cave the next day after I made this discovery; and I found it much easier to dig a great hole there,

药和多余的枪支，包括两支鸟枪和三支火枪。我在城堡里只留了五支枪，都像大炮一样架在外面的一道围墙上，随时可以射击，如果外出时需要，也可以顺便取下来。

在这次转移弹药过程中，我顺便打开了那桶从海里捞上来的潮湿了的火药；我发现桶里的火药有三四英寸被海水浸透了，结成了硬块，但里面的部分却保存得很好，就像果壳保全果仁一样：这样一来，我从那桶的中间弄到了六十磅上好的火药；这发现让我高兴了好一阵子；我把火药都搬了过去，再也不在我的城堡里保留两三磅以上的火药，以免发生任何意外。我又把我做子弹的铅全部搬了过去。

我觉得我现在很像古代的那些巨人，住在山洞岩穴里，谁也无法攻击他们。这里的情况使我相信，即使有五百个野人到处搜寻我，也别想找到，就算他们找到了，也不敢大胆攻过来。

在我发现这洞穴的第二天，那只奄奄一息的老公羊死在了洞口；我觉得，要把它拖出去太困

and throw him in, and cover him with earth, than to drag him out; so I interred him there, to prevent offense to my nose.

I was now in my twenty – third year of residence in this island, and was so naturalized to the place, and to the manner of living, that I could have but enjoyed the certainty that no savages would come to the place to disturb me. I could have been content to have capitulated for spending the rest of my time there, even to the last moment, till I had laid me down and died, like the old goat in the cave. By now I had kept a number of tame animals. My dog was a very pleasant and loving companion to me for no less than sixteen years of my time, and then died of mere old age; as for my cats, they multiplied, to that degree, that I was obliged to shoot several of them at first to keep them from devouring me and all I had; but at length, when the two old ones I brought with me were gone, and after some time continually driving them from me, and letting them have no provision with me, they all ran wild into the woods, except two or three favorites, which I kept tame, and whose young, when they had any, I always drowned, and these were part of my family. Besides these, I always kept two or three household kids about me, which I taught to feed out of my hand; and also more parrots which talked pretty

难，不如挖个大坑，把它埋起来方便些；我把它埋进了土中，免得以后臭气熏人。

如今我在这岛上已住了二十三个年头了，已完全适应了这儿的环境，习惯了这种生活方式，只要确保野人不来这儿骚扰，我将接受这种安排毫无怨言地在此地度过余生，直到咽下最后一口气，像山洞里那头老羊似的，寿终正寝，倒地而死。但是现在我有许多驯养动物，狗是给我带来了很多快乐的可爱伴侣，它陪伴了我至少十六年，后来老死了；至于我的猫，它们繁殖太快，以至于我不得不射杀几只，免得它们吃光我的东西，甚至他们会有一天把我本人也吃了。但后来时间久了，我带上岸的两只老猫死了，后来我不断地把它们从我身边赶走，不给它们东西吃，这些猫都跑到林子里，成了林子里的野猫，剩下有两三只是我特别喜欢的，还养在家里，成为这家庭的成员。当它们生了小猫，我就把小猫淹死。除了这些以外，我总是在家里养两三只小羊，教它们在我手里吃东西；还有几只鹦鹉，它们话讲得不

well, and would all call Robin Crusoe, but none like my first; nor indeed did I take the pains with any of them that I had done with him. I had also several tame sea – fowls, whose names I know not, which I caught upon the shore, and cut their wings; and the little stakes, which I had planted before my castle wall, being now grown up to a good thick grove, these fowls all lived among these low trees, and bred there, which was very agreeable to me, so that, I began to be very well contented with the life I led, if it might but have been secured from the dread of the savages.

Chapter 15 Savages' Visit

It was now December, and this being the southern solstice, for winter I cannot call it, but it was the partic- ular time of my harvest, and required my being pretty much abroad in the fields. When going out pretty early in the morning, I was surprised with seeing a light of some fire upon the shore, at a distance from me of about two miles, towards the end of the island, where I had observed some savages had been before; but not on the other side; but to my great affliction, it was on my side of the island.

I was indeed terribly surprised at the sight, and

错，都会说"鲁宾逊·克鲁索"，但都不如先前那一只。而且，说实在的，我在它们身上花的工夫也不如原来那只鹦鹉。我还在海边捉到过几只海鸟，不知道是什么鸟，我剪了它们的翅膀，当家禽养；我在城堡墙外插的木桩已长成了茂密的矮树丛，这些海鸟就栖息其中并在那儿繁衍生息，让我十分高兴。因此只要确保那些野人不来侵扰我，我对这样的日子就很满意了。

第十五章　野人来访

当时正是十二月冬至前后。当然，这儿的十二月，根本不能算是冬天，但对我来说，这是收获庄稼的特殊季节。我必须经常出门到田里去。一天清晨，天还未大亮，我就出门了。忽然，只见小岛尽头的海岸上一片火光，那儿离我大约有两英里远。这使我惊恐万分，那儿我也发现过野人到过的痕迹。但使我更苦恼的是，火光不是在岛的另一边，而是在我这一边。

看到这个情景，我着实吃惊不小。我立即停

stepped short within my grove, not daring to go out. If these savages, in rambling over the island, should find my corn standing, or cut, or any of my works and improvements, they would immediately conclude that there were people in the place, and would then never give over till they had found me out. In this extremity I went back directly to my castle, pulled up the ladder after me, having made all things without look as wild and natural as I could.

Then I prepared myself within, putting myself in a posture of defense. I loaded all my muskets, which were mounted upon my new fortification, and all my pistols, and resolved to defend myself to the last gasp; not forgetting seriously to commend myself to the divine protection and earnestly to pray to God to deliver me out of the hands of the barbarians; and in this posture I continued about two hours, but began to be mighty impatient for intelligence abroad, for I had no spies to send out.

After sitting a while longer, and musing what I should do in this case, I was notable to bear sitting in ignorance longer; so setting up my ladder to the side of the hill there was a flat place, as I observed before, and then pulling the ladder up after me, I set it up again, and mounted to the top of the hill; and pulling out my perspective glass, which I had taken on purpose, I laid

住脚步，留在小树林里，不敢再往外走，惟恐受到野人的突然袭击。可是，我心里怎么也无法平静了。我怕那些野人万一在岛上走来走去，发现我的庄稼，看到有些已收割了，有些还没有收割，或者发现我其他的一些设施，他们马上会断定岛上有人。那时，他们不把我搜出来是决不会罢休的。在这危险关头，我立即跑回城堡，收起梯子，并把围墙外的一切东西尽量弄成荒芜自然的样子。

然后，我在城堡内做好防御野人袭击的准备。我把所有的手枪和架在防御工事上的炮全都装好弹药。做好了这些准备，我决心抵抗到最后一口气。同时，我也没有忘记把自己托付给神的保护，挚诚地祈求上帝把我从野蛮人的手里拯救出来。在这种心情和状态下，我大约等了两小时，就又急不可耐地想知道外面的情况，因为我没有探子派出去为我打听消息。

我又在家里坐了一会儿，琢磨着该怎样应付当前的情况。最后，我实在坐不住了，因为我迫切需要知道外面的情况。于是，我便把梯子搭在山岩旁边。前面我曾提到过，山岩边有一片平坎，我登上那片平坎，再把梯子抽上来放在平坎上，

me down flat on belly on the ground, and began to look for the place. I presently found there was no less than nine naked savages sitting round a small fire they had made; not to warm them, for they had no need of that, the weather being extreme hot, but, as I supposed, to dress some of their barbarous diet of human flesh, which they had brought with them, whether alive or dead I could not know.

They had two canoes with them, which they had hauled up upon the shore; and it was then tide of ebb, they seemed to me to wait for the return of flood to go away again. It is not easy to imagine what confusion this sight put me into, especially seeing them come on my side the island, and so near me too; but when I observed their coming must be always with the current of the ebb, I began afterwards to be sedate in my mind, being satisfied that I might go abroad with safety all the time of tide of flood, if they were not on shore before; and having made this observation, I went abroad about my harvest work with more composure.

As I expected, so it proved, for as soon as the tide made to the westward, I saw them all take boat, and row all away. I should have observed that for an hour and more before they went off, they went dancing, and I could easily discern their postures and gestures by my

然后登上山顶。我平卧在山顶上，取出我特意带在身边的望远镜，向那一带地方望去。我立即发现，那儿大约有十来个赤身裸体的野人，围着他们燃起的一小堆火坐在地上。他们生火显然不是为了取暖，因为毫无必要——天气很热，根本用不着取暖。我想，他们一定是带来了战俘在烧烤人肉，至于那些战俘带上岛时是活是死，我就不得而知了。

他们有两只独木舟，已经被拉到岸上。那时正好退潮，他们大概要等潮水回来后再走。看到这一情景，不难想象我内心慌乱极了。尤其是发现他们到了小岛的这一边，离我住所那么近，很难想象我是多么惊慌失措啊！但我后来注意到，他们一定得趁着潮水才能够上岛。这一发现使我稍稍安心了一点。因为只要他们不在岸上，我在涨潮期间外出是绝对安全的，这一点还是较令我满意的。知道了这一点，我以后就可以外出安心收获我的庄稼了。

事情果然不出所料。当潮水开始回流时，他们就上船划桨离去了。我还发现，在离开前，他们还跳了一个多小时的舞。从我的望远镜里，可

glasses: I could not perceive, by my nicest observation, but that they were stark naked, and had not the least covering upon them; but whether they were men or woman, that I could not distinguish.

As soon as I saw them shipped and gone, I took two guns upon my shoulders, and two pistols at my girdle, and my great sword by my side, without a scabbard; and with all the speed I was able to make, I went away to the hill, where I had discovered the first appearance of all. And as soon as I got thither, which was not less than two hours, I perceived there had been three canoes more of savages on that place; and looking out farther, I saw they were all at sea together, making over for the main.

This was a dreadful sight to me, especially when going down to the shore, I could see the marks of horror which the dismal work they had been about had left behind it, namely, the blood, the bones, and part of the flesh of human bodies, eaten and devoured by those wretches with merriment and sport. I was so filled with indignation at the sight, that I began now to premeditate the destruction of the next that I saw there.

It seemed evident to me that the visits which they thus made to this island were not very frequent; for it was above fifteen months before any more of them came on shore there again, that is to say, I never saw them,

以清清楚楚地看到他们手舞足蹈的样子。我还可以看到他们都赤身裸体，一丝不挂，可是究竟是男是女，怎么仔细看也分辨不出来。

一见他们上船离开了，我就拿了两支枪背在肩上，两支手枪挂在腰带上，又取了一把没鞘的大刀悬在腰间，尽快向靠海的那座小山上跑去。正是在那地方，我第一次发现了那群野人，我足足用了一个多钟头才到达那里。我一上小山就看到，除了我刚才看到的两只独木舟外，还有另外三只停泊在那儿。再往远处看去，只见他们在海面上会合后往大陆方向驶去了。

对我来说，这真是一个可怕的景象。尤其是我走到岸边，看到他们所干的惨绝人寰的残杀所遗留下来的痕迹，更令人可怕！那血迹，那人骨，那一块块人肉！可以想象，那些残忍的家伙一边吞食，一边寻欢作乐。看见这些情况，我义愤填膺。这不禁使我预先考虑：下次再碰到他们过来干此罪恶勾当，非把他们斩尽杀绝不可，不管他们是什么部落，也不管他们来多少人。

但我发现，他们显然并不经常到岛上来。我第二次碰到他们在那里登岸，是一年零三个月之后的事。这就是说，一年多时间中，我从未再见

or any footsteps or signals of them in all that time; and I found they did not come in the rainy season; yet all this while I lived uncomfortably, by reason of the constant apprehensions I was in of their coming upon me by surprise.

In the middle of May, it blew a very great storm of wind all day, with a great deal of lightning and thunder, and a very foul night it was. I know not what the particular occasion of it, but as I was reading the Bible, and taken up with serious thoughts about my present condition, I was surprised with the noise of a gun, as I thought, fired at sea.

This was, to be sure, a surprise of quite a different nature from any I had met with before, for the notions that this put into my thoughts were quite of another kind. I started up in the greatest haste imaginable, and, in a trice, clapped up my ladder in the middle place on the rock, and pulled it after me, and mounting it the second time, got to the top of the hill; that moment a flash of fire bade me listen for a second gun, which, accordingly, in about half a minute I heard, and by the sound, knew that it was from that part of the sea where I was driven out with the current in my boat.

I immediately considered that this must be some ship in distress, and that they had some other ship in

到过他们，也没有见过他们的脚印或其他任何上岛的痕迹。看来，在雨季，他们肯定是不会出门的，至少不会跑到这么远的地方来。然而，在这一年多中，我却时刻担心遭到他们的袭击，所以日子过得很不舒畅。

五月十六日这一天刮起了暴风雨，整天雷声隆隆，电光闪闪，直至晚上，依然风雨交加，整夜不停。我也说不清事情究竟是什么时候发生的，正是在那儿我第一次发现野人的踪迹。我费了两只记得当时我正在读《圣经》，并认真地考虑着自己当前的处境。忽然，我听到一声枪响，好像是从海上发出的。这真大大出乎我的意料。

这个意外事件与我以前碰到的任何事件完全不一样，因而在我头脑里所产生的反应也完全不一样。听到枪声后，我一跃而起，转眼之间就把梯子竖在半山上，登上半山的平坎后，又把梯子提起来架在平坎上，最后爬上了山顶。就在这一刹那，我看见火光一闪，知道第二枪又要响了。果然不出所料，半分钟之后，又听到了枪声。从那声音判断，知道枪声正是从我上回坐船被急流冲走的那一带海上传来的。

我立即想到，这一定是有船只遇难了，而且，他们一定有其他船只结伴航行，因此放枪发出遇

company, and fired these guns for signals of distress, and to obtain help. I had this presence at that minute, as to think, that though I could not help them, it may be they might help me; so I brought together all the dry wood I could get at hand, and making a good sized pile, I set it on fire upon the hill; the wood was dry, and blazed freely, and though the wind blew very hard, yet it burnt fairly out, so that I was certain, if there was any such thing as a ship, they must see it, and no doubt they did, for as soon as my fire blazed up, I heard another gun, and after that several others, all from the same quarter. I plied my fire all night long, till day broke, and when it was broad day, and the air cleared up, I saw something at a great distance at sea, full east of the island, whether a sail, or a hull, I could not distinguish, no, not with my glasses, the distance was so great, and the weather still being hazy also: at least it was so out at sea.

I looked frequently at it all that day, and soon perceived that it did not move; so I presently concluded that it was a ship at anchor, and being eager, you may be sure, to be satisfied, I took my gun in my hand and ran towards the southeast side of the island, to the rocks, where I had been formerly carried away with the current, and getting up there, the weather by this time being per-

难的信号，请求救援。我这时非常镇定，我想，即使我无法救助他们，他们倒可能帮助我。于是，我把附近能找得到的干柴通通收集起来，在山上堆成一大堆点起了火。木柴很干，火一下子就烧得很旺。虽然风很大，火势依然不减。这样，我确信，只要海上有任何船只，他们一定看得见。事实是，他们确实也看到了。因为我把火一烧起来，马上又听见一声枪声，接着又是好几声枪响，都是从同一个方面传来的。我把火烧了一整夜，一直烧到天亮。天大亮后，海上开始晴朗起来。这时，我看到，在远处海面上，在小岛正东方向，仿佛有什么东西，不知是帆，还是船。我怎么看也看不清楚。用望远镜也没有用，因为距离实在太远了，而且，天气还是灰蒙蒙的。至少海面上雾气还很浓。

整整一天，我一直在眺望着海面上那东西，不久便发现它一直停在原处，一动也不动。于是我断定，那一定是一条下了锚的大船。可以想象，我多么急于把事情搞个水落石出，所以，我就拿起枪向岛的南边跑去，跑到我上次被急流冲走的那些岩石前面。当到了那里的时候，天气已完全

fectly clear, I could plainly see, to my great sorrow, the wreck of a ship cast away in the night upon these concealed rocks, which I found when I was out in my boat, and which rocks, as they checked the violence of the stream, and made a kind of counter stream, or eddy, were the occasion of my recovering then from the most desperate, hopeless condition, that ever I had been in.

Thus, what is one man's safety is another man's destruction; for it seems these men, whoever they were, being out of their knowledge, and the rocks being wholly under water, had been driven upon them in the night; the wind blowing very hard at E. and E. N. E. Had they seen the island, as I must necessarily suppose they did not, they must, as I thought, have endeavored to have themselves on shore by the help of their boat; but the firing of their guns for help, especially when they saw, as I imagined, my fire, filled me with thoughts.

It was now calm, and I had a great mind to venture out in my boat to this wreck, not doubting but I might find something on board that might be useful to me; and possibly there might be yet some living creature on board, whose life I might not only save, but might comfort my own to the last degree; and this thought clung so to my heart, that I could not be quiet night or day, but I must venture out in my boat on board this wreck; and

晴朗了。我一眼就看到，有一只大船昨天夜里撞在暗礁上失事了。这真是叫我痛心。因为事实上，我上次驾舟出游时，就发现了那些暗礁。正是这些暗礁。挡住了急流的冲力，形成了一股逆流或是漩涡，使我那次得以死里逃生。这是我生平从最绝望的环境里逃出性命的经历。

由此可见，同样的险境，对这个人来说是福音，对另一个来说则可能意味着毁灭。我想，这些人无论他们是谁，由于不熟悉地形，那些暗礁又都隐藏在水底下，再加上昨天晚上的东北风很大，所以船触上了暗礁。如果他们发现这个小岛，我想他们一定会用船上的救生艇竭尽全力划到岸上来的。但看来他们一定没有看到小岛，只是鸣枪求救，尤其是他们看到我燃起的火光后，更是多次放枪。由此我头脑里出现了种种设想。

这时，海面上已风平浪静，我很想冒险坐小船上那失事的船上看看。我相信一定能找到一些对我有用的东西。此外，我还抱着一个更为强烈的愿望，促使我非上那艘破船不可。那就是希望船上还会有活人。这样，我不仅可以救他的命，更重要的是，如果我能救他活命，对我将是一种莫大的安慰。这个念头时刻盘踞在我心头，使我日夜不得安宁，只想乘小船上去看看。我想，这

committing the rest to God's providence, I thought the impression was so strong upon my mind, that it could not be resisted, that it must come from some invisible direction, and that I should be wanting to myself if I did not go.

Under the power of this impression, I hastened back to my castle, prepared everything for my voyage, took a quantity of bread, a basket full of raisins, and thus loading myself with everything necessary, I went down to my boat, got the water out of her, and got her afloat, loaded all my cargo in her, and then went home again for more. My second cargo was a great bag full of rice, the umbrella to set up over my head for a shade, another pot full of fresh water, and about two dozens of my small leaves, or barley cakes, more than before, and a bottle of goat's milk, and a cheese; all which, with great labor and sweat, I brought to my boat, and praying to God to direct my voyage, I put out; and padding the canoe along the shore, I came at last to the utmost point of the island on that side. And now I was to launch out into the ocean, and either to venture, or not venture. I looked on the rapid currents which ran constantly on both sides of the island at a distance, and which were very terrible to me, from the remembrance of the hazard I had been in before, and my heart began to fail me; for I

种愿望如此强烈，自己已到了无法抵御的地步，那一定是有什么隐秘的神力在驱使我要去。这种时候，我如果不去，那就是对不起自己。

在这种愿望的驱使下，我匆匆跑回城堡做出航的准备。我拿了不少面包和一满筐葡萄干。这样，我把一切必需品都背在身上，就走到我藏小船的地方。我先把船里的水舀干，让船浮起来。然后把所有的东西都放进船里。接着，我又跑回家去取些其他东西。这一次我拿了一大口袋米，还有那把挡太阳的伞，又取了一大罐淡水，二十多只小面包——实际上是一些大麦饼，这次拿得比上次还多。另外又拿了一瓶羊奶，一块干酪。我费了不少力气，流了不少汗，才把这些东西通通运到小船上。然后，我祈祷上帝保佑我一路平安，就驾船出发了。我沿海岸先把小舟划到小岛的东北方向最后到了正对着目的地的岛边。现在，我得把独木舟驶入大洋中去了；要么冒险前进，要么知难而退。当我遥望着远处海岛两边日夜奔腾的两股可怕的急流，回想起上次遭到的危险，不由得有点害怕了。因为我可以想见，只要被卷

foresaw, that if I was driven into either of these currents, I should be carried a vast way out to sea, and perhaps out of reach or sight, of the island again; and that, as my boat was but small, if any little gale of wind should rise, I should be inevitably lost.

These thoughts so oppressed my mind, that I began to give over my enterprise, and having hauled my boat into a little creek on the shore, I stepped out, and sat me down upon a little spot of rising ground, very pensive and anxious, between fear and desire, about my voyage; when, as I was musing, I could perceive that the tide was turned, and the flood came on, upon which my going was for so many hours impracticable. Upon this it presently occurred to me, that I should go up to the highest piece of ground I could find, and observe, if I could see how the sets of the tides or currents lay when the flood came in, that I might judge whether, if I was driven one way out, I might not expect to be driven another way home, with the same rapidness of the currents. This thought was no sooner in my head, but I cast my eye upon a little hill, which sufficiently overlooked the sea both ways, and from whence I had a clear view of the currents, and which way I was to guide myself in my return. Here I found that as the current of the ebb set out close by the south point of the island, as the current of

入这两股急流中的任何一股，小舟一定会被冲进外海，到那时，我就再也看不到小岛，再也回不到小岛了。我的船仅仅是一只小小的独木舟，只要大海上稍刮起一阵风，就难免覆没了。

　　我思想压力很大，不得不开始考虑放弃原定的计划。我把小船拖进沿岸的一条小河里，自己迈步上岸，在一块小小的高地上坐下来沉思，心里一直不能平静，对这次出航我是既害怕，又想前去探个究竟。正当我沉思默想之际，只见潮流起了变化，潮水开始上涨。这样，我一时肯定走不成了。这时，我忽然想到，应该找一个最高的地方，上去观察一下潮水上涨时那两股急流的流向，从中我可以作出判断：万一我被一股急流冲入大海，是否有可能被另一股急流冲回来。正想着，我注意到附近有一座小山，从山上可以看到左右两边的海面，并对两股急流的流向可以一目了然，从而可以确定我回来时应走哪一个方向。到了山上，我发现那退潮的急流是沿着小岛的南

the flood set in close by the shore of the north side; and that I had nothing to do but to keep to the north of the island in my return, and I should do well enough.

Encouraged with this observation, I resolved the next morning to set out with the first of the tide; and reposing myself for that night in the canoe, under great watch – coat I mentioned, I launched out in the morning. Having a strong steerage with my paddle, I went directly for the wreck, and in less than two hours I came up to it.

It was a dismal sight to look at: the ship, which by the building was Spanish, stuck fast jammed in between two rocks; all the stern and quarter of her was beaten to pieces with the sea; and as her forecastle, which stuck in the rocks, had run on with great violence, her main-mast and foremast were brought by the board, broken short off; but her bowsprit was sound, and the head and bow appeared firm. When I came close to her, a dog appeared upon her, who, seeing me coming, yelped and cried; and as soon as I called him, jumped into the sea to come to me; and I took him into the boat, and found him almost dead for hunger and thirst. I gave him a cake of my bread, and he ate it like a ravenous wolf that had been starving for a fortnight in the snow. I then gave the poor creature some fresh water, with which, if I would

部往外流的，而那涨潮的急流是沿着小岛的北部往里流的。这样，我回来时，小舟只要沿着北部行驶，自然就可以被涨潮的急流带回来。

经过观察，我大受鼓舞，决定第二天早晨乘第一次潮汐出发，我把水手值夜的大衣盖在身上，在独木舟里过了一夜。第二天一早，我就驾舟出发了。我以桨代舵，使劲掌握航向，朝那失事的大船飞驶过去。不到两小时，我就到了破船跟前。

眼前的景象一片凄凉。从那条船的构造外形来看，是一条西班牙船，船身被紧紧地夹在两块礁石之间。船艉和后舱都被海浪击得粉碎，那搁在礁石中间的前舱，由于猛烈撞击，上面的前桅和主桅都折断倒在了甲板上，但船艏的斜桁仍完好无损，船头也还坚固。我靠近破船时，船上出现了一条狗。它一见到我驶近，就汪汪吠叫起来。我向它一呼唤，它就跳到海里，游到我的小船边来，我把它拖到船上，只见它又饥又渴，快要死了。我给了它一块面包，它就大吃大嚼起来，活像一只在雪地里饿了十天半月的狼。我又给它喝淡水，它喝得很猛，要是我不制止它的话，真的

have let him, he would have burst himself.

After this I went on board. The first sight I met with was two men drowned in the cook – room of the ship, with their arms fast about one another. I concluded, as is indeed probable, that when the ship stuck, it being in a storm, the sea broke so high, and so continually over her, that the men were not able to bear it, and were strangled with the constant rushing in of the water, as much as if they had been under water. Besides the dog, there was nothing left in the ship that had life, or any goods that I could see, but what were spoiled by the water. There were some casks of liquor, whether wine or brandy I knew not, which lay lower in the hold, and which, the water being ebbed out, I could see, but they were too big to meddle with. I saw several chests, which I believe belonged to some of the seamen, and I got two of them into the boat, without examining what was in them.

I found, besides these chests a little cask of liquor, of about twenty gallons, I got into my boat with much difficulty. There were several muskets in the cabin, and a great powder – horn, with about four pounds of powder in it: as for the muskets, I had no occasion for them, so I left them, but took the powder – horn. I took a fire – shovel and tongs, which I wanted extremely; as also two

可以喝得把肚子都胀破。

接着，我就上了大船。我第一眼看到的是两个淹死的人，他们紧紧地抱在一起，躺在前舱的厨房里。看来，极可能是船触礁时，海面上狂风暴雨，巨大的海浪接连不断地打在船上，以致于船上的人就像被埋在水里一样，实在受不了，最后随着不断涌入的海水窒息而死。除了那条狗，船上没有任何其他生还的生物。船上所有的货物，也都让海水给浸坏了，只有舱底下几桶酒因海水已退而露在外面。也不知道是葡萄酒还是白兰地。但是那些酒桶很大，我没法搬动它们。另外，我还看见几只大箱子，可能是水手的私人财物。于是，我搬了两只到我的小船上，也没有来得及检查一下里面究竟装的是什么东西。

除了那两只箱子，我还找到了一小桶酒，约有二十加仑。我费了九牛二虎之力，才把酒桶搬到小船上。船舱里还有几支短枪和一只盛火药的大角筒，里面大约有四磅火药。短枪对我来说已毫无用处。因此我就留下了，只取了盛火药的角筒。另外我又拿了一只火炉和一把火钳，这两样正是我十分需要的东西。我还拿了两把小铜壶，

little brass kettles, a copper pot to make chocolate, and a gridiron; and with this cargo and the dog I came away, the tide beginning to make home again; and the same evening, about an hour within night, I reached the island again, wearied and fatigued to the last degree.

The other chest I found had some clothes in it, but of little value; but by the circumstances it must have belonged to the gunner's mate, though there was no powder in it, but about two pounds of glazed powder in three small flasks, kept, I suppose, for charging their fowling – pieces on occasion. Upon the whole, I got very little by this voyage that was of much use to me, for, as to the money, I had no manner of occasion for it, it was to me as the dirt under my feet, and would have given it all for three or four pairs of English shoes and stockings, which were things I greatly wanted, for I had not had a pair on my feet for many years. I had, indeed, gotten two pairs of shoes now, which I took off the feet of the two men whom I found drowned in the wreck; and I found two pairs more in one of the chests, which were very welcome to me; but they were not like our English shoes, either for ease or service, being rather what we call pumps than shoes. I found in this seaman's chest about fifty pieces of eight in royals, but no gold; I suppose this belonged to a poorer man than the other, which seemed

一只煮巧克力的铜锅和一把铁的烤肉架。我把这些东西装进我的小船，再带上那只狗，就准备回家了。时值退潮，天黑后不到一小时，我就回到了岸上，人已劳累得疲倦不堪了。

在一只大箱子里找到一些衣服，但对我来说都没有多大用处。看样子，这只箱子是属于船上的副炮手的。箱子里没有很多火药，只有两磅压成细粒的火药，装在三只小瓶里。我想大概是装鸟枪用的。总的来说，我这趟出海弄到的东西有用的不太多。至于钱币，对我当然毫无用处，真是不如粪土！我宁愿用全部金币银币来换三四双英国袜子和鞋子，因为这些都是我迫切需要的东西，我已经好几年没有鞋袜穿了。不过，我还是弄到了两双鞋子，那是我从遇难船上两个淹死的水手的脚上脱下来的。另外，在这只大箱子里还找到两双鞋，这当然也是求之不得的。但这两双鞋子都没有英国鞋子舒适耐穿，因为不是一般走路穿的鞋子，只是一种便鞋而已。在这只船员的箱子里，我另外又找到了五十多枚西班牙银币，但没有金币，我想这只箱子的主人一定比较贫寒，

to belong to some officer.

Having now brought all my things on shore, and secured them, I went back to my boat, and rowed her along the shore to her old harbor, where I laid her up, and made the best of my way to my old habitation, where I found everything safe and quiet; so I began to repose myself, live after my old fashion, and take care of my affairs, and for a while I lived easy enough, only that I was more vigilant than I used to be, looked out oftener, and did not go abroad so much: and if any time I did stir with any freedom, it was always to the east part of the island, where I was pretty well satisfied the savages never came, and where I could go without so many precautions, and such a load of arms and ammunition as I carried with me if I went the other way.

One night in the rainy season, in March, I had the following dream: I was going out in the morning, as usual, from my castle, I saw upon the shore two canoes, and eleven savages coming to land, and that they brought with them another savage, whom they were going to kill, in order to eat him, when on a sudden the savage that they were going to kill, made his escape, and ran for his life; and then I thought in my sleep, that he came running into my little grove, before my fortification, to hide himself; and that I, seeing him, and not perceiving that

而另一只箱子的主人一定是位高级船员。

我把所有的东西运到岸上安置妥当后，就回到小船上。我沿着海岸，划到原来停泊的港口，把船缆系好。然后，我拖着疲惫的身子回到了我的老住所。到了那里，只见一切平安无事。于是我开始休息，并又像过去一样照常度日，料理家务。有这么一段短短的时期，我日子过得非常悠闲自在，只是比以前更谨慎罢了。我时时注意外面的动静，也很少外出。即使有时大胆到外面活动，也只是到小岛的东部走走，因为我确信野人从未到过那儿，因此用不着处处提防，也用不着带上许多武器弹药。要是到其他地方去，只带少许武器弹药就不行了。

在三月份雨季的一天晚上，我做了一个梦，梦见自己像往常一样，一大早走出城堡，走到岸边，看到有十一个野人划着两只小船向海岸靠近，他们还带着另一个野人，他们准备把他杀了吃掉。突然，他们要杀害的那个野人一下子跳起来，开始拼命奔逃。睡梦中，我恍惚见他很快就跑到我城堡外的小树林里在那里躲起来。当我发现只有

the others sought him that way, showed myself to him, and encouraged him, that he kneeled down to me, seeming to pray me to assist him; upon which I showed him my ladder, made him go up, and carried him into my cave, and he became my servant; and that as soon as I had got this man, I said to myself, "Now I may venture to the main – land, for this fellow will serve me as a pilot, and tell me what to do, and where to go for provisions, and where not to go for fear of being devoured; places to venture into, what to escape." I awoke with this thought, and was under such inexpressible impressions of joy at the prospect of my escape in my dream, that the disappointment I felt upon coming to myself, and finding it was no more than a dream, was really extravagant the other way, and threw me into a very great dejection of spirits.

Upon this, however, I made this conclusion, that my only way to go about an attempt for an escape, was to try to get a savage in my possession; and, if possible, it should be one of their prisoners, whom, they had condemned to be eaten.

Chapter 16   My Man Friday

With these resolutions in my thoughts, I set myself

他一个人，其他野人并没有过来追他，我便走出城堡，叫他不要怕。他急忙跪在地下，仿佛求我救救他。于是，我向他指指我的梯子，叫他爬上去，并把他带到我住所的洞穴里。从此，他就成了我的仆人。我一得到这个人，心里就想，现在，我真的可以冒险去大陆了。这个野人可以做我的向导，告诉我该如何行动，什么地方可以弄到食物，什么地方不能去，以免被野人吃掉；他还会告诉我什么地方可以去，什么地方不可以去。正这样想着，我就醒来了。一想到自己大有获救的希望，高兴得无法形容；当然这只是黄粱美梦一场，及至清晨到来，发现原来不过是一场梦境，不禁又极度失望，懊丧不已。

但是，这个梦境却给了我一个启示：我若想摆脱孤岛生活，惟一的办法就是尽可能弄到一个野人；而且，如果可能的话，最好是一个被其他野人带来准备杀了吃掉的俘虏。

第十六章　忠实朋友

怀着这样的决心，我开始在岛上巡逻，以便

upon the scout, as often as possible, till I was heartily tired of it. I was not at first more careful to shun the sight of these savages, and avoid being seen by them, I was now eager to be upon them.

Besides, I fancied myself able to manage one, nay, two or three savages, if I had them, so as to make entirely slaves to me, to do what I should direct them, and to prevent their being able at any time to do me any hurt. It was a great while that I pleased myself with this affair; but nothing still presented, all my fancies and schemes came to nothing, for no savages came near me for a great while.

About a year and a half later, I was surprised one morning early with seeing no less than five canoes all on shore together, on my side of the island, and the people who belonged to them all landed. The number of them broke all my measures, for seeing so many, and knowing that they always came four, or sometimes more in a boat, I could not tell what to think of it, or how to take my measures to attack twenty or thirty men, single – handed, so still in my castle, perplexed and discomforted. However, I put myself into all the postures for an attack that I had formerly provided, and was just ready for action, if anything had presented. Having waited a good while, listening to hear if they made any noise, at

找个野人，我不厌其烦地一天天地巡逻着。我不是像当初那样，小心翼翼地想躲开那些野人的视线，不让他们看见，而是希望能靠近他们。

除此之外，我想象着如果能捉住这些人，我会控制一个，不，两个或三个，使他们完全成为我的奴隶，服从我的命令，防止他们任何时候对我造成伤害的可能。很长一段时间我都为此兴奋不已，然而，所有幻想和阴谋都化为泡影，好长一段时间没有什么野蛮人出没。

大约一年半以后的一天，我们一大早起来，我吃惊地发现在岛上我所居住的这块地方有不下五只小船一并停泊在岸上，乘船而来的人们也都登陆了。他们的人数乱了我的方寸，本想着他们总是乘一只船来四个人，有时更多，结果看见那么多人，我一时半会儿脑子里一片空白，简直不知道赤手空拳怎样才能打败这二三十个人，我悄悄地呆在城堡里，静静地等待着，不知所措，沮丧不已。不过我还是进入了准备攻击的整个状态之中，因为在这之前我就有所防备，一有风吹草动，我就会立即采取行动来对付这帮家伙。听着动静，等了好一会儿，看他们是否有什么行动，

length, being very impatient, I set my guns at the foot of my ladder, and clambered up to the top of the hill by my two stages, as usual, standing so, however, that my head did not appear above the hill; so that they could not perceive me by any means. I here observed, by the help of my perspective glass, that they were no less than thirty in number, that they had a fire kindled, and that they had meat dressed; how they cooked it, that I knew not, or what it was; but they were all dancing, in I know not how many barbarous gestures and figures, round the fire.

While I was thus looking on them, I perceived, by my perspective glass, two miserable wretches dragged from the boats, where, it seems, they were laid by, and were now brought out for the slaughter. I perceived one of them immediately fall, being knocked down, I suppose, with a club, or wooden sword, for that was their way; and two or three others were at work, cutting him open for their cookery, while the other victim was left standing by himself till they should be ready for him. In that very moment, the poor wretch, seeing himself a little at liberty, nature inspired him with hopes of life, and he started away from them, and ran with incredible swiftness along the sands, directly towards me, I mean towards that part of the coast where my habitation was.

最后我不耐烦了，把枪放在梯子底部，像往常一样沿着两个台阶爬上山顶，站在那儿，头不敢露出山顶，这样他们怎么也发觉不了我。借着望远镜我窥探到他们不少于三十人，燃着篝火在烧烤着肉食，但不知道是什么肉，也不知道他们怎么个做法，只看见他们围着篝火跳着舞，在火的影映下，显示了他们狂野的姿势和体态。

这时我透过望远镜发现两个悲惨的可怜虫被从小船上拖了下来，他们开始在那儿搁着，现在被揪出来面临杀戮。我发现，其中一个即刻被砸倒在地，大概是用棍棒或木刀，那是他们惯用的方式，另外两三个正忙着把他劈开用以烹食，看着这血腥的场面着实让我吓了一跳，而那另一个牺牲品独自站在那儿等着挨人家的刀子。就在那一瞬间，那可怜的人静静地看到自己或许多少有点自由的机会，出于求助的本能，从他们身边溜走了，他撒开腿飞一般地跑过沙滩，直接朝我，朝我住的这块海滨疯狂奔来。

I was dreadfully frightened when I perceived him to run my way, and especially when, as I thought, I saw him pursued by the whole body; and I expected that part of my dream was coming to pass, and that he would take shelter in my grove; but I could not depend, by any means, upon my dream for the rest of it, namely, that the savages would not pursue him there, and find there. However, I kept my station and my spirits began to recover when I found that there were not above three men that followed him; and still more was I encouraged, when I found that he outstripped them exceedingly in running, and gained ground of them, so that if he could but hold out for half an hour, I saw he would fairly get away from them all.

There was between them and my castle, the creek, this I knew he must necessarily swim over, or the poor wretch would be taken there; but when the savage who was escaping came there, he made nothing of it, though the tide was then up, but plunging in, he swam through it in about thirty strokes, or thereabouts, landed and ran on with exceeding strength and swiftness. When the three pursuers came to the creek, I found that two of them could swim, but the third could not, and that he, standing on the other side, looked at the others, but went no farther, and soon after went softly back again.

看见他朝我这边跑来，当时我害怕极了，特别是一想到后面还有很多人在追捕他；我预料到他将在我的小树林里栖身以躲避野人的追捕，我的美梦马上就要实现了；但无论如何美梦不等同于现实，毕竟很难说那些野蛮的家伙会不会再追他到林子里，再次将他捕获。然而当我发现顶多有三个人在追捕他时，之前惴惴不安的情绪又恢复过来；看到那个人跑得快了很多，把追赶的人拉下长长一段距离，我更加兴奋了，只要他这样坚持半小时，我想他就一定会摆脱他们所有人。

一条小溪淌过我的城堡前方，这是他们的必经之道，那不幸儿必须游过来才可能逃生，否则他就必定会落难，只见他临近小溪，不以为意，立马跳了进去，尽管此时正值涨潮之际，约摸划了三十来下他就游上岸来，鼓起气力以迅捷无比的速度跑向前方。三个追赶的人跑到小溪边，其中只有两个会游泳，那另外一个注视着同伴们，在潺潺水流前停住了脚步，片刻后窘迫地离开了。

I observed that the two who swam were yet twice as long swimming over the creek as the fellow was that fled from them. It came now very warmly upon thoughts, and indeed, irresistibly, that now was my time to get me a servant, and perhaps, a companion or assistant, and that I was called plainly by Providence to save this poor creature's life. I immediately got down the ladders, fetched my two guns, for they were both at the foot of the ladders, getting up again with the same haste to the top of the hill. I crossed towards the sea; and, having a very short cut, and all down hill, clapped myself in the way between the pursuers and the pursued, hallooing aloud to him that fled, who, looking back, was at first as much frightened at me as at them; meantime, I slowly advanced towards the two that followed; then rushing at once upon the foremost, I knocked him down with the stock of my piece; I was loath to fire, because I would not have the rest to hear, thought at that distance it would not have been easily heard, and being out of sight of the smoke, too, they would not have known what to make of it.

Having knocked this fellow down, the other who followed him, stopped, as if he had been frightened, and I advanced a pace towards him; but as I came near-er, I perceived presently he had a bow and arrow, and

我发现这两个淌溪而过的追捕者比他们的猎物游得慢了许多，至少慢了一半的时间。此时我突然想起一件事，而这个想法是如何也挥之不去的。我一定要为自己争得一个仆人，或者是同伴，或者是助手，神意召唤着我应该去挽救这个可怜的生灵。我即刻爬下扶梯，抓起梯脚的两支枪，同样仓促地再次攀上山顶。我沿着下山的路，抄捷径冲往海的方向，挡在他们追捕与被追捕人的之间，冲着逃跑的人高喊，他转过身来看了看我，那极其恐惧的神色绝不亚于看着那些追他的人，这时我不慌不忙地踱向两位追赶者，然后倏地冲向前面那位野人，一枪柄把他打倒在地，我不想开枪，因为我不愿意其他人听见，虽然知道在如此近的距离开枪，也没有人会听到枪声，也没有人会看到浓烟，也一定不会有人明白所发生的事情。

砸倒这个家伙之后，跟在他身后的同伴停了下来，一副被吓着的样子，我迅速上前，突然发现他手持弓箭，弯弓急于向我射击，我情急之下

was fitting it to shoot at me, so I was then necessitated to shoot at him first, and killed him at the first shot. The poor savage who fled, but had stopped, though he saw both his enemies fallen, and killed, yet was so frightened with the noise and fire of my piece, that he stood stock – still, and neither came forward nor went backward, he seemed rather inclined to fly still, than to come on. I hallooed again to him, and made signs to him to come forward, which he easily understood, and came a little way, then stopped again, and then a little farther, and stopped again; then he stood trembling, as if he had been taken prisoner, and had just been to be killed, as his two enemies were.

I beckoned to him again to come to me, and gave him all the signs of encouragement that I could think of; and he came nearer and nearer, kneeling down every ten or twelve steps, in token of acknowledgement for saving his life. I smiled at him, and looked pleasantly, and beckoned to him to come still nearer. At length he came close to me, and then he kneeled down again, kissed the ground, and, taking my foot, set it upon his head; this, it seems, was in token of swearing to be my slave forever. I took him up, and made much of him, and encouraged him all I could. But I perceived the savage whom I knocked down was not killed, but stunned with the

马上抢先给了他一枪，结果了他的性命。听到枪响，逃命落难的那个人停了下来，尽管他的仇敌昏的昏、死的死、伤的伤，他还是耽于枪支的巨响和弹火的威力而惊恐不已，呆若木鸡，既不敢上前，也不敢后退，看样子他很可能还想要逃走，而不是乖乖地跟过来。我又冲他喊了喊，示意他过我这边来，他很容易就弄懂了我的意思，但却走走，停停，停停，走走，继而站在那儿发抖，就像被人劫持，面临同追捕者一样的生死劫难的命运。

我再次唤他过来，使出所有我能想出的各种姿势来鼓励他，他愈来愈近，每十步或是十二步跪倒一次，以示对我救他性命的不尽感激。我微笑着，显得兴高采烈，招呼他再走近一些。最后他终于来到我身边，又跪在地下，吻着地面，将我的一只脚举起压在他的头顶上，意思好像是说他将永远效忠我成为我的奴隶。我扶他起来，行为举止无不渗透着对他无比的重视和珍惜，尽我最大努力来安慰他。但是我发现刚刚倒在地上的粗蛮人还没有被打死，只是被打昏了而已，现在

blow, and began to come to himself. So I pointed to him, showing him the savage, that he was not dead; upon this he spoke some words to me, and though I could not understand them, yet I thought they were pleasant to hear, for they were the first sound of a man's voice that I had heard, for above 25 years. But there was no time for such reflections now. The savage who was knocked down recovered himself so as to sit upon the ground, and I perceived that my savage began to be afraid; but when I saw that, I presented my other piece at the man, as if I would shoot him; upon this my savage made a motion to me to lend him my sword, which hung naked in a belt by my side; so I did. He no sooner had it than he ran to his enemy, and, at one blow, cut off his head so cleverly. When he had done this, he came laughing to me in sign of triumph, and brought me the sword again, and laid it down, with the head of the savage he had killed, just before me.

I took him home for shelter. Here I gave him bread, and a bunch of raisins to eat and a draught of water. Having refreshed him, I made signs for him to go to sleep. As he was very tired from running and swimming, he laid down and fell asleep soon. He was a comely handsome fellow, perfectly well made, tall, and well – shaped, and, as I reckon, about twenty – six years of

正在渐渐清醒过来。因此我指指他，示意那人还活着，他于是说了几句话，虽然我没大听懂，但对我来说这些话令人内心十分愉快，因为这是二十五年来我第一次听到人的嗓音。但此刻不是动那心思的时候。被击倒在地的野人回过神来坐正，我看到我的奴隶害怕极了。看到这一幕，我举起另一支枪瞄准他，想要开枪打死他。我的粗蛮人示意我将光秃秃的挂在侧皮带一面的武器交给他，我照办了。他拿着刀，立即冲向仇敌，一刀下去那人已身首异处，做完这些，他冲着我笑了笑，一副得胜者的喜悦，然后把刀交还于我，同刚才死去的粗蛮人一同放在我前方的地面上。

我领他回家来，给了他几片面包、一串葡萄和一些水。吃这些东西，帮他恢复过来精力之后，我示意他赶快上床睡觉。疲于白天的长跑和游泳，他躺下来很快就睡着了。这时我才有机会仔细端详一下我的粗蛮人，他是个英俊标致的男人，长得很细致，高高的个儿，身材匀称，估计有二

age. He had a very good countenance, not a fierce and surly aspect, but seemed to have something very manly in his face, and yet he had all the sweetness and softness of an European in his countenance too, especially when he smiled. His hair was long and black, not curled like wool, his forehead very high and large, and a great vivacity and sparkling sharpness in his eyes. The color of his skin was not quite black, but very tawny, and yet not of an ugly, yellow, nauseous tawny, as the Brazilians, and Virginians, and other natives of America are, but of a bright kind of dun olive color that had in it something very agreeable, though not very easy to describe. His face was round and plump, his nose small, not flat like the Negroes, a very good mouth, thin lips, and his teeth fine, well set, and white as ivory. After he had slumbered about half an hour, he waked, and came out of the cave to me very thankful, and I let him know I was well pleased with him. In a little time I began to speak to him, and teach him to speak to me; and first, made him know his name should be Friday, which was the day I saved his life. I likewise taught him to say, "Master," and then let him know that was to be my name. I also taught him to say, "Yes," and "No," and to know the meaning of them. I gave him some milk in an earthen pot, and some bread, and let him see me

十六岁的样子。他眉清目秀，面容姣好，不是杀气腾腾的威慑，而是眉宇间流淌着的男子阳刚之美，还有欧洲人特有的甜蜜和温柔，尤其是在他笑的时候。他头发又黑又长，不是像羊毛一样拳起来的那种，额头非常宽阔，目光中神采奕奕。肤色褐黄而不显黑，并非巴西、弗吉尼亚等美国居民龌龊的令人作呕的黄，而是一种难以用语言形容却令人惬意的明亮的淡橄榄色。他的脸浑圆丰实，鼻头小巧，不像黑人的塌鼻儿，长着很不错的一张嘴，嘴唇薄薄的，牙齿也整齐美观，白如象牙。酣睡了大约半小时之后，他醒过来走出山洞，感激地告诉我他对我很知足。我也让他懂得我对他也非常满意，很快我就开始对他讲话，教他说话给我听。首先告诉他我为他取名"星期五"，那就是我救他的日子，因为那天是星期五。我还教他学说"主人"，并给他解释"yes"和"no"的含义，他跟着我学着说着，而且学得很快。我还教给他怎样从陶罐里往出倒牛奶，怎样

drink some before him, and sop my bread in it, which he quickly imitated, and made signs that it was very good for him.

I kept there with him all that night; but as soon as it was day, I took him away with me. As we went by the place where he had buried the two men, he pointed exactly to the spot, and showed me the marks he had made to find them again, making signs to me that we should dig them up and eat them; at this I appeared very angry, expressed my abhorrence of it, made as if I would vomit at the thought of it, and beckoned with my hand to him to come away, which he immediately did, with great submission. I then led him to the top of the hill, to see if his enemies were gone, and pulling out my glass, I looked, and saw plainly the place where they had been, but no appearance of them or their canoes; so they were quite gone.

I then took my man Friday with me, giving him the sword in his hand, with the bow and arrows, at his back, which I found he could use very dexterously, making him carry one gun for me, and I two for myself, and away we marched to the place where these creatures had been. When I came there, my very blood ran chill in my veins, and my heart sank within me at the horror of the spectacle. Indeed, it was a dreadful sight; the

取面包，当着他的面喝牛奶给他看，然后把面包蘸进去，他理解了我的意思迅速模仿，并做手势表示做这些他感觉不错。

我整夜与他呆在一起，天刚蒙蒙亮，我就带着他出去。当我们走过他埋葬那两具尸体的地方，他指了指，让我看他留下的记号示意很容易找到他们，并示意我应该将其挖出来吃掉。听到这些话，我很生气，表露了我想起来这些东西就恶心的痛恨之情，并且打手势唤他赶快离开，他马上顺从地随着我离开了。我带着他登上了山顶，看看他的敌人可曾离去，遂取出望远镜，我清清楚楚地看到他们呆过的地方，却不见他们的小舟和人影，因此，我断定，他们真的走了。

随后我带着我的仆人星期五，把刀递到他的手里，枪箭架在他的背上，这些器具他使用起来游刃自如，所以我让他替我挂一杆枪，我扛了两杆，我们一起挺进这些怪物所在的地方。到了那儿我的血几乎都快要凝滞了，因为看到这骇人惨状，令我悲莫能名，不知该说什么好，也不知该做什么好。这的确是幕非常可怕的情景，尸体横

place was covered with human bones, the ground dyed with the blood, great pieces of flesh left here and there, half eaten, mangled, and scorched, and in short, all the tokens of the triumphant feast they had been making there, after a victory over their enemies. I saw three skulls, five hands, and the bones of bodies; and Friday, by his signs, made me understand that they brought over four prisoners to feast upon, that three of them were eaten, and that he, pointing to himself, was the fourth; that there had been a great battle between them and their next king, whose subjects it seems he had been one of, and that they taken a great number of prisoners, all of which were carried to several places by those that had taken them in fight, in order to feast upon them, as was done here by these wretches.

I caused Friday to gather all the bones and flesh that remained, and lay them together in a heap, and burned them to ashes. I found that he had still a hankering stomach after the flesh, and was still a cannibal in his nature, but I displayed such abhorrence at the very thoughts of it, that he durst not discover it, for I let him know that I would kill him if he offered it.

The next day after I came home to my hut with him, I began to consider where I should lodge him; so I made a little tent for him in the vacant place between the

陈，地面被野人的鲜血渗得绯红，肉块随处可见，吃的吃，毁的毁，焦的焦，简直一幅战胜敌人后欢庆胜利的丰宴之像。我看到三具颅骨，五双手和一些尸骨。星期五示意我用我的那些家伙掳来四个囚犯喂肚子，其中三个已经被干掉了，第四个嘛，他指了指，就是他自己，他们曾为国王的子民，为了保卫国王赴疆场，流热血，他们曾打了很多胜仗，也曾把战败的俘虏带到各地用来作美餐，这正是那几个不幸的人们的下场。

我吩咐星期五将余下的残骨烂肉集中起来堆成一堆烧为灰烬。我发觉他对人肉依然充满贪婪的欲望，还是个彻头彻尾的食人者，不过我对他那非分之想表现出深恶痛绝，他于是也不敢有丝毫放肆，他要真敢那么做我会宰了他，这他能看出来。

和他一起回小屋的第二天我开始琢磨该怎么安顿他，在两个要塞间给他搭个小帐篷，里面是

two fortifications, in the inside of the last, and in the outside of the first. I barred it up in the night, taking in my ladders, too; so that Friday could in no way come at me in the inside of my innermost wall, without making so much noise in getting over.

But I needed none of these precautions, for never was a more faithful, loving, sincere servant than Friday was to me; without passions, sullenness or designs; his very affections were tied to me, like those of a child to its father, and, I dare say, he would have sacrificed his life for the saving of my own, upon any occasion whatever.

I was greatly delighted with him, and made it my business to teach him everything that was proper and useful, and especially to make him speak, and understand me when I spoke; and he was a very apt scholar, and he was so merry, so diligent, and so pleased when he could understand me, or make me understand him, that it was very pleasant for me to talk to him. And now my life began to be very easy and happy.

Two or three days later, I took him out with me one morning to the woods, and I saw a she – goat lying down in the shade, and two young kids close by her. I killed one of the kids. The poor creature who had, at a distance indeed, seen me kill the savage, his enemy, but

杉树，外围是最外端的防御物。夜间我把帐篷封严，门窗紧闭，移走梯子，这样星期五就没法来到我最里层墙壁之内，也就不会在翻爬时弄出那么多嘈杂声响。

但我不需要这样的预防措施，因为从未有过一个仆人像星期五对我那样忠实、亲密而诚挚，没有任何愠怒、郁闷和矫揉造作，他那感情紧紧地系着我，如同孩子对父亲的爱，我敢说在任何情况下他都会不惜一切甚至牺牲自己以保全我的性命。

我因为他的存在而欢乐无比，潜心教他所有得体并且有用的东西，特别是教他在我说话的时候能理解我并开口回应。他是个颇具潜力的学者，一懂得我的意思或者是我懂得了他要表达的东西就兴高采烈，更加一丝不苟的连我都乐此不疲地想不断跟他说下去。生活变得舒适愉快。

两三天之后我在清晨带着他去森林里，看到两只小山羊躺在树阴它们的母亲身旁，我杀死了其中的一只小山羊。可怜的东西隔着一段距离见过我杀死他野蛮的敌人，却不知也无法想象他们

did not know, nor could imagine how it was done, was sensibly surprised, trembled, and shook, and looked so amazed, that I thought he would have sunk down. He came and kneeled down to me, and embracing my knees, said a great many things I did not understand, but I could see that his meaning was to pray to me not to kill him.

I soon found a way to convince him that I would do him no harm; and, taking him up by the hand, laughed at him, and, pointing to the kid I had killed, beckoned to him to run and fetch it, which he did; and while he was looking to see how the creature was killed, I loaded my gun again, and by and by I saw a great fowl, like a hawk, sit upon a tree within shot; so, to let Friday understand a little what I would do, I called him to me again, pointing at the fowl, which was a parrot. I fired, and bade him look, and immediately he saw the parrot fall. He stood like one frightened again, notwithstanding all I had said to him; and I found he was the more amazed, because he did not see me put anything into the gun; but thought there must be some wonderful fund of death and destruction in that thing, able to kill man, beast, bird, or any other thing near or far off; and I believe, if I would have let him, he would have worshipped me and my gun; as for the gun itself, he would not so

是怎样被我杀死的，他大吃一惊，浑身发抖，蜷缩成一团简直吓呆了，我当时都担心他会瘫在地上。他过来向我跪下，抱着我的膝盖，说了一大堆我根本听不懂的话，意思似乎是恳求我不要杀死他。

　　很快我想出了一个办法确保他相信我不会伤害他，扶他起来，笑话他那样子，指着死去的小羊羔召唤他跑去拿过来，他很听话。当然他正想看看这只小羔羊是如何被杀死的，我已重新背起枪，忽然看见好大的一只禽鸟，鹰一般的个头，正伏坐在射程内的一棵树上，为了让星期五明白几分我要做的事情，我叫他回来，指着那只鹦鹉。我开火了，命令他快看，片刻间那只鹦鹉扑通落地。他又战战兢兢地呆立着，我白给他说了那么多，看来这些话对他一点也没有起作用。他的惊愕胜过之前，因为他没看到我往枪里放什么，想着这东西里一定有什么毁灭性的物质能够致人、兽、鸟和其他任何远近之物于死命。我确信，如果我给他枪他一定会崇拜我和枪的。至于那把枪，

much as touch it for several days after, but would speak to it, and talk to it, as if it had answered him, which as I afterwards learned of him, was to desire it not to kill him.

After we lived side by side together for quite some time, I tried to bring Friday off from his horrid way of feeding, and from the relish of a cannibal's stomach, I ought to let him taste other flesh and things. Having thus fed him with boiled meat and broth, I was resolved to feast him the next day with roasting a piece of the kid; this I did by hanging it before the fire in a string, as I had seen many people do in England. This Friday admired much; but when he came to taste the flesh, he took so many ways to tell me how well he liked it, and at last he told me he would never eat man's flesh any more.

The next day I set him to work to beat some corn out, and sift it in the manner I used to do; and he soon understood how to do it as well as I. I began now to consider having two mouths to feed instead of one, I must provide more ground for my harvest, and plant a larger quantity of corn than I used to do, so I marked out a larger piece of land, and began the fence in the same manner as before, in which Friday not only worked very hard, but very cheerfully; and I told him that it was for

他好多天之后连碰都不敢碰一下，只是对它说呀讲呀的，就像枪回应他了一样，后来我才了解到他是请求它不要杀死他。

在我们一起生活一段时间之后，我试图挽救星期五，使他摆脱他那可怕的吃饭方式和可怕的食人的胃口，我该让他尝尝别的肉和美味。给他吃煮熟的肉和汤之后，我决意第二天给他吃一次烤嫩羊，我把羊肉穿在篝火旁的线绳上，因为很多英国人都是这样做的。星期五挺羡慕的，品尝烤嫩羊之后费了好大劲儿告诉我他有多么喜欢那种烤肉味，最后给我说他再也不吃人肉了。

次日我安排他捶打玉米粒，然后照着我的样子筛选。他很快就学会了。我开始想着要有更大块的庄稼地，种更多的玉米来填两张嘴而不是一张嘴，于是开垦出一块更大的土地，像以前一样打上篱笆。星期五不但勤劳务实，扎实肯干，而且干得很出色。我告诉他玉米是我们用来糊口的，

corn to make more bread.

This was the pleasantest year of all the life I led in this place. Friday began to talk pretty well, and understand the names of almost everything I had occasion to call for, and of every place I had occasion to send him to, and talk a great deal to me; so that, in short, I began to have some use for my tongue again. Besides the pleasure of talking to him, I had a singular satisfaction in the fellow himself; his simple, unfeigned honesty appeared to be more and more every day, and I began really to love the creature; and I believe he loved me as much as possible.

I had a mind once to try if he had any lingering inclination to his own country; and having taught him English so well that he could answer me almost any questions, I asked him whether the nation that he belonged to was conquered in battle.

From what Friday told me, I came to understand that my man Friday had formerly been among the savages, who had used to come on shore on farther parts of the island, on the said man – eating occasions that he had been now brought for; and some time after, when I took courage to carry him to that side, he presently knew the place, and told me he was there once when they ate up twenty men, two women, and one child.

所以对我们俩的生存很重要。

这是我在这个地方度过的光阴中最快乐的一个年头。星期五开始很好的讲话，理解所有我在适当时候教的东西的名儿，所有我派他去的地方，而且他给我讲很多的话，因此很快我的口舌大显身手了。除了对他说话的愉悦之外，对于他自身我就有一种奇特的满足感。他朴实真挚的诚意与日俱增，我真正的爱上了这个动物，我也相信他在深深地爱着我。

我曾有过惮虑，他是否还残存着对自己祖国深深的眷顾之情，英文如此出色的他几乎能够回答我所有的问题，我问他他所属的那个民族是否从未打过凯旋之仗。

从星期五的话里我得知，我的忠实朋友星期五以前曾跻身于那帮野蛮人之间，他们在岛的远处登岸，来到所谓他被带到的吃人地。过后我鼓起勇气带他去那里，他即刻认出了那地方，说他有一次在那儿，他们吃了二十个男人、两个女人和一个孩子。

After I had had this discourse with him, I asked him how far it was from our island to the shore; whether the canoes were not often lost? He told me that there was no danger, no canoes ever lost; but that, after a little way out to sea, there was a current, and a wind always one way in the morning, the other in the afternoon.

This I thought to be no more than the sets of the tide, as going out or coming in; but I afterwards understood it was occasioned by the great draught and reflux of the mighty river Oroonoque; in the mouth of which river, as I thought afterwards our island lay; and that this land, which I perceived to the W. and N. W was the great island Trinidad, on the north point of the mouth of the river. I asked Friday a thousand questions about the country, the inhabitants, the sea, the coast, and what nations were near; he told me all he knew, with the greatest openness imaginable. I asked him the names of the several nations of his sort of people, but could get no other names than Caribs; from whence I easily understood that these were the Caribbees, which our maps place on that part of America which reaches from the mouth of the river Oroonoque to Guiana, and onwards to St. Martha. He told me that up a great way beyond the moon, which must be west from their country, there dwelt white, bearded men like me, and pointed to my

当我们有过这次交谈之后我问他岛距海滨有多远，小船是否不常迷失，他说没有什么危险，小船从不迷失航向，不过向海驶一段就会有湍流，而且一般情况下，流向是清早一个样，午后一个样。

我以为那只不过是潮涨潮落而已，后来我才明白是由于大河奥沦诺克的顺流和倒流而引起的现象，我们的岛坐落于奥沦诺克的河口，这也是我以后才想到的。这块被我感知为 W 和 N 的土地竟是河口北端的大岛特里尼达。我问了星期五不能再多的问题，比如说，国家、居民、大海、海滨以及附近的民族等等。他以最坦率的态度仔细地告诉我他所知道的一切。我问他那帮人所在诸国的国名，但他只提到加勒比人。我于此得知这些是加勒比地区的人，在地图上属于美洲地区，它们的范围由奥沦诺克河河口延伸至圭亚那，再延伸到圣马萨。他还告诉我月亮落下去那边好远的地方就是他的国家，在他们国家的西面住着白人，他们有着像我一样的络腮胡子，他说着，指

great whiskers. By all this I understood he meant the Spaniards, whose cruelties in America had been spread over whole countries, and were remembered by all the nations from father to son.

I inquired if he could tell me how I might come from this island, and get among those white men? He told me yes, I might go in 'two canoe.' I could not understand what he meant by 'two canoe,' till at last, with difficulty, I found he meant that it must be a large boat, as big as two canoes. This part of Friday's discourse began to relish with me very well; and from this time I entertained some hopes that, one time or other, I might find an opportunity to make my escape from this place, and that this poor savage might be a means to help me to do it.

Chapter 17 Preparation for Departure

I was now wanting to lay a foundation of religious knowledge in Friday's mind; particularly I asked him one time who made him. The poor creature did not understand me, but thought I had asked him who was his father. But I took it another way, and asked him who made the sea, the ground he walked on, and the hills and woods. He told me it was one old Benamuckee, that

着我的络腮胡。我知道他指的就是西班牙人，因为在美洲他们的杀戮遍布每个角落，所有的民族的祖祖辈辈对此刻骨铭心。

我问他可否告诉我怎样从这座岛上前往白人的居住地。他说我乘两只小木舟就可以去，我问他两只小木舟意味着什么，最后才费力地弄懂大概是一只大船，顶两只木舟大小。星期五的这些话令我十分愉悦，从此时起希望在我心中萌生悸动，早晚有一天我会有机会逃离此地，这个可怜的蛮人将成为我借以实现夙愿的得力助手。

第十七章　归心似箭

我此时此刻很想给星期五灌输一些宗教知识，尤其是我问他谁赋予他生命时，他竟然误解了我，还以为我想知道谁是他的父亲。于是，我换另外一种方式重新问他是谁创造了大海，是谁创造了他借以行走的地面，又是谁创造了山脉和森林。他告诉我是一位叫贝纳木基的长者，此人很了不

lived beyond all. He could describe nothing of this great person, but that he was very old; much older, he said, than the sea or the land, than the moon or the stars. I asked him then, if this person had made all things, why did not all things worship him? He looked very grave, and with a perfect look of innocence said, "All things should respect him." I asked him if the people who die in his country went away anywhere. He said, yes, they all went to Benamuckee. Then I asked him whether those they eat up went there, too. He said, "Yes."

From these things I began to instruct him in the knowledge of the true God. I told him that the great Maker of all things lived up there, pointing up towards the heaven; that he governs the world by the same power and providence by which he had made it; that he was omnipotent, could do everything for us, give everything to us, take everything from us, and thus, by degrees, I opened his eyes. He listened with great attention, and received with pleasure the notion if Jesus Christ being sent to redeem us, and of the manner of making our prayers to God and his being able to hear us, even into heaven. He told me one day, that if our God could hear us up the sun, he must be a greater God than their Benamuckee, who lived but a little way off, and yet could not hear till they went up to the great mountains

起，生活在很久以前，与海天可以媲美，与星月可以同辉。于是我又问他既然是长者创造了万事万物，万事万物就应该对他顶礼膜拜才对呀！此刻星期五显得很严肃，满脸无辜地对我说到："万物当然都崇敬他了。"我问他在这个地方辞世的人们是否都往他那去报到，他说他们当然都要去拜贝纳木基，然后我又问他是否那些活着的人们也去贝纳木基那儿礼拜，他说，"是的。"

通过以上事例，我开始给星期五传授"主"的知识。我告诉他万物真正的创造者生活在天堂；他用天意主宰着他创造的世界；他能呼风唤雨，替我们做好一切事情，赋予我们一切东西；当然他也能剥夺掉我们所拥有的一切。这样，渐渐地，我揭开了蒙住星期五双眼的面纱。他聚精会神地听着，满怀快乐地接受了这一事实：耶稣是上帝派来拯救我们的，是来引导我们祈祷者去信仰上帝的。虽然他住在天国依然能听到我们的祈祷和祝福。于是，有一天星期五告诉我，上帝住在天国还能听见我们的话语，比起贝纳木基他才是最至高无上的神灵。因为贝纳木基跟我们住得很近，而且只有人们爬到他居住的那座大山上跟他讲话

where he dwelt, to speak to him.

Sending him for something a great way off, I seriously prayed to God that he would enable me to instruct this poor savage, assisting by his Spirit the heart of the poor ignorant creature to receive the light of the knowledge of God in Christ, reconciling him to himself, and would guide me to speak so to him from the world of God, as his conscience might be convinced, his eyes opened, and his soul saved with him upon the subject of the redemption of man, by the Savior of the world, and of the doctrine of the gospel preached from heaven, namely, of repentance towards God, and faith in our blessed Lord Jesus. I then explained to him, as well as I could, why our blessed Redeemer took not on him the nature of angels, but the seed of Abraham, and how, for that reason, the fallen angels had no share in the redemption; that he came only to the lost sheep of the house of Israel, and the like.

I had great reason to be thankful that ever he came to me; my grief sat lighter upon me, my habitation grew comfortable to me beyond measure, and when I reflected, that, in this solitary life which I had been confined to, I had not only been moved myself to look up to heaven, and to seek to the hand that brought me there, save the life, and, for aught I knew, the soul, of a poor sav-

时，他才能听得清。

我开始一本正经地祈祷上帝赐给我能力去教导这个可怜的野人；愿凭借他的精神，去帮助这个既可怜又无知的生灵享受耶稣上帝知识的沐浴，愿上帝接受了星期五，愿上帝引导我去给星期五讲述上帝的知识：救世主用来自天国的信条教导他，使他对上帝进行悔悟，使他诚信基督教耶稣。这样，他的良知又能受到启发，他的视野变得开阔，他的灵魂在人类赎罪的这个基础上得到拯救。然后我再尽我自己所能把这些知识传授给他。比如：我们祈祷的上帝一定会善待每一个人，他教会人们不要生气；作为亚伯拉罕的子孙，生气对赎罪是毫无裨益的，他只是只迷途的羔羊跨入了以色列的大门等等。

我真的打心眼儿里感谢星期五闯入了我的生活，我的忧伤渐渐地减轻，岛上的生活给我带来了无法形容的舒适和乐趣。一想起被困于荒岛那与世隔绝的生活，我禁不住感动地抬头仰望苍天，寻求恩赐于我的那双手，渴望得到神的指点，我要给星期五这个可怜的生灵灌输宗教知识，去拨

age, and bring him to the true knowledge of religion, and of the Christ doctrine, that he might know Christ Jesus.

In this thankful frame I continued all remainder of my time and the conversation between Friday and me for three years, during which we lived there together, perfectly and completely happy. The savage was now a good Christian. I always applied myself to reading the Scriptures, and to let him know, as well as I could, the meaning of what I read.

After Friday and I became more intimately acquainted, and that he could understand almost all I said to him, and speak fluently, though in broken English to me, I acquainted him with my history. I let him touch gun – power and bullets, and taught him how to shoot. I gave him a knife, which he was wonderfully delighted with, and I made him a belt with a frog hanging to it, such as in England we wear hangers in, and in the frog, instead of a hanger, I gave him a hatchet.

I described to him the countries of Europe, and particularly England, which I came from; how we lived; how we worshipped God, how we behaved to one another, and how we traded in ships to all parts of the world. I gave him an account of the wreck which I had been on board of, and showed him, as near as I could, the place

动他理解基督信条的心弦，这样他才可能理解基督耶稣。

怀着对星期五的无比感谢，我和他相濡以沫地度过这后来的三年时光。这三年是我们度过的最幸福最快乐的时光，过去的野蛮人如今成了基督教的最好臣民。因为我总是尽我所能给他阅读《圣经》，而且竭力让他懂得我所阅读的真正含义。

渐渐地我和星期五越来越亲密无间，他不但能理解我给他所说的一切事情，能流利地说出一些英语，尽管对我来说这些英语并不连贯，而且还能熟知我的经历。我让他用我的枪和子弹，然后教他学习射击。我给了他一把刀子，这使得他很高兴；我又给他戴了一个带有花扣的皮带；最后再给他一把斧头。

我给他描述欧洲的国家，讲的最多的是我土生土长的英国，我告诉他我们在英国所过的生活，我们如何对上帝显示敬意，我们之间打交道的方式以及我们用什么方法跟世界各地的船只进行贸易。我还给他描述了我乘坐的那艘轮船的残骸的状况，并且还把他领到了曾经停泊过船的地方，

where she lay; but she had all been gone long ago. I showed him the ruins of our boat, which we lost when I escaped, and which was now fallen almost to pieces. Upon seeing this boat, Friday stood musing some time, and said nothing. I asked him what he studied upon; at last, said he, "Me see such boat like this come to place at my nation."

I did not understand him a good while; but at last, when I had examined farther into it, I understood by him, that a boat, such as that had been, came on shore upon the country where he lived, that is, as he explained it, was driven there by stress of weather. I presently imagined that some European ship must have been cast away upon their coast, and the boat might get loose, and drive ashore; but was so dull that I never once thought of men making their escape from a wreck there, much less whence they might come, so I only inquired after a description of the boat.

Friday described the boat to me well enough; but brought me better to understand him when he added, with some warmth, "We save the white men from drown." Then I presently asked him if there any white men, as he called them, in the boat. "Yes," he said, "the boat full of white men." I asked him, "How many?" He told me upon his fingers, seventeen. I asked

但不久前，船已经被海浪卷走了。我又把他带到了我逃生时遗弃的那艘小船前，但这艘小船已经支离破碎了。看着这艘船，星期五站在那儿苦苦地思索了一会儿，啥都没说，我问他在想什么，他说："我看到这样的船就想起了我的国家。"

我起初并没听懂他的意思，但最后，当我进一步深究时，我才理解，他刚才所见的这样一艘船是从他生活的那个国家的海岸边驶来的，也就是说正如他所解释的那样是由风等自然因素把船推过来的。我此刻想象着一定是某艘欧洲轮船从他们的海岸启程，途中遭遇风暴，但船没有被摧毁，就飘到了这个海岸上，但是情况并不乐观，所以我从来就没想到会有人从这艘残船上逃生，更不用说会有人来到这座岛上，所以我就不再打探关于人的情况，只是想了解这艘船的情况。

星期五给我详细地描述了船的情况，但是他随后又满怀热情地给我讲述了另一件事，这使我倍感高兴。他说："我们还救了那些快要淹死的白种人。"我马上就问："船上真的有白种人？"他说："是的，满船都是白种人。"我问："有多少？"他举起手指告诉我，十七个，我接着问，"他们的

him, "What became of them ?" He told me, "They live, they dwell at my nation."

This put new thoughts into my head again, for I presently imagined that these might be the men belonging to the ship that was cast away in my island, and who, after the ship was struck on the rock, and they saw her inevitably lost, had saved themselves in their boat, and were landed upon that wild shore among savages. Upon this I inquired of him more critically, what became of them; he assured me they still lived there, that they had been there about four years, that the savages let them alone, and gave them victuals to live. I asked him how it came to pass that they did not kill them, and eat them. He said, "No, they make brother with them, they no eat any men, but when make the war, fight."

It was after this, some considerable time, that being on the top of the hill, at the island, from whence I had, in a clear day, discovered the main, or continent of America, Friday, the weather being very serene, looked very earnestly towards the main – land, and in a kind of surprise fell a jumping and dancing, and called out to me; I asked him what was the matter. "O joy!" said he, "O glad! These see my country ! there my nation!"

I observed an extraordinary sense of pleasure appear

情况如何?"他说:"他们都活着呢,还住在我的国家里。"

这些话让我重新思索起来,因为此刻我想象着这些人可能就是从我的小岛上漂走的那艘船上的人,他们亲眼目睹了轮船触礁,又看着她沉没;然后依靠这艘小船逃生,着陆在野人居住的荒岛上。因此,我更加关切地询问起星期五这些人情况到底怎么样,他向我保证说他们依然住在那儿,大约有四年了,而野人们也听之任之,还给他们供应生存所需的食物,我继续问他事情怎么会是这样,野人们既不杀他们,也不吃他们。他说,"不,他们还跟他们称兄道弟,他们没吃一个人,只是等着发生战争时,进行作战。"

此后,激动人心的时刻终于到来了。在一个晴朗的日子里,在岛上的山顶上,我发现了一块陆地,即或是美洲大陆,星期五对这块陆地充满了急切之情,他既惊又喜,手舞足蹈,朝我大喊,我问他什么事,他说:"太高兴,太快乐了,我看见了我的祖国和人民。"

我发现星期五面露极度的喜悦之色,他的双

in his face, his eyes sparkled a strange eagerness, as if he had a mind to be in his own country again; and this observation of mine put a great many thoughts into me, which made me at first not so easy about my new man Friday as I was before; and I made no doubt, but that if Friday could get back to his own nation again, he would not only forget all his religion, but all his obligations to me. But I wronged the poor honest creature very much, for which I was very sorry afterwards; however, as my jealousy increased, and held me some weeks, I was a little more circumspect, and not so familiar and kind to him as before, in which I was certainly in the wrong.

From this time, I confess, I had a mind to venture over, and see if I could possibly join with these bearded men, who, I made no doubt, were Spaniards or Portuguese; not doubting but, if I could, we might find some method to escape from thence, being upon the continent, and a good company together, better than I could from an island, forty miles off shore, and alone without help. So, after some days, I took Friday to work again, by way of discourse, and told him I would give him a boat to go back to his own nation; and accordingly carried him to my frigate, which lay on the other side of the island, and having cleared it of the water, I brought it out, showed it him, and we both went into it.

眼迸出了一种奇怪的渴望之火花，好像又回到了自己的国土。我观察着这一细微的变化，思绪万千，我不能像从前那样小看星期五了，毫无疑问，如果星期五又一次重返家园，他不但会把他的宗教信仰抛到九霄云外去，而且还会忘记他对我的义务。以后我才发现我冤枉了这个可怜的小东西，为此我感到十分的抱歉。然而随后的好几个礼拜我都妒火中烧，不像从前那些样善待星期五，跟他打得火热了，而是小心从事。这一点我应该受到责备。

我承认这段时间我总想进行一次冒险，尝试是否能跟那些长着络腮胡的男人们混熟，毫无疑问那些男人是西班牙抑或是葡萄牙人。如果我真能如愿以偿，我们就可能从那块陆地上找到逃生的方法，一起结伴而行逃离这个远离海岸四十海里外的海岛。这总比我一个人只身冒险要好得多吧。所以，过了些日子，我说服星期五跟我一起执行这个计划，告诉他我可以给他弄艘船让他重返自己的国家。于是，我把他带到了泊在海岛边的那艘小救生艇旁，拨开水面，我们俩一起坐了进去。

I found he was very dexterous at managing it, and would make it go almost as swift again as I could; so I said to him, "Well, now, Friday, shall we go to your nation?" He looked very dull at my saying so, which, it seems, was because he thought the boat was too small to go so far. I told him then I had a bigger one; so the very next day I went to the place where the first boat lay, which I had made, but which I could not get into the water. He said that was big enough; but as I had taken no care of it, and it had lain 22 or 23 years there, the sun had split and dried it, that it was in a manner rotten. Friday told me that such a boat would do very well, and would carry 'much enough vittle, drink, bread.'

Upon the whole, I was by this time so fixed upon my design of going over with him to the continent, that I told him we would go and make one as big as that, and he should go home in it. He answered not one word, but looked very grave and sad. I asked him what was the matter with him. He asked me again thus: "Why you angry mad with Friday? What me done?" I asked him what he meant; I told him I was not angry with him at all. "No angry! No angry!" said he, repeating the words several times, "why send Friday home away to my nation?" "Why," said I, "Friday, did you not say you wished you were there?" "Yes, yes," said he, "wish we

我觉着星期五划船的技法熟练，他能够把船划的像我一样身轻如燕。于是我给他说："星期五，我们现在就可以去你们国家了。"听我这么说，星期五感到一片茫然，因为他认为这艘船似乎太小了一点，经不起这么遥远的路途颠簸。看到这，我告诉他说，我还有一艘大船。于是，第二天我把他领到了放第一艘船的那个地方，这艘船是我亲手做的，但我还没使用过。他说这艘船还可以。但是由于我没有能好好地照料这艘船，经过二十二三年日晒雨淋，它已经有点破碎了。星期五告诉我这样的船能修缮完好，还可以带足够的食物及贮备品。

直到这时，一切准备就绪，我决定执行我的计划，我告诉他我想把他带到那块陆地去，在那儿我们可以做一只跟这艘船一样大小的船。然后，他就可以坐这艘船回家。他一句话也没说，一脸的严肃和悲愤。我问他为啥这样。他却反问道："你为什么跟星期五生气了？星期五到底做错什么事了？"我问他这话是什么意思，我告诉他我根本没和他生气。"没生气！没生气！"他把这话重复了一遍又一遍。"那你为什么要把星期五送回他的老家？""为什么？"我问，"星期五，你自己不是渴望回家吗？""是的，我渴望回家，但我不是渴

both there no wish Friday there, no master there." In a word, he would not think of going there without me. "You shall go without me; leave me here to live by myself as I did before." He looked confused at this, and running to one of the hatchets which he used to wear, he took it up hastily, and gave it to me. "What must I do with this?" said I to him. "You take kill Friday." Said he. "What must I kill you for?" said I again. He returned very quick. "What you send Friday away for? Take kill Friday; no send Friday away." As he spoke, tears stood in his eyes, and I was so affected, that I said I would never send him away, if he was willing to stay with me.

I found that all the foundation of his desire to go to his own country was laid in his ardent affection to the people, and his hopes of my doing them good: a thing , which as I had no notion of myself, so I had not the least thought, or intention, or desire of undertaking it. But still I found a strong inclination to attempting an escape. I went to work with Friday, to find out a great tree proper to fell, and make a large canoe, for the voyage. After searching some time, Friday at last pitched upon a tree, for I found he knew much better than I what kind of wood was fittest for it; nor can I tell, to this day , what wood to call the tree we cut down, except that it was

望一个人回家，而是渴望和你一起回家，我不能没有主人。"一句话，他从来没有想过要和我分开。"你可以自己回去，让我还和从前一样在此生活吧。"他听到此话，感到一脸迷茫，跑过去抓起他曾经用过的一把斧头，举起来，塞到我手上。我问，"你用斧头做什么？""你把星期五杀了吧！"他说。"我为什么要杀你？""那你为什么要把星期五打发走，如果这样，你就把星期五杀了吧！"说着说着，眼眶布满了泪水。我为此深深感动，告诉他，如果他愿意跟我呆着，那就呆着吧。

星期五想要回家的这种愿望纯粹出于对他国人民的一种热切的爱。他希望我能帮助他的人民。而这事我还从来没有形成一种概念。所以对此事这至少还没考虑过，或者还没有任何企图或愿望去接受这项任务。然而，我此刻非常想逃走。我继续跟星期五工作着，想砍伐一棵大树，准备为这次航行做一个大的独木舟，找了一段时间后，星期五终于瞄准了一棵大树，将它砍倒。我发现，在识别木料方面，星期五是内行，他比我更熟悉哪种木料更适合做独木舟。到今天我还说不出我们砍倒的那棵树叫什么，只知道它有点像我们所

very like the tree we call fustic, or between that and the
Nicaragua wood, for it was much of the same color and
smell. Friday was for burning the hollow or cavity of this
tree out, to make it into a boat; but I showed him how
rather to cut it with tools, which after I showed him how
to use he did it very handily, and in about a month's
hard labor we finished it, and made it very handsome,
especially when with our axes, which I showed him how
to handle, we cut and hewed the outside into the true
shape of a boat. After this, however, it cost us near a
fortnight's time to get her along, as it were, inch by
inch, upon great rollers, into the water; but when she
was in, she would have carried twenty men with ease.

It amazed me to see with what dexterity, and how
swift my man Friday would manage her, turn, and paddle her along. So I asked him if he would, and if we
might venture over in her. "Yes," he said, "me venture
over in her very well, though great blow wind." However, I had a farther design that he knew nothing of, and
that was to make a mast and a sail, and to fit her with an
anchor. I set Friday to work to cut down a cedar – tree,
which I found near the place, and gave him directions
how to shape and order it; but as to the sail, that was
my particularly care. I knew I had pieces of old sails,
but as I had had them now twenty – six years by me, and

说的"法丝特苟"树，或者是介于"法丝特苟"和"尼加拉瓜"树之间的一种树，因为它与这两种树有同样的气味和颜色。星期五想把这棵树的中空部分用火烧一下制成船；我却教他如何使用工具进行制造。后来他做的相当熟练，大约用了一个月的工夫，凭借我们的斧头，我们终于做成了一艘外形跟真船一样的漂亮的小船。随后，我们又花了大约两周的时间，把船一点一点地慢慢地挪进了水里，船在水中可以轻松地装载二十多人。

星期五手脚麻利，身段敏捷地撑着这艘船，这让我大开眼界。于是我问他我们是否可能驾驭这艘船进行冒险，"当然，我完全可以驾驭它，哪怕是遇到大风大浪。"然而，此刻我有了更新的计划，而星期五对此却一无所知，那就是我想做一个船桅和一个主帆，使我们的船可以非常轻松的停泊。我开始让星期五就地取材砍倒一棵雪松树，指导他如何做船桅。但我最关心的还是如何去弄主帆。我有一些旧帆，但它们已经陪伴我二十六

not being very careful to preserve them, they were nearly all rotten. However, I found two pieces which appeared pretty good, and with a great deal of pains and awkward, tedious stitching, for want of needles, I at length made a three – cornered ugly thing, like what we call in England a shoulder – of – mutton sail, to go with a boom at the bottom, and a little short sprit at the top.

I was near two months in rigging and fitting out my mast and sails, for I fitted them very complete, making a small stay, and a sail, or foresail to it, to assist, if should turn to windward; and, which was more than all, I fixed a rudder to the stern of her to steer with, and though I was but a bungling shipwright, yet, as I knew the usefulness and even necessity of such a thing, I applied myself with so much pains to do it, that at last I brought it to pass.

After all this was done, I had my Friday to teach as to what belonged to the navigation of my boat; for though he knew very well how to paddle the canoe, he knew nothing what belonged to a sail and a rudder, and how the sail gibbed, and filled this way or that way, as the course we sailed changed; I say, when he saw this, he stood like one astonished and amazed. However, with a little use, I made all these things familiar to him, and he became an expert sailor, except that as to the com-

年了。由于对他们保存不妥，现在已经开始剥落了，但我还是能找出两片稍微好的，由于没有针，缝起来不仅吃力而且非常不方便，我最后做成了一个三种颜色混杂的样子难看的主帆。正如我们英语里所说的"羊肩帆"，主帆从桅杆底部升起，够不到桅杆的顶部。

两个月来，我一直在装备着这艘船，试着我的船桅及主帆，完成之后我先进行试航，检测它是否能经受得起风暴；当这一切办妥后，我在船的尾部安装了一个船舵，尽管造船方面我并不算高明，但我深深知道拥有这样一艘船对我来说是何等必要，我花了这么多时间和经历去做它，直到最后我才试行通过。

所有这一切准备就绪，我开始教星期五如何进行航海。当然星期五只精通驾驶脚踏独木舟，他对主帆和船舵的知识一无所知，尤其当航线改变时，主帆应该如何变化，他脑中一片空白。当看到这些装备时，他站在那儿傻眼儿了。然而，使用了几次后，他摸出了这些装备的使用窍门，成了一名出色的海员，只是我要让他明白罗盘针

pass I could make him understand very little of that; but there was not much occasion for the compass in these parts.

I now entered on the 27th year of my captivity in this place; though the last three years that I had this creature with me ought rather to be left out of the account, my habitation being quite of another kind than in all the rest of the time. I kept anniversary of my landing here with the same thankfulness to God for his mercies as at first; and if I had such cause of acknowledgement at first, I had much more so now, having such additional testimonies of the care of Providence over me, and the great hopes I had of being effectually and speedily delivered; for I had an invincible impression upon my thoughts, that my deliverance was at hand, and that I should not be another year in this place. However, I went on with all my work as usual.

Chapter 18   The Fighting

The rainy season was in the mean time upon me, when I kept more within doors than at other times; so I had stowed our new vessel as secure as we could, bringing her up into the creek, and thus we waited for the months of November and December, in which I designed

的用途有些吃力。但是罗盘针在这个地方还派不上多大用场。

我在此已经生活了二十七年了，尽管这最后的三年我有这个小东西陪伴着我，生活也还算过得去，但要我将我的后半生定居于此，那就要另当别论了。首先，我每年都要举行一次"着陆于此"纪念活动，借机来感谢上帝对我的恩赐。如果让我说明这样做的原因的话，千言万语都道不清说不明。托上帝的福，我所有的希望都能产生预期的结果，而且会迅速实现，此时此刻，我隐隐约约地感到实际上我不会在这个地方呆多久了，但我还是一如既往地从事着我的工作。

第十八章　白刃之战

雨季到了，这几天在家里呆着的时间相对长些，我把刚造好的船拉到先前的那条小河里，尽力把它藏严实，然后就等待十一月、十二月的到

to make my adventure.

When the settled season began to come in, the first thing I did was to lay by a certain quantity of provisions, being the store for our voyage; and I intended in a week or a fortnight's time to open the dock and launch out our boat. I was busy one morning upon something of a kind, when I called to Friday and bade him go to the sea – shore, and see if he could find a turtle. Friday had not been long gone, when he came running back, and flew over my outward wall, and cried out to me, "O master! O master! O sorrow! O bad!" "What's the matter, Friday?" said I. "O yonder," says he, "one, two, three canoe!" "Well, Friday," said I, "do not be frightened;" so I heartened him up as well as I could. However, I saw the poor fellow, was most terribly scared, for something ran in his head that they came to look for him, and would cut him in pieces and eat him; and the poor fellow trembled so, that I scarce knew what to do with him. I comforted him as well as I could, and told him I was in as much danger as he, and that they would eat me as well as him. "But," said I, "Friday, we must resolve to fight them. Can you fight, Friday?" "Me shoot," said he "but there come many great number." "No matter for that," said I again, "our guns will fright them that we do not kill." So I asked him whether, if I

来，我打算到那时去做一次冒险。

好天气一到，我做的第一件事就是为旅程储备一些食物，我还准备用一两周时间来开辟一个船坞，好让船头一次出海成功。一天早晨，我一边为这类事情忙活着，一边把星期五叫过来，打发他去海边瞧瞧能不能找到海龟。星期五出去没多久，就一路飞跑回来，一下子从外墙上翻了进来，对我使劲地嚷道："噢，主人，主人！太可怕，太可恶了！""怎么啦？星期五？"我问。"噢，那么，一、二、三只船……""好了星期五，别怕！"我尽力给他鼓气。但是这个可怜的家伙一时被惊吓过度，抖得像筛糠一样。我都不知道该对这个吓坏的家伙怎么办好了。我接着尽力用心去安慰他，并且告诉他，我们的处境一样都非常危险，他们吃了他也一定会吃了我。"但是，"我说，"星期五，我们必须下决心斗争打败我们的敌人，我们才能保命，你会打仗吗？""我，打枪。"他说，"但是他们人好多。""那没关系，"我又说，"我们可以吓跑那些没杀死的敌人。"于是我又问

resolved to defend him, he would defend me, and stand by me, and do just as I bade him. He said, "Me die when you bid die master." So I gave him a good dram of rum; and when he had drunk it, I made the two fowling – pieces, and loaded them with swan – shot, as big as small pistol – bullets; then I took four muskets, and loaded them with two slugs and five small bullets each; and my two pistols I loaded with a brace of bullets each. I hung my great sword, as usual, naked by side, and gave Friday his hatchet.

When I had thus prepared myself I took my per- spective glass, and went up to the side of the hill to see what I could discover, and I found quickly by my glass that there were twenty – one savages, three prisoners, and three canoes; and that their whole business seemed to be the triumphant banquet upon these three human bodies; but nothing more than as I had observed as usual with them.

They landed, not where they had done when Friday made his escape, but nearer to my creek, where the shore was low, and where a thick wood came close al- most down to the sea. This, with the abhorrence of the inhuman errand these wretches came about, so filled me with indignation, that I came down to Friday, and told him I resolved to go down to them and kill them all, and

如果我坚决保卫他，他会不会也坚决保卫我，和我站在一起，照我的吩咐去做。他说，"主人，你让我去死，我也会去死的。"我给了他一点朗姆酒让他喝下去，这样可以使他壮壮胆。然后，我开始收拾那两杆鸟枪；装上像手枪子弹一样的大号弹丸。我接着又取来了四杆滑膛枪，每个滑膛枪里面装了两个子弹和五个小子弹。我的手枪也分别装上了两颗子弹，我像往常一样，挂上我的没有刀鞘的大刀，让星期五把他的斧子带上，准备跟我出发。

一切准备妥当之后，我带上望远镜，爬上小山坡看能否发现什么情况，很快我透过望远镜看到二十一个野人，三个俘虏和一条小船。这些野人想做的事情似乎就是用这三个俘虏开一个丰盛的人肉宴，并没发现有什么其他特别的企图。

他们上岸的地方并不是星期五逃回来的那个地方，但却靠近我们的船坞，那里水位非常浅，一片浓密的树林几乎延伸到海里。这种情形再加上对这些坏蛋的毫无人性的行径的憎恶，使我怒火万丈，恨不得把他们全部干掉。我下来对星期五说，我决定去把他们干掉，问他是否愿意和我

asked him if he would stand by me. He had now gotten over his fright, and his spirit being a little raised with the dram I had given him, he was very cheerful, and told me as before, "He would die when I bid die."

I entered the wood with all possible wariness and silence with Friday close at my heels and marching till I came to the skirt of the wood, on the side which was next to them, only that one corner of the wood lay between me and them. Here I called softly to Friday, and showing him a great tree, which was just at the corner of the wood, I bade him go to the tree, and bring me word if he could see there plainly what they were doing. He did so, and came immediately back to me, and told me they might be plainly viewed there; that they were all about the fire, eating the flesh of one of their prisoners, and that another lay bound upon the sand, a little from them, whom, he said, they would kill next, and which fired the very soul within me. He told me it was not one of their own nation, but one of the bearded men whom he had told me of, that came to their country in the boat. I was filled with horror at the very naming the white, bearded man, and going to the tree, I saw plainly by my glass a white man, who lay upon the beach of the sea, with his hands and feet tied with flags, or things like rushes, and that he was an European, and had clothes

一块去战斗。这时，他已经战胜了恐惧，而且喝了我给他的朗姆酒，胆量也大了些，他很兴奋，仍像上次一样说让他死，他也去死。

我悄悄地，小心翼翼地走进林子里，星期五紧紧跟在我后面，我们一直走到林子的边上，这里正靠近那伙野人，和他们仅隔着一角林子。走到那里，我轻轻叫住星期五，我指着林角上的一棵大树示意让他上去，然后回来告诉我，他能不能看清楚他们在干什么，他跑了过去，很快又回来向我汇报说，可以看到他们，那伙人正围着一堆火，吃着其中一个俘虏的肉，另外一个俘虏被绑了起来，放在沙滩下，离他们有点距离，星期五说下一个就轮到吃那个家伙了。这更激起了我的怒火。他还告诉我，那人并不是来自他的部落，而是一个他曾对我说过的长胡子的白人，这人曾经乘船到过他的部落。一提到白人这个名称我心里就充满了恐惧。于是爬到树上，用望远镜清清楚楚地看到一个白人，躺在海边河滩下，手脚用烂草蔓捆着，可以看出他是个欧洲人，身上穿着

on.

I had not a moment to lose, for nineteen of the dreadful wretches sat upon the ground, all close huddled together, and had just sent the other two to butcher the poor Christian, and bring him, perhaps limp by limp, to their fire, and they stooped down to untie the bands at his feet. I turned to Friday: "Now, Friday," said I, "do as I bid you." Friday said he would. "Then, Friday," said I, "do exactly as you see me do; fail in nothing." So I set down one of the muskets and the fowling – piece upon the ground, and Friday did the like by his; and with the other musket I took my aim at the savages, bidding him do the like: then asking him if he was ready, he said, "Yes." "Then fire at them," said I, and the same moment I fired also.

Friday took his aim so much the better than I, that on the side he shot he killed two of them and wounded three more; and, on my side, I killed one and wounded two. They were in a dreadful consternation; and all of them who were not hurt jumped up upon their feet immediately, but did not know which way to run or which way to look, for they knew not from whence their destruction came. Friday kept his eyes close upon me, so, as soon as the first shot was made, I threw down the piece and took up the fowling – piece, and Friday did the like; he

衣服。

我一分钟也不能浪费了。因为十九个可憎的恶棍紧紧围坐成一堆，派了另外两个去宰杀那可怜的基督教徒，要把他架到火旁来。现在两个家伙正弯下腰合伙把他的脚捆紧。我转身对星期五说："现在，星期五，照我的吩咐去做。"星期五说他会的。我说："星期五，照我的样子去做，别落下。"然后，我把其中一杆滑膛枪和鸟枪放下，星期五也照我的样子去做，我把另外一杆滑膛枪瞄向那些野人，并让星期五也照我样子做，我问他，"准备好了吗?"他说："好了。""朝他们开火!"我说着自己也开始射击。

星期五的准头一点儿也不比我差，在整个战斗中他一共射死两个人，射伤了三个。我则打死一个，打伤了两个，那些野人惊恐万状，没有伤的都一下子跳起来，抱头鼠窜，但不知道头该往哪里看，人该往哪里逃。因为他们不知道这突如其来的灾难是从哪里降临的。星期五紧紧注视着我，看着我的一举一动，射完一阵后，我放下滑膛枪拿起鸟枪，星期五也照我的样子去做。他看

sees me cock and present; he did the same again. "Are you ready, Friday?" said I. "Yes," said he. "Let fly, then," said I; and with that I fired again among the amazed wretches, and so did Friday, and as our pieces were now loaded with what I call swan – shot, or small pistols bullets, we found only two drop; but so many were wounded, that they ran about yelling and screaming like mad creatures, all bloody and wounded most of them, and three more fell quickly after, but not quite dead.

"Now, Friday," said I, laying down the discharged pieces and taking up the muskets, which was yet loaded, "follow me," which he did with a deal of courage; upon which I rushed out of the wood and showed myself and Friday close at my foot. As soon as I perceived they saw me, I shouted as loud as I could, and bade Friday do so too; and running as fast as I could, I made directly towards the poor victim. The two butchers, who were just going to work with him, had left him at the surprise of our first fire and fled, in a terrible fright, to the seaside, and had jumped into a canoe, and three more of the rest made the same way. I turned to Friday, and bade him step forwards and fire at them. He understood me immediately, and, running about forty yards to be nearer them, he shot at them, and I thought he had

我上枪瞄准，也上枪瞄准。"准备好了，星期五?"我问。"好了。""开火!"我说着再次朝那些受了惊吓的恶棍开火，星期五也同样射击起来，朝那些家伙开火，我们的枪里装着被我叫做弹丸或小手枪子弹的东西。我们只浪费了两颗。就让那么多的人都受了伤，使得他们像一群疯了的动物叫喊着哭号着到处乱跑。大多数野人身上受了伤，流着血，其中三四个很快倒下了，但并没有死。

"现在，星期五，"我说着放下刚刚射完的滑膛枪，拿起了装上子弹的鸟枪。"照我的样子去做!"他做的时候表现得十分勇敢。其时，我一下子冲出树林，出现在他们面前，星期五也紧随其后出现在他们面前，一看到他们发现了，我便扯开嗓子大声地叫喊着，也让星期五像我一样大声叫喊着，我使劲地跑，一直奔向那个可怜的俘虏。正准备宰他的两个屠夫，受到我们枪声和喊声的惊吓，把他撇下不管，惊恐万分地跑到海边，已经跳上木船，剩下有三个人也朝那个方向跑去。我转身让星期五跟上他们，朝他们开枪，他立刻领会了我的意思，跑到离他们只有四十码的地方开始朝他们射击，我以为他把他们都干掉了，因

killed them all, for I saw them all fall on a heap in the boat, though I saw two of them up again quickly. However, he killed two of them, and wounded the third, so that he lay in the bottom of the boat as if he had been dead.

While Friday fired at them, I pulled out my knife and cut the flags that bound the poor victim; and loosing his hands and feet, I lifted him up, and asked him, in the Portuguese tongue, what he was, but he was so weak and faint, that he could scarce stand or speak. I took my bottle out of my pocket and gave it him, making signs that he should drink, which he did; and I gave him a piece of bread, which he ate. Then I asked him what countryman he was, and he said, "Espagniole;" and, being a little recovered, let me know, by all the signs he could possibly make, how much he was in my debt for his deliverance. I said, in as good Spanish as I could, "We will talk afterwards, but we must fight now; if you have any strength left, take the pistol and sword that lay about you." He took them very thankfully, and no sooner had he the arms in his hands, but, as if they had put new vigor into him, he flew upon his murderers like a fury, and had cut two or three in pieces in an instant, for they were so surprised and frightened, that they could make no resistance, nor attempt to escape.

枪，我把一个猎枪给了他，他拿上猎枪就去追两个野人，并把他们俩打伤。由于他身心疲惫不能快跑，他们还是从他手中逃到树林子里去了。星期五就在林子里追他们，并且杀死了其中一个野人，另外一个野人实在太敏捷，虽然受了伤，还是一下子跳进海里，全力朝着上了船的那几个人的方向游去。

上了船的那几个人拼命地躲着子弹，虽然星期五朝他们开了两三枪，但没有打中一个。星期五愿意划着他们带来的船只去追他们。事实上，他们的逃跑令我很焦急，惟恐他们把消息带回去，然后带两三百艘船的人来，利用人多势广把我们一举消灭。因此，我赞同和星期五划船去追他们，跑到其中的一个船边，我跳了进去，并让星期五紧跟上来，进去之后我们才惊讶地发现，里面躺着一个可怜的还没死的家伙，手脚被捆着，这个西班牙人被这次屠杀几乎快吓死了。还不知道到底发生了什么事，连抬眼看看船外的力气都没有，他脖子、脚跟都绑得很紧，而且又被绑了这么长的时间，已经奄奄一息剩不了几口气了。

I immediately cut the twisted flags that bound him, and would have helped him up; but he could not stand or speak, but groaned most piteously, believing, it seems, still, that he was only unbound in order to be killed. When Friday came, I bade him speak to him, and tell him of his deliverance; and pulling out my bottle, made him give the poor wretch a dram, which, with the news of being delivered, revived him, and he sat up in the boat. But when Friday came to hear him speak, and looked in his face, it would have moved any one to tears to have seen how Friday kissed, jumped about, danced, sang, and then cried again, wrung his hands, beat his own face and head, and then sang and jumped about again, like a distracted creature. It was a good while before I could make him speak to me, or tell me what was the matter; but when he came a little to himself, he said that it was his father.

It is not easy for me to express how it moved me, to see what ecstasy and filial affection had worked in this poor savage, at the sight of his father, and of his being delivered from death: nor indeed can I describe half the extravagance of his affection after this, for he went into the boat and out of the boat a great many times. When he went in to him, he would sit down by him, open his breast, and hold his father's head close to his bosom

我立刻砍掉绑在他手脚上的草蔓，想扶他站起来，但是他仍然站不起来，也讲不出话，只是痛苦地呻吟着，好像觉得把他松开只是为了杀掉他。我让星期五过来跟他讲话，告诉他他已经获救了，并拿出酒瓶给这个可怜的家伙。喝了点酒，听到被解救的消息，他回过神了，并在船里站了起来。星期五过来听了听他讲话，看了看他的脸，这之后的情景会让每一个见到的人都会热泪盈眶。星期五疯狂地亲吻着那人，跳着，又舞又唱，然后大声哭着绞着双手，拍着对方的脸和头，再唱再叫，像个发狂的动物。过了好大一会儿，我才使他静下来，给我讲话，告诉我发生了什么事——当他恢复过神来，他告诉我那就是他的父亲！

　　看到这个可怜的野人发现自己的父亲，发现自己的父亲被从死神手中解救出后表现出来的如此的孝心和感情，难以描述当时我对此是多么地感动。这之后他那夸张的情感也很难让我说清楚，他一会儿上船一会儿下船这样重复了好几次，他进船来靠在父亲的身边坐下，敞开怀抱，把他父亲的头紧紧放在胸脯上以支撑着他，这样一呆

half an hour together, to nourish it; then he took his arms and ankles, which were numbed and stiff with the binding, and chafed and rubbed them with his hands; and I perceiving what the case was, gave him some rum out of my bottle to rub them with, which did them a deal of good. This action put an end to our pursuit of the canoe with the other savages, who had now gotten almost out of sight; and it was happy for us that we did not, for it blew so hard within two hours after, and before they could be gotten a quarter of their way, and continued blowing so hard all night, which was against them, that I could not suppose their boat could live, or that they ever reached to their own coast.

But to return to Friday, he was so busy about his father, that I could not find in my heart to take him off for some time: but after I thought he could leave him a little, I called him to me, and he came jumping and laughing, and pleased to the highest extreme. Then I asked him to give his father some water, which revived his father more than all the rum or spirits I had given him, for he was just fainting with thirst.

When his father had drunk, I called to Friday to bring some bread and water to the poor Spaniard too, who was indeed very weak, and was reposing himself upon a green place, under the shade of a tree, and whose

就是半个小时，然后拿起他那由于捆绑变得麻木僵硬的胳膊和膝盖并用手揉擦，按摩。看到这种情形，我从瓶里倒出些酒来让他用酒搓，这使它们好了许多。这一变故使我们不能继续追赶船上的那些野人。那时他们也几乎逃得无影无踪了。没有继续追倒是我们的一件幸事，随后的两个小时风刮得很猛，他们大概走不到四分之一的路程，整个晚上风都刮得很猛，而且是逆着他们走的方向吹，我都难以想象他们是否能活下来并且到达自己的海岸。

再来看看星期五，他忙碌着照顾他的父亲，什么东西都不可能让他转移一下注意力，哪怕是一瞬间，但我认为应该让他离开一会儿。于是我把星期五叫过来，他过来时，边跳边笑，极度兴奋达到极点。我让他给他父亲喝点水，水对他父亲的恢复会比酒和精神力量更加有效，因为我知道他父亲都快渴晕了。

他父亲喝了水之后，我让星期五也拿一些水和面包给那个西班牙人，他的确也很虚弱，正躺在树阴下的一片绿地上，由于他被粗暴地捆绑过，

limbs were also very stiff, and very much swelled with
the rude bandage he had been tied with. When I saw
that, upon Friday's coming up to him with the water, he
sat up and drank, and took the bread and began to eat,
I went up to him and gave him a handful of raisins. He
looked up in my face with all the tokens of gratitude and
thankfulness that could appear in any countenance; but
was so weak, notwithstanding he had so exerted himself
in the fight, that he could not stand upon his feet. He
tried to do it two or three times, but was really not able,
his ankles were so swelled and so painful to him; so I
bade him sit still, and caused Friday to rub his ankles,
and bathe them with rum, as he had done his father's.

As soon as I had secured my two weak, rescued
prisoners, and given them shelter, and a place to rest
upon, I began to think of making some provision for
them; and the first thing I did, I ordered Friday to take
a yearling goat out of my particular flock, to be killed.
Then I cut off the hinder quarter, and chopping it into
small pieces, I set Friday to work to boiling and stewing,
and made them a very good dish of flesh and broth, and
we all enjoyed it and ate heartily. After we had dined,
or rather supped, I ordered Friday to take one of the canoes and go and fetch our muskets and other fire – arms
from the place of battle; and the next day I ordered him

四肢非常僵硬，而且肿胀起来并且肿得十分厉害。我看到星期五拿水过去给他，他坐起来喝水，接过面包，开始吃了起来，我也走过去给了他一把葡萄干，他抬起头看着我，脸上充满了无限的感激之情。但是他实在太虚弱了，而且在打斗中使尽了浑身的力气，几乎站都站不起来，十分吃力的试了两三次，确实不行。他的膝盖又肿又疼，我让他坐着别动并让星期五过去给他揉揉膝盖，并用酒擦擦膝盖，就好像对待他自己的父亲那样。

救醒这两个被我们营救来的奄奄一息的俘房后，我给他们收拾了一个住处，可以临时休息的地方，然后开始想怎么给他们弄点吃的，这是我首先要做的。我先让星期五去我们的牲口棚牵了一头长了一年的山羊，把它杀了，然后我把山羊后半部切下来，剁成小块，并让星期五去烧水把这些山羊肉好好地炖一炖，最后做成了一锅让人垂涎三尺的美味的肉汤，所有的人都狼吞虎咽，好好享用了一番这锅美味佳肴。用完午餐，应该算是用完晚餐，我让星期五划条船去战场上把我们的猎枪及其他武器取回来。第二天，我又让

to go and bury the dead bodies of the savages and I also ordered him to bury the horrid remains of their barbarous feast.

But I was under continual apprehensions for some time, and kept upon my guard, I and all my army; for, as we were now four of us, I would have ventured upon a hundred of them in the open field. In a little time, however, no more canoes appearing, the fear of them coming wore off, and I began to take my former thoughts of a voyage to the main into consideration, being likewise assured, by Friday's farther, that I might depend upon good usage from their nation, in his account, if I would go.

But my thoughts were a little suspended, when I had a serious discovery with the Spaniard, and when I understood that there were sixteen more of his countrymen and Portuguese, who having been cast away, and made their escape to that side, lived there at peace indeed with the savages, but were very sore put to it for necessaries, and indeed for life. I asked him all the particulars of their voyage, and found they were a Spanish ship, bound from the Rio de la Plata to the Havannah, being directed to leave their loading there, which was chiefly hides and silver, and to bring back what European goods they could meet with there; that they had five

他把野人的尸体统统埋了，还有野人宴上剩下的令人发指的人肉也埋了。

但是有一段时间我一直感觉忐忑不安，为我以及拥有我的这一小队人马保持高度警觉。现在我们已经是拥有四个人的小团体，在外面的空地上或许能和百十号野人干上一仗。然而，一时也没有船来，萦绕在我脑中的恐惧也慢慢消失了，脑子里重新又想着如何才能回到大陆，对这个我最关心的问题星期五的父亲又一次向我保证，如果我愿意，可以用他们部落的力量来协助我。

我当时有点儿犹豫，因为我从西班牙人那里得到一个重要消息，了解到有至少十六个葡萄牙人和西班牙人在船上遇难后，逃到了那边的岛上，和野人一块过起了平静安详的生活，但日常必需品极度缺乏，实际生活十分艰辛。我询问了他有关他们出海的细节，了解到他们乘的是一艘西班牙人的船，从拉普拉塔开到哈瓦那。他们奉命把船上的货物——大多是些兽皮和银子——运到欧洲，换回他们在那里能见到的所有东西。上面还

Portuguese seamen on board, whom they took out of another wreck; that five of their own men were drowned when first their ship was lost; and that these escaped through infinite dangers and hazards, and arrived, almost starved, on the cannibal coast, where they expected to be devoured every moment.

He told me they had some arms with them, but they were perfectly useless, for they had neither powder nor ball, the washing of the sea having spoiled their powder, but a little, which they used at their first landing to provide themselves some food. I asked him what he thought would become of them there, and if they had formed no design of making an escape. He said they had many consultations about it, but having neither vessel, nor tools to build one, nor provisions of any kind, their counsel always ended in tears and despair. I asked him how he thought they would receive a proposal from me, which might tend towards an escape; whether, if they were all here, it might not be done.

He told me they were all under the greatest distress imaginable, and if I would undertake their relief, they would live and die by me. Upon these assurances, I resolved to venture to relieve them, if possible, and to send the old savage and the Spaniard over to them to treat. But when he had gotten all the things in readiness

有五个葡萄牙船员，他们是从另一艘失事的船上被解救下来的。第一艘船失事时，五个他们的人淹死在海里了。从极度危险的环境中逃出来的人都饿得头晕目眩，最后他们来到了一个野人居住的海岸上，在那里随时都会面临着生命危险。

他告诉我那些人手中有些武器，但一点儿用也没有，因为他们既没火药也没子弹，而且海水浸湿了火药，剩下一点儿能用的，也在他们刚上岸时用来打猎找食了。我问他如何看待他们，他们是否都没了逃跑的意图。他说他们一块儿商讨过这个问题很多次，但是因为他们一没有船，二没有造船的工具，也没有造船的材料。所以每次开会他们都是以眼泪和绝望而告终。我问他觉得那些人会不会接受我逃跑的建议；如果他们都来了，事情就办不成了，这就会破坏我的全盘计划了。

他说那些人正遭受着常人难以想象的痛苦和折磨，如果我能让他们解脱这种痛苦逃出这个地方，他们定会对我生死相随。得到这些保证，我决定冒险去解救他们，如果可能的话就派这个老野人和西班牙人去协商。但是当一切准备就绪，

to go, the Spaniard himself started an objection, which had so much prudence in it on the one hand, and so much sincerity on the other hand, that I could not but well satisfied in it; and, by his advice, put off the deliverance of his comrades for at least half a year. The case was thus: He had been with us now about a month, during which time had let him see in what manner I had provided, with the assistance of Providence, for my support; and he saw evidently what stock of corn and rice I had laid up, which, as it was more than sufficient for myself, so it was not sufficient, at least without good husbandry, for my family, now it was increased to the number of four; but much less would it be sufficient, if his countrymen, who were, as he said, fourteen, still alive, should come over; and, least of all, would it be sufficient to victual our vessel, if we should build one, for a voyage to the Christian colonies of America. So he told me he thought it would be more advisable to let him and the two others dig and cultivate more land as much as I could spare seed to sow; and that we should wait another harvest, then we might have a supply of corn for his countrymen, when they should come; for want might be a temptation to them to disagree, or not think themselves delivered, otherwise than out of one difficulty into another.

我们马上就要启程时，西班牙人提出反对意见，他的意见既出于谨慎又出于真诚，让我万分高兴，对他的建议非常满意。根据他的建议，我们应当推迟至少半年再去营救他的那些同行者。事情是这样的：他已经和我们呆了一个月，看到了在上帝保佑和我的支撑下，我们是如何维持生计的，很明显他知道我贮存的玉米和大米，对我一个人来说肯定是足够的，但要维持两个人的生活就难了。现在我们已增长到四口人，那就更不够吃了。如果照他所说的，他那十四个同胞仍然活着，如果到了这边，更供给不了整船的人。当然了，假如我们能够造出这艘船驶向美国那个基督教征服的殖民地的话事情就好办多了。所以他告诉我让他和另外两个人多开些荒地，多种些粮食这样做会更合适些。等到下次收获庄稼的时候，如果他的同胞来，我们也可以供应他们一些粮食了，而且这些必需品对他们来说也具有一种诱惑感，使他们不至于认为自己从一个困境到了另外一个困境。

His caution was so reasonable, and his advice so good, that I could not but be very well pleased with his proposal, as well as I was satisfied with his fidelity. So we fell to digging, all four of us, as well as the wooden tools we were furnished with permitted; and in about a month's time, by the end of which it was seed – time, we had gotten as much land cured, and trimmed up, as we sowed twenty – two bushels of barley on, and sixteen jars of rice, which was, in short, all the seed we had to spare.

At the same time, I contrived to increase my little flock of tame goats as much as I could; and to this purpose I made Friday and the Spaniard go out one day, and myself with Friday the next day, for we took our turns; and, by this means, we got about twenty young kids to breed up with the rest; for whenever we shot the dam we saved the kids, and added them to our flock. But, above all, the season for curing the grapes coming on, I caused such a prodigious quantity to be hung up in the sun, and this, with our bread, was a great part of our food.

It was now harvest, and our crop in good order. It was not the most plentiful increase I had seen in the island; but, however, it was enough to answer our end, for, from our twenty – two bushels of barley, we brought in and thrashed out above two hundred and twenty bush-

他的担心合情合理，建议也很好，对于他的提议，我很高兴，对于他的忠诚我也十分满意。于是我们开始使用所能找到的木制工具来翻地，直干到四个人都筋疲力尽为止。因为一个月后的月底就是播种时间，到时我们就得把地翻好并且平整好，然后种下二十二蒲式耳大麦，十六坛子大米，也可以说种下我们能够省下的所有的粮食。

同时，我们又尽量去繁殖羊群。为了这件事情，我让星期五和西班牙人出去一天，星期五和我第二天再出去。我们轮着来。这样，除了原有的羊，我们羊群里又增加了二十只小羊，因为射死母羊之后，我们总是把留下幼崽，把它们放到羊群里以增加我们羊群的数量。接着，最重要的收获葡萄干的季节到来了，我晒了大量的葡萄干，加上原有的面包，现在已经有不少食物供我们食用了。

现在，收获的季节到了，我们的庄稼收成也很好，但却不是在这岛上我见到的增产最多的一次，但也算对得起我们的付出的劳动了。因为种下的那二十二蒲式耳大麦，我们收回来后打出了

els, and the like in proportion of the rice, which was store enough for our food to the next harvest, though all the fourteen Spaniards had been on shore with me; or, if we had been ready for a voyage, it would very plentifully have victualled our ship to have carried us to any part of the world. When we had thus housed and secured our magazine of corn, we fell to work to make more wicker work, namely, great baskets in which we kept it; and the Spaniard was very handily and dexterous at this part.

And now, having a full supply of food for all guests I expected, I gave the Spaniard leave over to the main, to see what he could do with those he had left behind him there. I gave him strict charge not to bring any man with him. Under this instruction, the Spaniard and the old savage, went away in one of the canoes. I gave each of them a musket, and about eight charges of powder and ball, charging them to be very careful of both, and not to use either of them, but upon very urgent occasions.

This was a cheerful work, being the first measure used by me, in view of my deliverance, for now twenty – seven years and some days. I gave them provisions of bread and of dried grapes, sufficient for themselves for many days, and sufficient for all their countrymen for about eight days; and wishing them a good voyage, I let them go, agreeing with them about a signal they should

二百二十多蒲式耳大麦，大米的增产率也差不多如此。这样，即使那十四个西班牙人全来了，贮存的食物也足够支撑到下一次收获的季节。如果我们准备出海，带上这些食物可以供我们走到世界任何地方。把粮食储存起来，掩藏好以后，我们开始用柳条编织，编成用来盛粮食的大篮子，那西班牙人编起来特别敏捷灵巧。

给客人的食物准备好后，我让西班牙人起身去那个大一些的岛，去看看被他落在那里的人，我命令他这次不要带任何人回来。带着这个嘱托，西班牙人和老野人乘一艘小船动身离开了。我给他们每人一把步枪，八颗子弹和小弹丸，嘱咐他们要小心谨慎使用，除非情况很紧急，否则不要用。

考虑到我马上就要解脱，我所采取的这第一步，是二十七年多以来一件十分令人高兴的事情。我让他们带了面包和葡萄干等食物，足够他们吃好几天的，足够他那些老乡维持八天的生计，给他们说了一路顺风的祝愿之后，我就让他们上路

hang out at their return, by which I should know them again, when they came back, at distance before they came on shore. They went away, with a fair gale, on the day that the moon was at the full, by my account, in the month of October, as near as I could tell.

Chapter 19   The Sighting of a Boat

It was no less than eight days I waited for them, when a strange and unforeseen occurrence intervened, of which the like has not, perhaps, been heard of in history. I was fast asleep in my hut one morning, when my Friday came running in to me, and called aloud, "Master, master, they are come, they are come!" I jumped up, regardless of danger, went out, as soon as I could get my clothes on, through my little grove; I went without my arms, which it was not my custom to do; but I was surprised, when, turning my eyes to the sea, I presently saw a boat a league and a half distance, standing in for the shore, with a shoulder – of – mutton sail, and the wind blowing fair to bring them in. Also, I observed, that they did not come from that side which the shore lay on, but from the southern – most end of the island. Upon this I called Friday in, and bade him lie close, for these were not the people we looked for, and that we did

了。商量好在他们回来时在船上挂一标记，我们可以在他们上岸前远远地看到他们。他们走了，正好顺风，那天月亮很圆，据我推算，应该差不多是十月份。

第十九章　柳暗花明

他们走后，我刚刚等到第八天，忽然发生了一件意外的事情。这件事那么奇特，那么出人意料，也许是有史以来闻所未闻的。那天早晨，我在自己的茅舍里睡得正香，忽然星期五跑进来，边跑边嚷："主人，主人，他们来了！他们来了！"我立即从床上跳起来，不顾一切危险，急忙披上衣服，穿过小树林，跑了出来。我说不顾一切危险，意思是我连武器都没有带就跑出来了。这完全违反了我平时的习惯。当我放眼向海上望去时，不觉大吃一惊。只见四五海里之外，有一只小船，正挂着一副所谓"羊肩帆"向岸上驶来。当时正好顺风，把小船往岸上送。接着我就注意到，那小船不是从大陆方向来的，而是从岛的最南端驶过来的。于是我把星期五叫到身边，叫他不要离开我。因为，这些人不是我们所期待的人，现在

not know yet whether they were friends or enemies.

In the next place, I went in to fetch my perspective glass, to see what I could make of them; and, having taken the ladder out, I climb up to the top of the till, as I used to do when I was apprehensive of anything, and to take my view plainer, without being discovered. I had scarce set my foot on the hill, when my eye discovered a ship lying at anchor, at about two leagues and a half distance from me, but not above a league and a half from the shore. It appeared plainly to be an English long – boat.

I cannot express the confusion I was in, though the joy of seeing a ship, and one which I had reason to believe was manned by my own countrymen, and consequently friends, was such as I cannot describe; but yet I had some secret doubts hanging about me, I cannot tell from whence they came, bidding me to be on my guard. I began to consider what business an English ship could have here; since it was not the way to or from any part of the world where the English had any traffic; and I knew there had been no storm to drive them in there, as in distress; and that if they were English really, it was probable they were here upon good design, and that I had better continue as I was than fall into the hands of thieves and murderers.

还不清楚他们是敌是友。

然后，我马上回家去取望远镜，想看清楚他们究竟是些什么人。我搬出梯子，爬上山顶。每当我对什么东西放心不下，想看个清楚，而又不想被别人发现，就总是爬到这山上来瞭望。我一上小山，就看见一条大船在我东南偏南的地方停泊着，离我所在的位置大约有七八海里，离岸最多四五海里。我一看就知道，那是一艘英国船，而那只小船样子也是一条英国小艇。

我当时混乱的心情实难言表。一方面，我看到了一艘大船，而且有理由相信船上有我的同胞，是自己人，心里有一种说不出的高兴。然而，另一方面，我心里又产生了一种怀疑。我不知道这种怀疑从何而来，但却促使我警惕起来。首先，我想，一条英国船为什么要开到这一带来呢？因为这儿不是英国人在世界上贸易往来的要道。其次，我知道，近来并没有发生过什么暴风雨，不可能把他们的船刮到这一带来。如果他们真的是英国人，他们到这一带来，一定没安好心。我与其落到盗贼和罪犯手里，还不如像以前那样过下去。

When they were on shore, I was fully satisfied they were Englishmen, at least most of them; one or two I thought were Dutch. There were in all, eleven men, whereof three I found were unarmed, and bound; and when the first four or five of them jumped on shore, they took these three out of the boat as prisoners. One of the three I could perceive using the most passionate gestures of entreaty, affliction, and despair, the other two lifted up their hands sometimes, and appeared concerned indeed, but not so much as the first.

I was perfectly confounded at the sight, and knew not what the meaning of it could be. Friday called out to me, "O master, you see English mans eat prisoners as well as savage mans." "Why," said I, "do you think they are going to eat them, then?" "Yes," says Friday, "they will eat them." "No, no," said I, "Friday, I am afraid they will murder them, indeed, but you may be sure they will not eat them."

All this while I had no thoughts of what the matter really was, but expected every moment the three prisoners would be killed; and once I saw one of the villains lift up his arm, with a great cutlass or sword, to strike one of the poor men, and I expected to see him fall every moment. I wished heartily now for my Spaniard, and the savage that was gone with him; or that I had any way to

他们上岸之后，我看出他们果然都是英国人，至少大部分是英国人。其中有一两个看样子像荷兰人，但后来证明并不是荷兰人。他们一共有十一个人，其中三个好像没有带武器，而且仿佛被绑起来了似的。船一靠岸，就有四五个人首先跳上岸，然后把三个人押下船来。我看到其中有一个正在那里指手画脚，做出种种恳求、悲痛和失望的姿势，其动作真有点过火。另外两个人我看到有时也举起双手，显出很苦恼的样子，但没有第一个人那样激动。

我看到这幅情景，真有点莫名其妙，不知他们究竟在搞什么名堂。星期五在旁边一直用英语对我喊道："啊，主人，你看英国人也吃俘虏，同野人一样！""怎么，星期五，"我说，"你以为他们会吃那几个人吗？""是的。""星期五，我看他们会杀死他们，但决不会吃他们，这我敢担保！"

这时，我不知道眼前发生的一切究竟是怎么回事，只是站在那里，看着这可怕的情景发抖，并一直担心那三个俘虏会给他们杀掉。有一次，我看到一个恶棍甚至举起一把水手们称为腰刀的那种长刀，向其中一个可怜的人砍去，眼看他就要倒下来了。这使我吓得不寒而栗。我真心希望西班牙人和那个野人赶快逃离，同时也希望我能

come undiscovered within shot of them, that I might have rescued the three men, for they had no firearms that I saw.

After I had observed the outrageous usage of the three men by the insolent seamen, I saw that the fellows ran scattering about the land, as if they wanted to see the country. I observed, also, that the three other men had liberty to go where they pleased, but that they sat down all three upon the ground, very pensive, and looked like men in despair.

It was just at the top of high water when these people came on the shore and while partly they stood parleying with the prisoners they brought, and partly while they rambled about to see what kind of place they were in, they had carelessly stayed till the tide was spent, and the water was ebbed considerably away, leaving the boat aground.

It was my design, as I said before, not to have made any attempt until it was dark; but about two o'clock, being the heat of the day, I found that they were all gone straggling into the woods, and, as I thought, all laid down to sleep. The three poor distressed men, too anxious for their condition to get any sleep, were, however, sat down under the shelter of a great tree, out of sight of any of the rest.

接近他们而不被发现， 这样我有可能拯救这三个人，因我看见他们未带任何武器。

我看到，那伙盛气凌人的水手把那三个人横暴地虐待一番之后，都在岛上四散走开了，好像想看看这儿的环境。同时，我也发现，那三个俘虏的行动也很自由，但他们三个人都在地上坐了下来，一副心事重重和绝望的样子。

海上风越来越大，把浪头掀得老高，这时这些人来到岸边。他们有些人和他们带来的俘虏谈话，有些则四处东游西逛，察看这个他们所到之处是什么样子，他们无所事事一直呆到海水退潮，风平浪静，船只被搁浅在海滩。

上面我已经说过，我不想在天黑之前采取任何行动。下午两点种左右，天气最热。我发现他们都三三两两地跑到树林里，大概去睡觉了。那三个可怜的人，深为自己目前的处境忧虑，睡也睡不着，只好在一棵大树的荫凉下呆呆地坐着，离我大约有一百多码远。而且，看样子其他人看不见他们坐的地方。

Upon this I resolved to discover myself to them, and learn something of their condition. I immediately I marched with my man Friday at a good distance behind me, as formidable for his arms as I, but not making quite so staring a specter – like figure as I did. I came as near them undiscovered as I could, and then, before any of them saw me, I called aloud to them, in Spanish, "What are ye, gentleman?"

They started up at the noise, but were ten times more confounded when they saw me, and the uncouth figure I made. They made no answer at all, but I thought I perceived them just going to fly from me, when I spoke to them in English: "Gentlemen," said I, "do not be surprised at me; perhaps you may have a friend near you when you do not expect it." "He must be sent directly from heaven, then," said one of them very gravely to me, and pulling off his hat at the same time, "for our condition is past the help of man." "All help is from heaven, sir," said I, "but can you put a stranger in the way now to help you, for you seem to be in some great distress? I saw you when you landed; and when seemed to make application to the brutes that came with you, I saw one lift up his sword to kill you."

The poor man, with tears running down his face, and trembling, looking like one astonished, returned.

看到这种情况，我决定走过去了解一下他们的情况。我马上向他们走过去。我上面说了，我的样子狰狞可怕；我的仆人星期五远远地跟在我后面，也是全副武装，样子像我一样可怕，但比我稍好一些，不像我那样，像个怪物。我稍稍走近他们，还没等到他们看见我，我就抢先用西班牙语向他们喊道："先生们，你们是什么人？"

　　听到喊声，他们吃了一惊，可看到我的那副怪模怪样，更是惊恐万分，连话都说不出来了。我见他们想要逃跑的样子，就用英语对他们说："先生们，别害怕。也许，你们想不到，在你们眼前的人，正是你们的朋友呢?!""他们一定是天上派下来的，"其中一个说，并脱帽向我致礼，神情十分认真，"因为我们的处境非人力所能挽救得了。""一切拯救都来自天上，先生，"我说，"你们看来正处于极大的危难之中，你们能让一个陌生人来帮助你们吗？你们上岸时，我早就看见了。你们向那些和你们一起来的蛮横的家伙哀求的时候，其中有一个人甚至举起刀来要杀害你们呢！这一切我都看到了。"

　　那可怜的人泪流满面，浑身发抖，显得惊异。

"Am I talking to God or man? Is it a real man, or an angel?" "Be in no fear about that, sir," said I, "if God had sent an angel to relieve you, he would have come better clothed, and armed after another manner, than you see me. Pray lay aside your fears; I am a man, an Englishman, and disposed to assist you, you see. I have one servant only; we have arms and ammunition, tell us freely, can we serve you? What is your case?"

"Our case, sir," said he, "is too long to tell you, while our murderers are so near; but, in short, sir, I was commander of that ship, my men have mutinied against me, they have been hardly prevailed upon not to murder me, and, at last, have set me on shore in desolate place, with these two men with me, one my mate, the other a passenger, where we expected to perish, believing the place to be uninhabited, and know not yet what to think of it."

"Where are those brutes, your enemies?" said I; "do you know where they are gone?" "There they are, sir," said he, pointing to a thicket of trees; "my heart trembles for fear they have seen us, and heard you speak; if they have, they will murder us all."

"Have they any fire – arms?" said I. He answered, "They had only two pieces, and one which they left in the boat." "Well, then," said I, "leave the rest to me.

他回答说："我是在对上帝说话呢，还是在对人说话？你是人，还是天使？""这你不用担心，先生，"我说，"如果上帝真的派一位天使来拯救你们，他的穿戴一定会比我好得多，他的武器也一定完全不一样。请你们放心吧。我是人，而且是英国人。你们看，我是来救你们的。我只有一个仆人。我们都有武器。请你们大胆告诉我们，我们能为你们效劳吗？你们到底发生了什么事？"

"我们的事，先生，"他说，"说来话长，而我们的凶手又近在咫尺。现在，就长话短说吧，先生。我是那条船的船长，我手下的人反叛了。我好不容易才说服他们不杀我。最后，他们把我和这两个人一起押送到这个岛上来。他们一个是大副，一个是旅客。我们想，在这个岛上，我们一定会饿死的。我们相信，这是一个没有人烟的荒岛，真不知道怎么办呢！"

"你们的敌人，那些暴徒，现在在什么地方？"我问，"你们知道他们到哪儿去啦？""他们正在那边躺着呢，先生。"他指着一个灌木林说，"我现在心里吓得直发抖。怕他们看到我们，听到你说话。要那样的话，我们没命了！"

"他们有没有枪支？"我问。他回答说，他们只有两支枪，一支留在船上了。"那就好了，"我说，"一切由我来处理吧。我看他们现在都睡着

I see they are asleep. It is an easy thing to kill them all; but shall we rather take them prisoners?" He told me there were two desperate villains among them, that was scarce safe to show any mercy to, but if they were secured, he believed all the rest would return to their duty. I asked him which they were. He told me he could not, at that distance, describe them; but he would obey my orders in anything I would direct. "Well," said I, "let us retreat out of their view or hearing, lest they awake, and we will resolve farther." So they willingly went back with me, till the woods covered us from them.

"Look you, sir," said I, "if I venture upon your deliverance, are you willing to make two conditions with me?" He anticipated my proposals, by telling me, that both he and the ship, if recovered, should be wholly directed and commanded by me in everything; and if the ship was not recovered, he would live and die with me, in what part of the world so ever I would send him, and the two others said the same.

"Well," said I, "my conditions are but two, first, that while you stay on this island with me, you will not pretend to any authority here; and if I put arms in your hands, you will, upon all occasions, give them up to me, and do no prejudice to me or mine, upon this island; and, in the mean time, be governed by my orde-

了，一下子就能全部干掉。不过，是不是活捉更好？"他对我说，其中有两个是亡命之徒，决不能饶恕他们。只要把这两个坏蛋解决了，其余的人就会回到自己的工作岗位上去。我问是哪两个人。他说现在距离太远，看不清楚，不过他愿意服从我的指挥。"那好吧，"我说，"我们退远一点，免得给他们醒来时看到或听到。回头我们再商量办法吧。"于是，他们高兴地跟着我往回走，一直走到树林后面隐蔽好。

"请你听着，先生，"我说，"我如果冒险救你们，你们愿意和我订两个条件吗？"他没等我把条件说出来，就先说，只要把大船收复回来，他和他的船完全听从我的指挥。如果船收复不回来，他也情愿与我共生死，同存亡；我要上哪儿就上哪儿。另外两个人也同样这样说。

"好吧，"我说，"我只有两个条件。第一，你们留在岛上期间，决不能侵犯我在这里的主权；如果我发给你们武器，无论什么时候，只要我向你们要回，你们就得交还给我。你们不得在这岛上反对我或我手下的人，并必须完全服从我的管

rs. Secondly, that if the ship is, or may be, recovered, you will carry me and my man to England passage free."

He gave me all the assurances that the invention and faith of man could devise, that he would comply with these most reasonable demands, and, besides, would own his life to me, and acknowledge it, upon all occasions, as long as he lived. "Well, then," said I, "here are three muskets for you, with powder and ball. Tell me next what you think is proper to be done." He showed all the testimony of his gratitude that he was able; but offered to be wholly guided by me. I told him I thought it was hard venturing anything, but the best method I could think of was to fire upon them at once, as they lay; and if any were not killed at the first volley, and offered to submit, we might save them, and so put it wholly upon God's providence to direct the shot.

Animated with this, he took the musket I had given him in his hand, and a pistol in his belt, and his two comrades with him, each man a piece in his hand. There were three more in the company, and one of them was also slightly wounded. By this time I came; and when they saw their danger, and that it was in vain to resist, they begged for mercy. The captain told them he would spare their lives, if they would give him any assurance of their abhorrence of the treachery they had

教。第二，如果那只大船收复回来，你们必须把我和我的仆人免费送回英国。"

他向我提出了种种保证，凡是想得到和使人信得过的保证，都提出来了。他还说，我的这些要求是完全合情合理的，他将会彻底履行；同时，他还要感谢我的救命之恩，终身不忘。"那好吧，"我说，"现在我交给你们三支短枪，还有火药和子弹。现在，你们看，下一步该怎么办？"他一再向我表示感谢，并说他情愿听从我的指挥。我对他说，现在的事情很棘手，不过，我认为，最好趁他们现在还睡着，就向他们开火。如果第一排枪放过后还有活着的，并且愿意投降，那就可以饶他们的命。至于开枪之后能打死多少人，那就只好听从上帝的安排了。

听了我的话，他受到激励，就把我给他的短枪拿在手里，又把一支枪插在皮带上。他的两个伙伴也跟着他一起去了，每人手里也都拿着一支枪。跟那两个水手在一起的还有其余三个人，其中有一个已经受了轻伤。就在这时，我也到了。他们看到了危险临头，知道抵抗已没有用了，就只好哀求我们饶他们一命。船长告诉他们，他可以饶他们的命，但他们得向他保证，表示痛恨

been guilty of, and would swear to be faithful to him in recovering the ship, and afterwards in carrying her back to Jamaica, from whence they came. They gave him all the protestations of their sincerity that could be desired, and he was willing to believe them, and spare their lives, which I was not against; only I obliged him to keep them bound, hand and foot, while they were upon the island.

While this was doing, I sent Friday, with the captain's mate, to the boat, with orders to secure her, and bring away the oars and sail, which they did. Three straggling men, that were parted from the rest, came back again upon hearing the guns fired; and seeing their captain, who was before their prisoner, now their conqueror, they submitted to be bound also.

It now remained that the captain and I should inquire into one another's circumstances. I began first, and told him my whole story, which he heard with an attention even to amazement, and particularly at the wonderful manner of my being furnished with provisions and ammunition; and, indeed, as my story is whole collection of wonder, it affected him deeply, but when he reflected from thence upon himself, and how I seemed to have been preserved there on purpose to save his life, the tears ran down his face, and he could not speak a

自己所犯的反叛的罪行，并宣誓效忠船长，帮他把大船夺回来，然后开回牙买加，因为他们正是从牙买加来的。他们竭力向船长表示他们的诚意，船长也愿意相信他们，并饶他们的命。对此我也表示并不反对，只是要求船长在他们留在岛上期间，应把他们的手脚绑起来。

与此同时，我派星期五和船长手下的大副到那小船上去，命令他们把船扣留下来，并把上面的几只桨和帆拿下来。他们都一一照办了。不一会儿，有三个在别处闲逛的人因听到了枪声，这时也回来了。他们看见他们的船长，不久前还是他们的俘虏，现在却一下子变成了他们的征服者，也就俯首就缚。

现在，船长和我已经有时间来打听彼此的情况了。我先开口，把我全部经历告诉了他。他全神贯注地听我讲着，显出无限惊讶的神情。特别是在我讲到怎样用奇妙的方式弄到粮食和军火时，更显得惊讶万分。他听了我的故事，大为感动，因为我的经历，实在是一连串的奇迹。可是当他从我的故事联想到自己的遭遇，想到上帝仿佛有意让我活下来救他的命时，他不禁泪流满面，泣

word more.

Upon this, I told him the first thing we had to do was to stave the boat, which lay upon the beach, so that they might not carry her off, and take everything out of her, leave her so far useless as not to be fit to swim. Accordingly we went on board, took the arms which were left on board out of her, and whatever else we found there.

When we had carried all these things on shore, we knocked a great hole in her bottom, that if they had come strong enough to master us, yet they could not carry off the boat.

Indeed, it was much in my thoughts that we could be capable to recover the ship; but my view was that if they went away without the boat, I did not much question to make her fit again to carry us away to the Leeward Islands, and call upon our friends the Spaniards in my way.

While we were thus preparing our designs, and had first, by main strength, heaved the boat up on the beach, so that the tide would not float her off at high – water mark; and besides, had broken a hole in her bottom too big to be quickly stopped, and sat down musing what we should do, we heard the ship fire a gun, and saw her make a waft, as a signal for the boat to come on

不成声了。

于是，我告诉他，我们首先应该把搁浅在沙滩上的那只小船凿破，把船上所有的东西都拿下来，使它无法下水，他们就无法把它划走。于是我们一齐上了小船，把留在上面的那支枪拿了下来，又把上面所能找到的东西通通拿下来。

我们把剩下的这些东西搬上岸之后，又在船底凿了一个洞。这样一来，即使他们有充分的实力战胜我们，也没法把小船划走。

说实话，我认为收复大船的把握不大。我的看法是，只要他们不把那只小船弄走，我们就可以把它重新修好。那样，我们就可乘它去利华德群岛，顺便把那些西班牙朋友也可带走。因为我心里还时刻记着他们。

我们立即按计划行事。首先，我们竭尽全力，把小船推到较高的沙滩上。这样，即使潮水上涨，也不致把船浮起来；何况，我们已在船底凿了个大洞，短时间内无法把洞补好。正当我们坐在地上，寻思着下一步计划时，只听见大船上放了一枪，并且摇动旗帜发出信号，叫小船回去。可是，

board; but no boat stirred, and they fired several times, making other signals for the boat.

At last, when all their signals and firings proved fruitless, and they found the boat did not stir, we saw them hoist another boat off, and row towards the shore and we found, as they approached, that there were no less than ten men in her, and that they had fire – arms with them.

As the ship lay almost two leagues from the shore, we had a full view of them as they came. The captain knew the persons and characters of all the men in the boat, of whom he said that there were three very honest fellows, who, he was sure, were led into this conspiracy by the rest, being overpowered and frightened, but that as for the boatswain, who was the chief officer among them, and all the rest, they were as outrageous as any of the ship's crew, and were, no doubt, made desperate in their new enterprise.

As soon as they got to the place where their other boat lay, they ran their boat into the beach, and came all on shore, hauling the boat up after them, which I was glad to see; for I was afraid they would rather have left the boat, and anchor some distance from the shore, with some hands in her to guard her, and so we should not be able to seize the boat.

他们看不见小船上有任何动静。于是，接着又放了几枪，并向小船又发出了一些别的信号。

最后，他们见信号和放枪都没有用处，小船还是没有任何动静，我们在望远镜里看见他们把另一只小船放下来，向岸上摇来。当他们逐渐靠近时，我们看出小船上载着不下十来人，而且都带着枪支。

那条大船停泊在离岸大约两海里的地方，他们来的时候，我们看得非常清楚。船长知道那条小船上所有的人，也说得出每个人的性格如何，他说其中有三个很老实的家伙，他相信他们是在其余人的胁迫下参与这阴谋的。至于那水手长，看起来是他们的头目，他和剩下的那几个都是船员中最凶悍的家伙，毫无疑问是要干到底了。

那批人来到头一只小船停泊的地方，马上把他们自己的小船推到沙滩上，船上的人也通通下了船，一齐把小船拉到岸上。看到这一情景，我心里非常高兴。因为我就怕他们把小船在离岸较远的地方下锚，再留几个人在船上看守。那样我们就没法夺取小船了。

Being on shore, they ran all to the other boat; and it was easy to see they were under a great surprise to find her stripped, and a great hole in the bottom.

After this, they set up a great shout; but it was all to no purpose, then they came all close in a ring, and fired a volley of their small arms, which indeed we heard, and the echoes made the woods ring, but it was all one; those in the cave we were sure could not learn, and those in our keeping, though they heard it well enough, yet durst give no answer to them.

They were surprised at this, as they told us afterwards, that they resolved to go all on board again to their ship, and let them know there that the men were all murdered, and the long boat staved; accordingly, they immediately launched their boat again, and got all of them on board. The captain was terribly amazed, and even confounded at this, believing they would go on board the ship again, and set sail, giving their comrades up for lost, and so he should still lose the ship, which he was in hopes we should have recovered, but he was quickly as much frightened the other way.

They had not been long put off with the boat, but we perceived them all coming on shore again; and they left three men in the boat, and the rest went up into the country to look for their fellows. This was a great disap-

一上岸，他们首先一齐跑去看前一只小船。不难看出，当他们发现船上空空如也，船底上有一个大洞时，个个都大吃一惊。

　　他们把眼前看到的情景寻思了一会儿，就一起使劲大喊了两三次，想叫他们的同伴听见。可是毫无结果。接着，他们又围成一圈，放了一排枪。这片枪声我们当然听见了，而且枪声的回声把树林都震响了。可是结果还是一样。那些关在洞里的，自然听不见；那些被我们看守着的，虽然听得很清楚，却不敢作任何反应。

　　这事大大出乎他们的意料，使他们万分惊讶。事后他们告诉我们，他们当时决定回到大船上去，告诉船上的人说，那批人都给杀光了，船也给凿沉了。于是，他们马上把小船推到水里，一齐上了船。看到他们的这一举动，船长非常吃惊，简直不知怎么办好了。他相信，他们一定会回到大船上去，把船开走，因为他们一定认为他们的伙伴都已没命了。那样的话，他原来想收复大船的希望就落空了。可是，不久，他看到那批人又有了新的举动，又一次使他惶恐不安起来。

　　他们把船划出不远，我们看到他们又一齐重新回到岸上。这次行动他们采取了新的措施，看来是他们刚才已商量好的。那就是，留三个人在小船上，其余的人一齐上岸，深入小岛去寻找他

pointment to us, for now we were at a loss what to do; for our seizing those seven men on shore would be of no advantage to us if we let the boat escape, because they would then row away to the ship, and then the rest of them would be sure to weigh, and set sail, and so our hope of recovering the ship would be lost.

However, we had no remedy but to wait and see what the issue of things might present. The seven men came on shore, and the three who remained in the boat put her off to a good distance from the shore, and came to an anchor, to wait for them, so that it was impossible for us to come at them in the boat.

Those that came on shore kept close together, marching towards the top of the little hill, under which my habitation lay, and we could see them plainly, though they could not perceive us.

The captain made a very just proposal to me upon this consultation of theirs, namely, that perhaps they would all fire a volley again, to endeavor to make their fellows hear, and that we should all sally upon them just at the juncture when their pieces were all discharged, and they would certainly yield, and we should have them without bloodshed. I liked the proposal, provided it was done while we were near enough to come up to them before they could load their pieces again.

们的伙伴。这使我们大失所望，简直不知怎么办才好。因为如果我们让小船开跑，即使我们把岸上的七个人统统抓住，那也毫无用处。那三个人必然会把小船划回大船，大船上的人必然会起锚扬帆而去，那我们收复大船的希望同样会落空。

可是，我们除了静候事情的发展，别无良策。那七个人上岸了。三个留在船上的人把船划得离岸远远的，然后下锚停泊等岸上的人。这样一来，我们也无法向小船发动攻击。

那批上岸的人紧紧走在一起，向那小山头前进。而那小山下，就是我的住所。我们可以把他们看得清清楚楚，可他们根本看不到我们。

船长向我提出一个建议，这建议确实合情合理。那就是，他们或许还会开一排枪，目的是想让他们的伙伴听见。我们应趁他们刚开完枪，就一拥而上。那时他们只好束手就擒，我们就可以不流一滴血把他们制服。我对这个建议很满意。但是，我们必须尽量接近他们，在他们来不及装上弹药前就冲上去。

But this event did not happen, and we lay still a long time, very irresolute what course to take; at length I told them there would be nothing to be done, in my opinion, till night; and then, if they did not return to the boat, perhaps we might use some stratagem with them in the boat to get them on shore.

We waited a great while, and were very uneasy; when we saw them all start up, and march towards the sea. It seemed they had such dreadful apprehensions upon them of the danger of the place, that they resolved to go on board the ship again, give their companions over for lost, and so go on their intended voyage with the ship.

I ordered Friday and the captain's mate to go over the little creek westward, towards the place where Friday was rescued, and at about half a mile distance, I bade them halloo as loud as they could, and as soon as they heard the seamen answer them, they should return it again, and then, keeping out of sight, take a round, and then wheel about again to me by such ways as I directed.

They were just going into the boat, when Friday and the mate hallooed, and they presently heard them, and answering, ran along the shore westward, towards the voice they heard, when they were stopped by the

可是，他们并没有开枪。我们悄悄地在那里埋伏了很久，不知怎么办才好。最后，我告诉他们，在我看来，天黑之前我们不能采取任何行动。但到了晚上，如果他们不回到小船上去，我们也许可以想出什么办法包抄到他们和海岸中间，用什么策略对付那几个小船上的人，引他们上岸。

我们又等了很久，心里忐忑不安，巴不得他们离开。只见他们商议了半天，忽然一起跳起来，向海边走去。这一下，我们心里真有点慌了。看来，他们很害怕这儿真有什么危险，并认为他们那些伙伴都已完蛋了，所以决定不再寻找他们，回大船上去继续他们原定的航行计划。

我命令星期五和那位大副越过小河往西走，一直走到那批野人押着星期五登陆的地方，并叫他们在半英里外的那片高地上，尽量大声叫喊，一直喊到让那些水手听见为止。我又交待他们，在听到那些水手回答之后，再回叫几声，然后不要让他们看见，兜上一个大圈子，一面叫着，一面应着，尽可能把他们引往小岛深处。然后，再按照我指定的路线迂回到我这边来。

那些人刚要上小船，星期五和大副就大声喊叫起来。他们马上听见了，就一面回答，一面沿海岸往西跑。他们朝着喊话的方同跑去。跑了一阵，他们就被小河挡住了去路。当时小河正值涨

creek, the water being up, they could not get over, and called for the boat to come and set them over, as, indeed, I expected.

When they had set themselves over, I observed that they took one of the three men out of her, and left only two in the boat, having fastened her to a stump of a little tree on the shore.

This was what I wished for; and immediately leaving Friday and the captain's mate to their business, I took the rest with me, and crossing the creek out of their sight, we surprised the two men before they were aware, one of them lying on the shore between sleeping and waking, and, going to start up, the captain, who was foremost, ran in upon him and knocked him down, and then called to him in the boat to yield or he was a dead man.

There needed very few arguments to persuade a single man to yield, when he saw five men upon him, and his comrade knocked down: besides, this was, it seems, one of the three men who were not so hearty in the mutiny as the rest of the crew, and, therefore, was easily persuaded, not only to yield but afterwards to join very sincerely with us.

In the mean time, Friday and the captain's mate so well managed their business with the rest, that they drew

水，他们没法过河，只好把那只小船叫过来，渡他们过去。一切都在我意料之中。

他们渡过河后，我发现他们从船上叫下一个人来跟他们一块走，所以现在船上只留下两个人了，他们把小船拴在一根小树桩上。

这一切正合我的心愿。我让星期五和大副继续干他们的事，自己马上带其余的人偷偷渡过小河，出其不意地向那两个人扑过去。当时，一个人正躺在岸上，一个人还在船里呆着。那岸上的人半睡半醒，正想爬起来，走在头里的船长一下冲到他跟前，把他打倒在地。然后，船长又向船上的人大喝一声，叫他赶快投降，否则就要他的命。

当一个人看到五个人向他扑来，而他的同伴已被打倒，叫他投降是用不着多费什么口舌的。而且，他又是被迫参加叛乱的三个水手之一，所以，他不但一下子就被我们降服了，而且后来还忠心耿耿地参加到我们这边来，跟我们一起干。

与此同时，星期五和大副也把对付其余几个人的任务完成得很出色。他们一边喊，一边应，

them, by hallooing and answering, from one wood to another, till they not only heartily tired them, but left them
where they were sure they could not reach back before it
was dark, and indeed they were heartily tired themselves
also by the time they came back to us.

It was several hours after Friday came back to me
before they came to their boat, and we could hear foremost of them long before they came quite up, calling to
those behind to come along, and could hear them answer, and complain how lame and tired they were, and
not able to come any faster, which was very welcome news to us. At length they came up to the boat, but it is
impossible to express their confusion when they found the
boat fast aground in the creek, and their two men gone;
we could hear them telling one another they were gotten
into an enchanted island; that either there were inhabitants in it, and they should all be murdered, or else there
were devils or spirits in it, and they should be carried
away and devoured.

They hallooed again, and called their two comrades
by their names, but got no answer. After some time, we
could see them by the little light there run about like
men in despair; and that sometimes they would go and
sit down in the boat to rest themselves, then come on
shore again, and walk about, and do the same thing over

把他们从一座小山引向另一座小山，从一片树林引向另一片树林，不但把那批人搞得精疲力竭，而且把他们引得很远很远，不到天黑他们是绝不可能回到小船上来的。不用说，就是星期五他们自己，回来时也已劳累不堪了。

星期五他们回来好几小时后，那批人才回到了他们小船停泊的地方。我们老远就能听到走在头里的几个向掉在后面的几个大声呼唤着，要他们快点跟上。又听到那后面的几个人一面答应着，一面叫苦不迭，说他们又累又脚痛，实在走不快了。这对于我们确实是一个好消息。最后，他们总算走到了小船眼前。当时潮水已退，小船搁浅在小河里，那两个人又不知去向，他们那种惊慌失措的样子，简直无法形容。我们听见他们互相你呼我唤，声音十分凄惨。他们都说是上了一个魔岛，岛上不是有人，就是有妖怪。如果有人，他们必然会被杀得一个不剩；如果有妖怪，他们也必然会被妖怪抓走，吃个精光。

他们又开始大声呼唤，不断地喊着他们那两个伙伴的名字，可是毫无回音。又过了一会儿，我们从傍晚暗淡的光线下看见他们惶惶然地跑来跑去，双手互扭，一副绝望的样子。他们一会儿跑到小船上坐下来休息，一会儿又跑到岸上，奔

again.

My men would have fallen upon them in the dark, but I was willing to spare them, and kill as few of them as I could, being unwilling to hazard the killing any of our men, knowing the others were well armed. I resolved to wait and make sure of them, and drew my ambuscade nearer, and ordered Friday and the captain to creep upon their hands and knees, and get as near them as they possibly could before they offered to fire.

They had not been long in that posture when the boatswain, who was the principal ringleader, had now shown himself the most dispirited of all the rest, walked towards them with two more of their crew. The captain was so eager at having the principal rogue so much in his power, that he could hardly have patience to let him come so near as to be sure of him, for he only heard his tongue before; but when they came nearer, the captain and Friday, starting up on their feet, let fly at them. The boatswain was killed on the spot, the next was shot through the body, and fell just by him, though he did not die till an hour or two after, and the third ran for it.

At the noise of the fire, I immediately advanced with my whole army, which was now eight men, namely, myself, generalissimo; Friday, my lieutenant – general; the captain and his two men; and the three prisoners of

来跑去。如此上上下下，反复不已。

　　这时，我手下的人恨不得趁着夜色立即向他们扑上去。可是我想给他们留一条生路，尽可能少杀死几个。我尤其不愿意我们自己人有伤亡，因为我知道对方也都是全副武装的。我决定等待着，因此，为了更有把握制服他们，我命令手下人再向前推进埋伏起来，并让星期五和船长尽可能贴着地面向前爬进，并在他们动手开枪之前，爬得离他们愈近愈好。

　　他们埋伏在那里没有多长时间，主要的叛乱头目——水手长和其余几个无精打采的船员出现在他们面前。船长总算找到了这个恶棍头子，气往上涌，他几乎没有耐心等到恶棍过来以确定其身份，因为以前只听过他的声音。这群流氓离我们越来越近，船长和星期五飞快朝他们奔去。那水手长当场给打死了。另一个身上中弹受伤，倒在水手长身旁，过了一两个小时也死了。第三个人拔腿就跑。

　　我一听见枪响，立即带领全军前进。我这支军队现在一共有八个人，那就是：我，总司令；星期五，我的副司令。另外是船长和他的两个部下。还有三个我们信得过的俘虏，我们也发给了

war, whom we had trusted with arms.

We came upon them indeed in the dark, so that they could not see our number; and I made the man they had left in the boat, who was now one of us, call them by name, to try if he could bring them to parley. In a word, they all laid down their arms, and begged their lives.

Our next work was to repair the boat. It now occurred to me that the time of our deliverance came, and that it would be a most easy thing to bring these fellows in to be hearty in getting possession of the ship. Since I gave them liberty and treated them in earnest and trusted them with arms, they were all grateful to me.

I asked the captain if he was willing to venture with those hands on board the ship; and he replied in affirmative.

Chapter 20 Return to Civilization

The captain now had no difficulty before him but to furnish his two boats, stop the breach of one, and man them. He made his passenger captain of one, with four other men: he himself, with his mate and five more, went in the other. And they contrived their business very well, for they came up to the ship about midnight. As

他们枪支和弹药。

趁着漆黑的夜色，我们向他们发动了猛攻。他们根本看不清我们究竟有多少人。那个被留在小船上的人，现在已是我们的人了。我命令他喊那些水手的名字，看看能否促使他们和我们谈判，强迫他们投降。简而言之，他们都放下了武器，请求饶命。

我们下一步工作就是把那凿破的小船修好。这时我忽然想起，我们获救的时刻到了。现在把这些人争取过来，让他们全心全意去夺取那只大船，已非难事。我把他们全部释放了，真心对待他们并给他们发了武器，他们感激我。

我问船长，他是否愿意冒险带领这些人去收复大船。他给了我肯定的回答。

第二十章　荣归故里

船长现在只要把两只小船装备好，把留在沙滩下的那只小船的洞补好，再分派人员上去，别的就没有什么困难了。他任命他的旅客做一条小船的船长，带上另外四名水手。他自己、大副和另外五名水手，上了另一条小船。他们的事情进行得很顺利。到了半夜，他们已到了大船旁。当

soon as they came within call of the ship, he made Robinson hail them, and tell them he had brought off the men and the boat, but that it was a long time before they had found them, and the like; holding them in chat till they came to the ship's side; when the captain and the mate, entering first with their arms, immediately knocked down the second mate and the carpenter with the butt-end of their muskets, being very faithfully seconded by their men. They secured all the rest that were upon the main and quarter-decks, and began to fasten the hatches to keep them down who were below, when the other boat, and the men entering the fore chains secured the forecastle of the ship, and the scuttle which went down into the cook-room, making three men they found there prisoners.

When this was done, and all safe upon the deck, the captain ordered the mate with three men to break into the round-house, where the new rebel captain lay; and he, having taken the alarm and gotten up, now stood with two men and a boy, having firearms in their hands; and when the mate, with a crow, split open the door, the new captain and his men fired boldly among them, and wounded the mate with a musket-ball, which broke his arm, and wounded two more of the men, but killed nobody.

他们划到能够向大船喊话时，船长就命令一个也叫鲁宾逊的水手同他们招呼，告诉他们人和船都已回来了，他们是花了好多时间才把人和船找回来的。他们一面用这些话敷衍着，一面靠拢了大船。当小船一靠上大船，船长和大副首先带枪上了船。这时，手下的人表现得很忠诚。在他们的协助下船长和大副一下子就用枪把子把二副和木匠打倒了。紧接着他们又把前后甲板上的其他人全部制服，并关好舱口，把舱底下的人关在下面。这时，第二只小船上的人也沿着船头的铁索爬上来，占领了船头和通厨房的小舱口，并把在厨房里碰到的三个人俘虏了。

这一切完成后，又肃清了甲板，船长就命令大副带三个人进攻艉楼甲板室，去抓睡在那里做了新船长的叛徒。这时，那新船长已听到了警报，从床上爬起来。他身边有两个船员和一个小听差，每人手里都有枪。当大副用一根铁撬杠把门劈开时，那新船长和他手下的人就不顾一切地向他们开火。一颗短枪子弹打伤了大副，把他的胳膊打断了，还打伤了其他两个人，但没有打死人。

The mate calling for help, rushed, however, into the roundhouse, wounded as he was, and, with his pistol, shot the new captain through the head, upon which the rest yielded, and the ship was taken effectually, without any more lives lost. As soon as the ship was thus secured, the captain ordered seven guns to be fired, which was the signal agreed upon with me, to give me notice of his success, which; you may be sure, I was glad to hear, having sat watching upon the shore for it till two o'clock in the morning.

Having heard the signal plainly, I laid me down, and being very much fatigued, I fell sound asleep, when shortly I was awoke by the noise of a gun; and starting up, I heard a man call me by the name of "Governor," and presently I knew the captain's voice, when climbing up to the top of the hill, there he stood, and pointing to the ship, he embraced me in his arms. "My dear friend and deliverer," said he, "there's your ship; for she is all yours, and so are we, and all that belongs to her." I cast my eyes to the ship, and there she rode, about half a mile off the shore, for they had weighed her anchor as soon as they were masters of her, and the weather being fair, had brought her to an anchor just against the mouth of a little creek, and the tide being up, they had brought the pinnace in near the place where I had first landed my

大副虽然受了伤，还是一面呼救，一面冲进船长室，用手枪朝新船长头上就是一枪。子弹从他嘴里进去，从一只耳朵后面出来，他再也说不出一句话了。其余的人看到这情形，也都投降了。于是大船就这样稳稳当当地夺了过来，再也没有死一个人。占领大船后，船长马上下令连放七枪。这是我和他约定的信号，通知我事情成功了。不用说，听到这个信号我是多么高兴。因为我一直坐在岸边等候这个信号，差不多一直等到半夜两点钟。

我把信号听得十分清楚，便倒下来睡觉。我整整忙碌了一天，已十分劳累，所以睡得很香。但刚睡了一会儿，就在梦中听到一声枪声，我被惊醒了。我马上爬起来，听到有人在喊我："总督！总督！"（他总是这样称呼我。）我一听是船长的声音，就爬上小山头，一看果然是他。他指了指大船，把我搂在怀里。"我亲爱的朋友，我的救命恩人，"他说，"这是你的船，它是你的，我们这些人和船上的一切也都是你的！"我看了看大船，只见它停泊在离岸不到半英里的地方。原来，船长他们夺回了大船后，看见天气晴朗，便起了锚，把船一直开到小河口上。这时正好涨潮，船长就把小船划到我当初卸木排的地方靠岸，也就

rafts, and so landed just at my door.

I was, at first, ready to sink down with surprise, for I saw my deliverance indeed visibly put into my hands, all things easy, and a large ship just ready to carry me away where I pleased to go. He perceived my situation, and immediately pulled a bottle out of his pocket, and gave me a dram of cordial, which he had brought on purpose for me. After I drank it, I sat down upon the ground, and it was a good while before I could speak to him.

After some time, I came to myself, and then I embraced him in my turn, as my deliverer, and we rejoiced together. I told him, I looked upon him as a man sent from heaven to deliver me, and that the whole transaction seemed to be a chain of wonders; and such things as these were the testimonies we had of a secret hand of Providence governing the world, and an evidence that the eyes of an infinite power could search into the remotest corner of the world, and send help to the miserable whenever he pleased; nor did I forget to return thanks to God for all his mercies.

When we had talked a while, the captain told me he had brought me some little refreshment, such as the ship afforded, and such as the wretches, who had been so long his masters, had not plundered him of. Upon

是正好在城堡门口上岸。

　　起初，这突如其来的喜事，使我几乎晕倒在地，因为我亲眼看到我脱险的事已十拿九稳，且一切顺利，而且还有一艘大船可以把我送到任何我想去的地方。有好半天，我一句话也答不上来。如果不是船长用手紧紧抱着我，我也紧紧靠在他身上，我早已倒在地上了。他给我喝了几口他特别为我带的提神酒。又过了好半天，才说得出话来。

　　过了好一段时间我才清醒过来，我把船长当做我的救命恩人并且拥抱了他。我们两个人都喜不自胜。我告诉他，在我看来，他是上天特意派来救我脱险的；又说这件事的经过简直是一连串的奇迹。这类事情证明，有一种天意在冥冥中支配着世界，证明上帝无所不在，并能看清天涯海角发生的一切，只要他愿意，任何时候都可以救助不幸的人。我也没有忘记衷心感谢上天。

　　船长跟我谈了一会儿，便告诉我，他给我带了一点饮料和食物。这些东西，只是暴徒们劫后残剩下来的，所以只能拿出这么一点儿了。说着，

this he called aloud to his men, and told them to bring the things ashore that were for the governor: and it was a splendid present.

After all things were brought into my little apartment, we began to consult what was to be done with the prisoners we had, and whether we might venture to take them away with us or no, especially two of them, whom we knew to be incorrigible and refractory to the last degree, and the captain said he knew that they were such rogues, that there was no obliging them; and if he did carry them away, it must be in irons, as malefactors, to be delivered over to justice at the first English colony he could come at.

Upon this, I told him I durst undertake to bring the men he spoke of to make it their own request that he should leave them upon the island, of which the captain said he should be very glad.

I accordingly sent for them, and entered seriously into discourse with them upon their circumstances. One of them answered in the name of the rest, that they had nothing to say but this, that when they were taken, the captain promised them their lives, and they humbly implored my mercy. But I told them I knew not what mercy to show them; for, as for myself, I had resolved to quit the island with all my men, and had taken passage with

他向小船高声喊了一声，吩咐他手下人把献给总督的东西搬上岸来。这实际上是一份丰厚的礼物。

送礼的仪式完毕，东西也都搬进了我的住所，我们便商议处置俘虏的问题。我们必须考虑是否冒风险把他们带走。尤其是他们中间有两个人，我们认为是绝对无可救药、顽固不化的暴徒。船长说，他知道他们都是坏蛋，没法对他们宽大。就算把他们带走，也必须把他们像犯人一样锁起来，只要他的船开到任何一个英国殖民地，就把他们送交法办。

对此，我告诉船长。如果他同意，我可以负责说服那几个人，让他们自己提出来请求留在岛上。他很高兴我能那样做。

我派人把他们叫来，根据他们的实际情况郑重其事地分析了目前的形势。他们中间有一个人出来说话了。他说，他们没有什么话可说的。只是他们被俘时，船长曾答应饶他们不死。他们现在只有低头恳求我的宽宥。可是，我告诉他们，因为我自己已决定带着手下的人离开本岛，跟船

the captain to go to England; and as for the captain, he would not carry them to England, but as prisoners in irons, to be tried for mutiny and running away with the ship; the consequence of which, they must needs know, would be the gallows: so that I could not tell which was best for them, unless they had a mind to take their fate in the island; if they desired that, I did not care, as I had liberty to leave it; I had some inclination to give them their lives, if they could shift on shore. They seemed very thankful for it; and said they would rather venture to stay there, than to be carried to England to be hanged.

I left them five muskets, three – fowling pieces, and three swords. I had about a barrel and a half of powder, which I left them. I gave them a description of the way I managed the goats, and directions to milk and fatten them, to make both butter and cheese. In a word, I gave them every part of my own story; and I told them I would prevail with the captain to leave them two barrels of gunpowder more, and some garden seeds, which I told them I would have been very glad of; also I gave them the bag of peas which the captain had brought me, and bade them to be sure to sow and increase them.

Having done this, I left them the next day, and went on board the ship. The next morning two of the five

长一起搭船回英国去，所以我不知道该如何宽宥他们。至于船长，他只能把他们当做囚犯戴上手铐脚镣关起来带回英国，并以谋反和劫船的罪名送交当局审判。其结果他们应该都知道，那必定是上绞架。所以，我实在也为他们想不出更好的办法，除非他们下定决心留在岛上，听任命运的安排。如果他们同意这个办法，我本人没有意见，因为我反正已经能离开本岛了。只要他们愿意留在岛上自谋生计，我可以饶他们不死。他们看起来感激涕零，说他们宁愿冒险留在这里，也不愿回英国被绞死。

我把枪支都留给了他们，其中包括五支短枪，三支鸟枪，还有三把刀。我留下了一桶半火药，还把养山羊的方法教给了他们，告诉他们怎样把羊养肥，怎样挤羊奶，做奶油，制乳酪。总之，我把自己的经历详详细细地告诉了他们。我还对他们说，我要劝船长再给他们留下两桶火药与一些菜种。我对他们说，菜种一直是我所求之不得的东西。我还把船长送给我的一袋豆子也留给了他们，嘱咐他们做种子用，播下去以便有更大的收获。

这些事情办完后，第二天我就离开他们上了大船。第二天一大早，那五个人中有两个人忽然

men came swimming to the ship's side, and making a most lamentable complaint of the other three, begged to be taken into the ship, for God's sake, for they should be murdered.

The captain pretended to have no power without me; but, after some difficulty, and after their solemn promises of amendment, they were taken on board, and were shortly after soundly whipped, after which they proved very honest and quiet fellows. Some time after this, I went with the boat on shore, the tide being up, with the things promised to the men, with which the captain, at my intercession, sent their chests and clothes, and were very thankful for, I also encouraged them, by telling them that if it lay in my way to send any vessel to take them in, I would not forget them.

When I quitted this island, I carried on board, for relics, the great goat – skin cap I had made, my umbrella, and one of my parrots; also I forgot not to take the money I had had laid by me so long useless.

And thus I left the island, the 19th of December, by the ship's account, in the year 1686, after I had been upon it twenty eight years, two months, and nineteen days; being delivered from the second captivity the same day of the month that I made my escape from among the Moors at Sallee. In this vessel, after a long

向船边泅来。他们诉说那三个人怎样歧视他们，样子甚为可怜。他们恳求我们看在上帝分上收留他们，不然准会给那三个人杀死。

船长看到这种情形，就假装自己无权决定，要征得我的同意才行。后来，经过种种留难，他们也发誓痛改前非，才把他们收容上船。上船后，每人结结实实地挨了一顿鞭子，打完后再用盐和醋搽伤处。从那以后，他们果然成了安分守己的人了。过了一会儿，潮水上涨了。我就命令把我答应给那三人的箱子和衣服一起送去。他们收到后，都千恩万谢，感激不尽。我又鼓励他们说，如果将来有机会派船来接他们，我一定不会忘记他们。

当我就要离开小岛的时候，我把自己做的那顶极大的羊皮帽、羊皮伞和我的那只鹦鹉都带上船，作为纪念。同时，我也没有忘记把钱拿走，那钱在这里放了许久，毫无用处。

这样，根据船上的日历，我在一六八六年十二月十九日，离开了这个海岛。我一共在岛上住了二十八年两个月零十九天。我第二次遇难而获救的这一天，恰好和我第一次从萨利的摩尔人手里坐小艇逃出来，是同月同日。我乘坐着这条船，

voyage, I arrived in England, the 11th of June, in the year 1687, having been thirty – five years absent.

When I came to England, I was as perfect a stranger as if I had never been known there. My benefactor and faithful steward, whom I left in trust with my money, was alive, but had had great misfortunes in the world, became a widow the second time, and was in very low circumstances. I made her easy as to what she owed me, assuring her I would give her no trouble; but, on the contrary, in gratitude to her former care and faithfulness to me, I relieved her as much as my little stock would afford, which at that time would indeed allow me to do but little for her; but I assured her I would never forget her former kindness to me; nor did I forget her when I had sufficient to help her at a future time.

I went down afterwards into Yorkshire; but my father was dead, and my mother, and all the family extinct, except two sisters, and two of the children of one of my brothers; and, as I had been long ago given over for dead, there had been no provision made for me, so that, in a word, I found nothing to relieve or assist me, and the little money I had would not do much for me, as to settling in the world.

I met with one piece of gratitude, indeed, which I did not expect; and this was, that the master of the

长途跋涉，终于在一六八七年六月十一日抵达英国。计算起来，我离开家乡已经三十五年了。

我回到英国，人人都把我当外国人，好像我从未在英国住过似的。我那位替我保管钱财的恩人和忠实的管家，这时还活着。不过她的遭遇非常不幸。她再嫁之后又成了寡妇，境况十分悲惨。我叫她不要把欠我的钱放在心上，并对她说，我决不会找她麻烦。相反，为了报答她以前对我的关心和忠诚，我又尽我微薄的财力给了她一点接济。当然，我现在财力有限，不能对她有多少帮助。可是，我向她保证我永远不会忘记她以前对我的好处，并告诉她，只要我将来有力量帮助她，我决不会忘记。这是后话了。

后来，我去了约克郡。我父亲已经过世，我母亲及全家也都已故去。我只找到了两个妹妹和我一位哥哥的两个孩子。因为大家都以为我早已不在世上了，所以没有留给我一点遗产。一句话，我完全找不到一点接济和资助，而我身上的一点钱，根本无法帮助我成家立业。

万万没有料到的是，在我这样窘迫的时候，却有人对我感恩图报。我意外救了船长，也救了

ship, whom I had so happily delivered, having given a very handsome account to the owners of the manner how I had saved the lives of the men and the ship, they invited me to meet them and some other merchants concerned, and all together made me a very handsome compliment upon the subject, and a present of almost two hundred pounds sterling.

But, after making several reflections upon the circumstances of my life, and how little way this would go towards settling me in the world, I resolved to go to Lisbon, and see if I could get any information of the state of my plantation in Brazil, and of what became of my partner, who, I supposed, had for some years now given me over for dead.

With this view, I took shipping for Lisbon, where I arrived in April following; my man Friday accompanying me very honestly in all these ramblings, and proving a most faithful servant upon all occasions. When I came to Lisbon, I found out by inquiry, and to my particular satisfaction, my old friend, the captain of the ship, who first took me up at sea, off the shore of Africa. He had now grown old, and had left off the sea, having put his son into the ship, and who still used the Brazil trade. The old man did not know me, and I scarcely knew him; but he soon recollected me when I told him who I was.

他的船和货物。这时，船长把我怎样救了全船和船上的人，详详细细地报告了那些船主。他们就把我邀请去，和他们以及几个有关的商人会面。他们对我的行为大大地赞扬了一番，又给了我两百英镑作为酬谢。

我对自己当前生活的处境反复考虑了好多次，感到实难在这个世界上安身立命，就决定到里斯本去一趟，看看能不能打听到我在巴西的种植园和那合股人的情况如何。我相信，那合股人一定以为我已死了多年了。

抱着这一希望，我搭上了开往里斯本的船，于第二年四月份到达了那里。当我这样东奔西跑的时候，星期五一直跟着我，诚实可靠，并证明无论何时何地，他都是我最忠实的仆人。到了里斯本，我几经打听，找到了我的老朋友，也就是把我从非洲海面上救起来的那位船长。这真使我高兴极了。船长现在年事已高，早就不再出海了；他让儿子当了船长，而儿子也已近中年了，仍旧做巴西生意。那老人家已经不认得我了。说实在话，我也几乎认不出他了。但当我告诉他我是谁之后，他也记起了我的面貌。

The old man then asked me if he should put me in a method to make my claim to the plantation. I told him I thought to go over to it myself. He said I might do so if I pleased; but that if I did not, there were ways enough to secure my right, and immediately to appropriate the profits to my use; and as there were ships in the river of Lisbon just ready to go to Brazil, he made me enter my name in a public register, with his affidavit, affirming, upon oath, that I was alive, and that I was the same person who took up the land for planting the said plantation at first.

This being regularly attested by a notary, and a procuration affixed, he directed me to send it, with a letter of his writing, to a merchant of his acquaintance at the place, and then proposed my staying with him till an account came of the return.

Never anything was more honorable than the proceedings upon this procuration; for in less than seven months I received a large packet from the survivors of my trustees, the merchants for whose account I went to sea; and as the Brazilian ships come all in fleets, the same ships which brought my letters brought my goods.

By these, it appeared I was now master, all on a sudden of above five thousand pounds sterling in money, and had an estate, as I might well call it, in Brazil, of

老人家问我，是不是要他替我想个办法，把我的种植园收回来。我告诉他，我想亲自去巴西走一趟。他说，如果我想去，那也好。不过，如果我不想去，也有不少办法保证我收回自己的产权，并马上把收入拨给我使用。目前，在里斯本的特茹河里，正有一批船要开往巴西。他劝我在官方登记处注册了我的名字，他自己也写了一份担保书，证明我还活着，并声明当时在巴西领取土地建立种植园的正是我本人。

我把本人的担保书按常规作了公证，又附上了一份委托书。然后，老人又替我写了一封亲笔信，连同上述两份文件，让我一起寄给了他所熟悉的一位巴西商人。这一切办完，他建议我在他家里静候回音。

这次委托手续真是办得再公正也没有了。不到七个月，我收到那两位代理人的财产继承人寄给我的一个大包裹，我正是为了那两位代理人才从事这次遇难的航行的。那些巴西船队，向来是成群结队而来，给我带来了信件的那支船队，也同时运来了我的货物。

突然间，我成了拥有五千英镑现款的富翁，而且在巴西还有一份产业，每年有一千镑以上的

above a thousand pounds a – year, as safe as any landed estate in England, in a word, I was in a condition which I could scarcely understand, or how to compose myself for its enjoyment.

The first thing I did was to recompense my original benefactor, my good old captain, who had been first charitable, to me in my distress, kind to me in the beginning, and honest to me at the end. I showed him all that was sent me. I told him that, next to the providence of Heaven, which disposes all things, it was owing to him; and that it now lay on me to reward him. So I sent for a notary, and caused him to draw a procuration, empowering him to be my receiver of the annual profits of my plantation, and appointing my partner to account to him, and make the returns by the usual fleets to him, in my name, adding a clause in the end, being a grant of one hundred moidores a year during his life, and fifty moidores a year to his son after him.

I was now to consider which way to steer my course next, and what to do with the estate that Providence had thus put into my hands; and, indeed, I had more care upon my head now than I had in my silent state of life on the island, where I wanted nothing but what I had, and had nothing but what I wanted.

As I had rewarded the old captain fully, and to his

收入，就像在英国的田产一样可靠。一句话，我目前的处境，连自己也莫名其妙，更不知道如何安下心来享用这些财富了。

我做的第一件事情，就是报答我最初的恩人，也就是那好心的老船长。当初我遇难时，他待我十分仁慈，此后自始至终对我善良真诚。我把收到的东西都给他看了。我对他说，我之所以有今天，除了主宰一切的天意外，全靠了他的帮助。现在，我既然有能力报答他，我就要百倍地回报他。我请来了一位公证人，请他起草了一份委托书，委任老船长作为我那种植园的年息管理人，并指定我那位合股人向他报告账目，把我应得的收入交给那些长年来往于巴西和里斯本的船队带给他。委托书的最后一款是，老船长在世之日，每年从我的收入中送给他一百葡萄牙金币；在他死后，每年送给他儿子五十葡萄牙金币。这样，我总算报答了这位老人。

我现在该考虑下一步的行动了，并考虑怎样处置上天赐给我的这份产业了。说实在话，与荒岛上的寂寞生活相比，现在我要操心的事更多了。在岛上，除了我所有的，就别无他求；除了我所需要的，也就一无所有。

我现在已充分报答了我从前的恩人老船长，

satisfaction, who had been my former benefactor, so I began to think of my poor widow, whose husband had been my first benefactor, and she, while it was in her power, my faithful steward and instructor. So the first thing I did I got a merchant in Lisbon to write to his correspondent in London, not only to pay a bill, but to go find her out, and carry her in money a hundred pounds from me, and to talk with her and comfort her in her poverty, by telling her she should, if I lived, have a farther supply. At the same time, I sent my two sisters in the country, each of them a hundred pounds, they being, though not in want, yet not in very good circumstances; one having been married, and left a widow, and the other having a husband not so kind to her as he should be. But, among all my relations or acquaintances, I could not yet pitch upon one to whom I durst commit the gross of my stock.

I had once a mind to have gone to Brazil, and have settled myself there, for I was, as it were, naturalized to the place, but that I really did not know with whom to leave my effects behind me; so I resolved at last to go to England with them, where, if I arrived, I concluded I should make some acquaintance or find some relations that would be faithful to me, and accordingly I prepared to go for England with all my wealth.

他也感到心满意足。所以，我开始想到那位可怜的寡妇了。他的丈夫是我的第一位恩人，而且，她本人在有能力时，一直是我忠实的管家，并尽长辈之责经常开导我。因此，我做的第一件事情是，我让一位在里斯本的商人写信给他在伦敦的亲戚，除了请他替我把汇票兑成现款外，还请他亲自找到她，替我把一百英镑的现款亲自交给她。我还要此人当面和她谈一下，因为她目前非常贫困，境况不佳，所以我要此人好好安慰她，并告诉她，只要我活在人世，以后还会接济她。另外，我又给我那两个住在乡下的妹妹每人寄一百。她们虽然并不贫困，但境况也不太好。一个妹妹结了婚，后来成了寡妇；另一个妹妹的丈夫对她很不好。可是在我所有的亲戚朋友中，我还找不到一个可以完全信托的人，把我的全部财产交付给他保管。

我一度也曾想到过在巴西安家落户，因为我从前入过巴西籍。我不知道该把我的财产托付给谁代管。所以，我决定带着我的钱和财产回英国去。到了那里，我相信一定可以结交一些朋友，或找到什么忠于我的亲戚。这样，我就决定带着我的全部财富回英国去。

Having settled my affairs, sold my cargo, and turned all my effects into good bills of exchange, my next difficulty was which way to go to England. I had been accustomed enough to the sea, and yet I had a strange aversion to go to England by sea at that time; and though I could give no reason for it, yet the difficulty increased upon me so much, that though I had once shipped my baggage in order to go, yet I altered my mind, and that not once but two or three times.

It is true I had been very unfortunate by sea, and this might be one of my reasons; but let no man strike the strong impulses of his own thoughts in cases of such moment. Two ships, each of which I had engaged to go in, but again withdrew my agreement, miscarried, namely, one was taken by the Algerines, and the other was cast away on the Start, near Torbay, and all the people drowned, except three; so that in either of those vessels I would have been made miserable, and in which most, it was hard to say.

Having been thus harassed in my thoughts, my old pilot, to whom I communicated everything, pressed me earnestly not to go by sea; but either to go by land to the Groyne, and cross over the Bay of Biscay to Rochelle, from whence it was but an easy and safe journey by land to Paris, and so to Calais and Dover; or go up to Mad-

就这样，我把该料理的事情都办了，把货也卖出去了，又把我的钱财换成可靠的汇票，下一步的难题就是走哪一条路回英国。海路我是走惯了，可是这一次不知什么原因，我就是不想走海路。我不愿意从海路回英国，尽管我自己也说不出什么理由，这种想法越来越强烈，以致有两三次，我把行李都搬到船上了，可是还是临时改变了主意，把行李从船上搬了下来。

我的航海生涯确实非常不幸，这也许是我不想再出海的理由之一。但这时，任何人也不应忽视自己内心这种突发的念头。我曾特别挑选过两条船，本来我是决定要搭乘的。其中有一条，我把行李都搬上去了；另一条，我也都和船长讲定了。可是，两条船我都没有上。后来，那两条船果然都出事了。一条给阿尔及利亚人掳了去；另一条在托贝湾的斯塔特岬角沉没了，除了三个人生还，其他人都淹死了。反正不管我上哪条船，都得倒霉；至于上哪条船更倒霉，那就很难说了。

我为这事心里烦透了，就去与老船长商量。他坚决反对我走海路，而劝我最好走陆路到拉科鲁尼亚，渡过比斯开湾到罗谢尔，再从罗谢尔走陆路到巴黎，既安全又舒适，然后再从巴黎到加来和多佛；或先到马德里，然后由陆路穿过法国

rid, and so all the way by land through France.

In a word. I was so prepossessed against my going to sea at all, except from Calais to Dover, that I resolved to travel all the way by land, which, as I was not in haste, and did not value the charge, was by much the pleasanter way; and to make it more so, my old captain brought an English gentleman, the son of a merchant in Lisbon, who was willing to travel with me; after which we picked up two more, who were English, and merchants also, and two young Portuguese gentlemen, the last going to Paris only, so that we were in all six of us and five servants; the two merchants, and the two Portuguese, contenting themselves, with one servant between two, to save the charge; and as for me, I got an English sailor to travel with me as a servant, besides my man Friday, who was too much a stranger to be capable of supplying the place of a servant upon the road.

In this manner we set out from Lisbon; and our company being all very well mounted and armed, we made a little troop, whereof they did me the honor to call me captain, as well because I was the oldest man as because I had two servants, and indeed was the originator of the whole journey.

Four French gentlemen, who had stopped on the French side of the passes, as we were now on the Span-

回到我的家乡。

总之，我不想走海路已成了一种先入为主的想法，怎么也无法改变了。惟一我不愿意坐船的一段路，又不在乎花钱，所以就决定全部走陆路，而且陆上旅行实在也是很愉快的。为了使这次旅行更愉快，我的老船长又给我找了一位英国绅士为伴。此人是在里斯本的一位商人的儿子，他表示愿意和我结伴同行。后来我们又找到了两位英国商人和两位葡萄牙绅士，不过这两位葡萄牙绅士的目的地是巴黎。这样，我们现在一共有六个旅伴和五个仆人——那两位英国商人和两位葡萄牙绅士为了节省开支，各共用一个听差。而我除了星期五之外，又找了一个英国水手当我路上的听差，因为星期五在这异乡客地，难以担当听差的职务。

我们就这样从里斯本出发了。我们都骑着好马，全副武装，成了一支小小的部队。大家都很尊敬我，称我为队长，一来是我年纪最大，二来我有两个听差。再说，我也是这次旅行的发起人哩。

大雪一直下个不停。正当我们在考虑另寻出路时，忽然来了四位法国绅士。他们曾经在法国

435

ish, had found out a guide, who had brought them over the mountains by such ways, that they were not much incommoded with the snow; and, where they met with snow in any quantity, they said it was frozen hard enough to bear them and their horses.

We sent for this guide, who told us that he would undertake to carry us the same way, with no hazard from the snow, provided we were armed sufficiently to protect us from wild beasts; for, he said, upon these snow regions it was common for wolves to show themselves at the foot of the mountains, being made ravenous for want of food, while the ground was covered with snow. We told him we were well enough prepared for such creatures as they were, if he would insure us from a kind of two legged wolves, from which we were told most danger was to be apprehended, especially on the French side of the mountains.

He satisfied us there was no danger of that kind in the way that we were to go. So we readily agreed to follow him, as did also twelve other gentlemen, with their servants, some French, some Spanish, who, as I said, had attempted to go, and were obliged to come back again.

Accordingly, we all set out from Pampeluna, with our guide, on the 15th of November; and, indeed, I

境内的山路上被雪所阻，正像我们在这儿西班牙境内的山路上被雪所困一样。但是，他们后来找到了一个向导，带他们绕过朗格多附近的山区，一路上没碰到什么大雪；即使在雪最多的地方，据他们说也冻得很硬，人和马通行是不成问题的。

我们就把那位向导找了来。他对我们说，他愿意从原路把我们带过去，不会遇到大雪的阻碍，但我们必须多带武器，防备野兽的袭击。因为，他说，在大雪覆盖的区域，经常有些狼在山脚下出没，因为遍地大雪，它们找不到食物已经饿慌了。我们告诉他，我们对狼这一类野兽已有充分的准备；不过，他能否保证我们不会遇到一种两条腿的狼，因为，我们听说，这一地区十分危险，经常会受到强人的抢劫，尤其是在法国境内的山区。

向导对我们说，在我们走的路上，没有强人袭击的危险。于是，我们马上同意跟他走。另外还有十二位绅士和他们的仆人决定和我们一起走。他们中间有法国人，也有西班牙人。我前边提到，这些人试图过境，但因大雪所阻，被迫折回来了。

于是，在十一月十五日，我们一行全体人马跟着我们的向导，从潘佩卢出发了。出乎我意料

was surprised, when, instead of going forward, he came directly back with us above twenty miles; on the same road by which we came from Madrid, when, having passed two rivers, and come into the plain country, we found ourselves in a warm climate again, where the country was pleasant, and no snow was to be seen; but, on a sudden, turning to the left, he approached the mountains by another way; and though, it is true, the hills and the precipices looked dreadful, yet he made so many tours, and meanders, and led us by such winding ways, that we insensibly passed the height of the mountains without being much encumbered with the snow; and. all on a sudden, he showed us the pleasant fruitful provinces of Languedoc and Gascoigne, all green and flourishing, though indeed they were at a great distance, and we had some rough way to pass yet.

We were a little uneasy, however, when we found it snowed so fast one whole day and night that we could not travel; but he bade us be easy, we should soon be past it all. We found, indeed, that we began to descend every day, and to come more north than before; and so, depending upon our guide, we went on.

It was about two hours before night, when our guide, being something before us, and not just in sight, out rushed three monstrous wolves, and after them a

的是，他并不往前走，而是带我们倒回头来，朝我们从马德里来的那条路上走回去。这样走了大约二十多英里，然后渡过了两条河，来到了平原地带。我们发现这儿气候暖和起来，且乡村的风景十分悦目，看不见一点雪。可是向导突然向左一转，从另一条路把我们带进了山区。这一路上尽是崇山峻岭、悬崖峭壁，看起来煞是可怕。可是，向导左转右转，曲折迂回，居然带着我们不知不觉地越过了最高的山头，路上并没有碰到什么大雪的困阻。突然，他叫我们向远处看，我们居然看到了风景美丽、物产丰富的朗格多和加斯科尼省。只见那儿树木繁茂，一片葱绿，但距离还相当远。我们还得走一程崎岖艰难的山路，才能到达那儿。

然而，使我们感到不安的是，这时下起了大雪，整整下了一天一夜，简直没法走路。向导叫我们放心，说我们不久即可通过这一地区。事实上，我们也发现，我们一天天地在下山，而且愈来愈往北走。因此，我们就跟着向导，继续前进。

天黑前两小时，我们的向导远远走在我们的前面；当时，我们已看不到他的身影了。突然，从左边密林深处的山坳里，冲出来三只凶猛的大

bear, out of a hollow way, adjoining to a thick wood. Two of the wolves flew upon the guide, and had he been half a mile before us, he would have been devoured, indeed, before we could have helped him. One of them fastened upon his horse, and the other attacked the man with that violence, that he had not time, or not presence of mind enough to draw his pistol, but hallooed and cried out to us most lustily. My man Friday being next to me, I bade him ride up, and see what was the matter. As soon as Friday came in sight of the man, he hallooed as loud as the other, "O master! O master!" but, like a bold fellow, rode directly up to the man, and, with a pistol, shot the wolf that attacked him through the head.

It was happy for the poor man that is was my man Friday, for he, having been used to that kind of creature in his country, had no fear upon him, but went up close to him, and shot him as above, whereas, any of us would have fired at a farther distance, and might, perhaps, have either missed the wolf, or shot the man.

But it was enough to have terrified a bolder man than I; and indeed it alarmed all our company, when, with the noise of Friday's pistol, we heard on both sides the most dismal howling of wolves, and the noise redoubled by the echo of the mountains.

My man Friday had delivered our guide, and when

狼，后面还跟着一头熊。有两只狼直向我们的向导扑去。如果他离我们再远点，就早给狼吞掉了，我们也来不及救他了。这时，一只狼向他的马扑去，紧紧咬住了马；另一只向他本人扑去，使他措手不及，不仅来不及拔出枪，甚至在慌乱中都没有想到要拔枪自卫，只是一个劲儿拼命朝我们大喊大叫。这时，星期五正在我的身旁。我就命令他策马向前，看看究竟发生了什么事。星期五一见到狼，也像向导一样大叫起来："主人！主人！"但他毕竟是个勇敢的男子汉，立即策马冲到向导跟前，拿起手枪，对着那只狼的头上就是一枪，结果了那畜牲的生命。

可怜的向导应该说运气不错，因为他碰上了星期五。星期五在他家乡与野兽打惯了交道，所以一点儿也不害怕。他能坦然地走到狼的跟前，一枪把它打死。要是换了别人，就不敢靠得那么近开枪了。而从远距离开枪，不是打不着狼，就是可能打着人。

即使像我这样胆大的人，见此情景也着实吓得心惊肉跳。说实在的，我们一行人都吓得魂不附体，因为，紧跟着星期五的枪声，我们就听见两边的狼群发出一片最凄惨的嚎叫，结果狼嚎和回声此起彼伏，犹如成千上万的狼在吼叫。

星期五救了向导的性命。当我们走上去的时

we came up he was helping him off from his horse, for the man was both hurt and frightened, and indeed the last more than the first.

We had one dangerous place to pass, of which our guide told us, if there were any more wolves in the country, we should find them there; and this was a small plain, surrounded with woods on every side, and a long, narrow defile or lane, which we were to pass, to get through the wood, and then we should come to a village where we were to lodge.

It was within half an hour of sunset when we entered the first wood; and a little after sunset we came into the plain. We met with nothing in the first wood, except that, in a little plain within the wood, which was not above two furlongs over, we saw five great wolves cross the road, full speed, one after another, as if they had been in chase of some prey they had in view. They took no notice of us, and were gone, and out of our sight in a few moments.

This gave us leisure to charge our pieces again, and that we might lose no time, we kept going; but we had little more than loaded our fusils, and put ourselves into readiness, when we heard a terrible noise in the wood on our left.

The night was coming on, and the light began to be

候，他正在帮助向导下马，因为向导受了伤，又受了惊吓，而且，看来惊恐甚于伤势。

向导对我们说，我们还要经过一个危险的地方。如果这一带还有狼的话，我们一定会在那里碰到。那地方是一片小小的川地，四周都是树林。要想穿过树林，就必须走一条又长又窄的林间小道，然后才能到达我们将要宿营的村庄。

当我们进入第一座树林时，离太阳落山仅半小时了，到我们进入那片平川，太阳已经下去了。在第一座树林里，我们什么也没有碰见，只在一块二百来码长的林间空地上，看见有五条大狼，一条跟着一条，飞快地在路上跃过，大概是在追赶一个什么小动物吧，因为那小动物就在他们前面。那些狼没有注意到我们，不到一会儿，就跑得无影无踪了。

这时，我们才有时间重新给枪装弹药。同时，我们抓紧时间继续前进。可是，我们刚装好枪准备上路时，又从左边原来的那座树林里传出了可怕的嚎叫声。这一次狼群离我们较远，但却在我们去路的正前方。

黑夜渐渐地来临了，光线变得暗淡起来。这

dusky, which made it the worse on our side; but the noise increasing, we could not perceive that it was the howling of those ravenous creatures; and, on a sudden, we perceived two or three troops of wolves, one on our left, one behind us, and one in our front, and we knew not what course to take; but the creatures resolved us soon, for they gathered about us; in hopes of prey; and I verily believe there were three hundred of them. It happened very much to our advantage, that, at the entrance into the wood there lay some large timber trees, cut down, and I drew my little troop in among these trees, and placing ourselves in a line, behind one long tree, I advised them all to alight, and keeping that tree before us for a breastwork, to stand in a triangle or three fronts, inclosing our horses in the center.

We did so; and it was well we did, for never was a more furious charge than the creatures made upon us in this place: they came on us with a growling kind of noise, and mounted the piece of timber, as if they were only rushing upon their prey; and this fury of theirs, it seems, was principally occasioned by their seeing our horses behind us, which was the prey they aimed at. I ordered our men to fire as before, every other man, and they took their aim so sure, that they killed several wolves at the first volley; but there was a necessity to

对我们更加不利。嚎叫声越来越响，我们不难辨别出，那是恶狼的嚎叫。突然，出现了两三群狼。一群在我们左边，一群在我们后边，还有一群在我们前面，看样子已经把我们包围起来了，想以我们一行人马果腹。我们知道没有路可逃了，这些狼我确确实实地相信，一共有三百来只。值得庆幸的是，在离树林入口处不远，正好堆着一大批木料，大概是夏天采伐下来堆在那里预备运走的。这对我们的行动非常有利。我把我这一小队人马开到那堆木料后面。那儿有一根木头特别长，我就把队伍在那根长木头后面一字排开。我让大家都下马，把那根长木头当做胸墙，站成一个三角形的阵线，把我们的马围在中央。

我们这样做了，而且也幸亏这样做了。因为这群饿狼向我们发动了攻击，其凶猛程度在狼害为患的当地也是罕见的。它们嚎叫着向我们扑来，蹿上了那根木头。前面我已提到，我们以此长木头作为胸墙。它们的目的只有一个，就是扑向猎物。从它们的行动判断，其目标主要是我们身后的那些马匹。我命令我的队伍像上次那样分两批开火，一批射击另一批做准备。他们都瞄得很准。第一排子弹开出去，就打死了好几只狼。可是，

keep a continual firing, for they came on like devils, those behind pushing on those before.

When we had fired the second volley of our fusils, we thought they stopped a little, and I hoped they would have gone off, but it was but a moment, for others came forward again, so we fired two volleys of our pistols, and, I believe, in these four firings, we killed seventeen or eighteen of them, and lamed twice as many; yet they came on again.

I was loath to spend our last shot too hastily; so I called my servant, not Friday, but my other man, and, giving him a horn of powder, I bid him lay a train all along the piece of timber, and let it be a large train. He did so; and had but just time to get away, when the wolves came up to it, and some got upon it, when I, snapping an uncharged pistol close to the powder, set it on fire. Those that were upon the timber were scorched with it, and six or seven of them fell, or rather jumped in among us, with the force and fright of the fire. We dispatched these in an instant, and the rest were so frightened with the light, that they drew back a little.

Upon which I ordered our last pistols to be fired off in one volley; and after that we gave a shout: upon this the wolves turned tail, and we sallied immediately upon near twenty lame ones, whose dreadful crying and howl-

我们不得不连续发火。这批恶狼犹如恶魔一样，前仆后继，不知死活地向前猛冲。

第二排枪放完后，我们以为狼群暂时停止了进攻，我也希望它已经逃走。但一会儿，后面的狼又冲上来了。我们又放了两排手枪子弹。而且，我相信，这四排枪杀死了十六至十七只狼，使三十二至三十四只狼残废。但这群狼又冲上来了。

我不想匆匆地浪费掉最后的子弹，我叫来自己的仆人。我没有叫星期五，而是叫了我新雇的那个水手。我给了他一角火药，命令他沿着那根长木头把火药撒下去撒成一条宽宽长长的火药线。他照着办了。他刚转身回来，狼群就冲了过来，有几只甚至已冲上了那根长木。我立即抓起一支没有放过的手枪，贴近火药线开了一枪，使火药燃烧起来。冲上木料的几只狼给烧伤了；其中有六七只由于火光的威力和惊恐，竟连跌带跳地落入我们中间。我们立即把它们解决了。其他的狼被火光吓得半死，加上这时天已黑下来，火光看起来就更可怕了，这才使那些狼后退了几步。

这时，我就下令全体人员用剩下的手枪一直开火，然后大家齐声呐喊。这才使那些狼掉转尾巴逃跑了。于是我们马上冲到那二十多只受伤的狼跟前。那些逃跑的狼听到它们同伴的惨叫声，

ing scared the rest, so that they all fled, and left us.

After this I had nothing uncommon to take notice of in my passage through France, nothing but what other travelers have given an account of, with much more advantage than I can. I traveled from Thoulouse to Paris, and, without any considerable stay came to Calais, and landed safe at Dover, the 14th of January, after having a severe cold season to travel in.

I had now come to the center of my travels, and had, in a little time, all my newly discovered estate safe about me, the bills of exchange which I had brought with me having been currently paid.

My principal guide and privy counselor was my good old widow, who, in gratitude for the money I had sent her, thought no pains too much, or care too great, to employ for me. I began to think of leaving my effects with this woman, and setting out for Lisbon, and so to the Brazils. But now another scruple came in my way, and that was religion; for, as I had entertained some doubts about the Roman religion, even while I was abroad, especially in my state of solitude, so I knew there was no going to the Brazils for me, much less going to settle there, unless I resolved to embrace the Catholic religion, without any reserve; except, on the other hand, I resolved to be a sacrifice to my principles, be a martyr

就吓得离开我们跑远了。

　　在法国的旅程，一路上没有什么特别的事情可记。即使有，也不过是许多其他旅行家已记过的事，而且他们肯定比我记得好得多。我从土鲁斯到巴黎，一路马不停蹄，直达加莱。随后，在一月十四日，平安渡过海峡到达多佛。这整整一个最严寒的冬季，我就在旅行中度过了。

　　现在已抵达旅行的终点了。在短短的几天里，我兑现了带来的几张汇票。我新获得的财产，也都安全地转到了我的手上。

　　我的长辈和良师益友，就是那位心地善良的老寡妇，她衷心感激我们汇给她的钱。因此，她不辞劳苦，对我关怀备至，尽心尽力为我服务。我对她也是一百个放心，把所有的财产都交托给她保管。我自己出发去里斯本，再从那里去巴西。但这时我有了另一个顾虑，那就是宗教问题。早在国外时，尤其是我在荒岛上过着那种孤寂的生活时，我对罗马天主教就产生了怀疑。因此，我若想去巴西，甚至想在那里定居，在我面前只有两种选择：要么我决定毫无保留地信奉罗马天主教，要么我决定为自己的宗教思想献出生命，作为殉教者在宗教法庭上被判处死刑。所以，我就

for religion, and die in the Inquisition; so I resolved to stay at home, and, if I could find means, to dispose of my plantation.

To this purpose I wrote to my old friend at Lisbon, who, in return, gave me notice that he could easily dispose of it there; but that, if I thought fit to give him leave to offer it in my name to the two merchants, the survivors of my trustees, who lived in the Brazils, and most fully understood the value of it, who lived just upon the spot, and whom I knew to be very rich, so that he believed they would be fond of buying it, he did not doubt but I should make four or five thousand pieces of eight more for it. Accordingly I agreed, gave him orders to offer it to them, and he did so; and in about eight months more, the ships then returned, he sent me an account that they had accepted the offer, and had remitted thirty – three thousand pieces of eight to a correspondent of theirs at Lisbon to pay for it.

In return, I signed the instrument of sale in the form which they sent from Lisbon, and sent it to my old man, who sent me bills of exchange for thirty – two thousand eight hundred pieces of eight for the estate, reserving the payment of one hundred moidores a – year to him, the old man, during his life, and fifty moidores afterwards to his son for his life, which I had promised

决定仍在本国，而且，如果可能的话，把我在巴西的种植园卖掉。

为此，我写了一封信给我在里斯本的那位老朋友。他回信告诉我，他可以很容易地在那儿把我在巴西的种植园卖掉。我若同意委托他经办此事，他可以以我的名义通知住在巴西的那两位商人，也就是我那两位代理人的儿子。他们住在当地，一定知道那份产业的价值，而且，我也知道他们很有钱。所以，他相信，他们一定会乐意买下来，他也毫不怀疑，我至少可以多卖四五千葡萄牙金币。我同意让他通知他们。他也照办了。大约八个月后，去巴西的那艘船又回到了里斯本。他写信告诉我，他接受了我的卖价，并已经汇了三万三千葡萄牙金币给他们在里斯本的代理人，嘱咐他照付。

我在他们里斯本寄给我的卖契上签了字，并把契约寄回给在里斯本的我那位老朋友。他给我寄来了一张三万二千八百块葡萄牙金币的汇票，那是我变卖那份产业所得的钱。我仍然履行了我先前许下的诺言，每年付给这位老人一百块葡萄牙金币，直到他逝世，并在他死后每年付给他儿子五十块葡萄牙金币作为终身津贴。原先这笔钱

them, and which the plantation was to make good as a rent charge.

And thus I had given the first part of a life of fortune and adventure, a life of Providence's checker – work, and of a variety, which the world will seldom be able to show the like of, beginning foolishly, but closing much more happily than I had ever any reason even to hope for.

Any one would think that, in this state of complicated good fortune, I was past running any more hazards; but I was inured to a wandering life, had no family, nor many relations, nor, however rich, had I contracted much acquaintance; and though I had sold my estate in the Brazils, yet I could not keep that country out of my head, and had a great mind to be upon the wing again, especially I could not resist the strong inclination I had to see my island.

My true friend, the widow, earnestly dissuaded me from it, and so far prevailed with me, that for almost seven years she prevented my running abroad; during which time I took my two nephews, the children of one of my brothers, into my carry. The eldest, having something of his own, I bred up as a gentleman, and gave him a settlement of some addition to his estate after my decease; the other I put out to the captain of a ship,

是我许诺从种植园的每年收益中支取的。

现在，我叙述完了我一生幸运和冒险经历的第一部分。我这一生犹如造物主的杰作，光怪陆离，浮沉不定，变化无常，实乃人间罕见。虽然开始时我显得那么愚昧无知，但结局却比我所期望的要幸运得多。

在这种情况下，任何人都以为我不会再出去冒险了。如果情况不是像后来发生的那样，我也确实会在家安享余年。可是，我现在的情况是，自己已过惯了游荡的生活，加上我目前一无家庭牵连，二无多少亲戚，而且，我虽富有，却没有结交多少朋友。所以尽管我把在巴西的种植园已经卖掉，可是我还常常想念那个地方，很想旧地重访，再作远游。我尤其想到我的岛上去看看。

我忠实的朋友，就是那位寡妇，竭力劝我不要再外出远游了。她真的把我劝住了。整整七年，她都不让我出游。在这期间，我领养了我的两个侄儿，他俩都是我一个哥哥的孩子。大侄儿本来有点遗产，我把他培养成了一个有教养的人，并且分给他了一点我的财产。我把另一个侄儿托付

and, after five years, finding him a sensible, bold, enterprising young fellow, I put him into a good ship, and sent him to sea. And this young fellow afterwards drew me in, old as I was, to farther adventures myself.

In the mean time, I in part settled myself here. For, first of all, I married, and had three children, two sons and one daughter. But my wife dying, and my nephew coming home, with good success, from a voyage to Spain, my inclination to go abroad, and his importunity prevailed, and I engaged to go in his ship as a private trader to the East Indies. In this voyage I visited my new colony in the island, saw my successors, the Spaniards; had the whole story of their coming to and adventures in the island, after my departure.

I may write later of all these things.

给一位船长。五年后，他已成了一个通情达理、有胆识、有抱负的青年，我就替他买了一条好船，让他航海去了。后来，正是这位小青年竟把我这个老头子拖进了新的冒险事业。

在此期间，我在国内也初步安居下来。首先，我结了婚，有了三个孩子：两个儿子和一个女儿。可是，不久我妻子就过世了。这时，我的侄子又正好从西班牙航海归来，获利甚丰。我出洋的欲望又强烈起来，加上我侄儿一再劝说，于是，我就以一个私家客商的身份，搭他的船到东印度群岛去。在这次航行中，我回到了我的岛上。现在，这座小岛已是我的新殖民地了。我看到了我的那些继承人——就是那批大陆上过去的西班牙人，并了解了他们的生活情况。

所有这些事情，我可能以后慢慢给你们讲述。